THE FUTURE OF AMERICAN HIGHER EDUCATION

A SASSO and DEVITIS BOOK
A project developed under the editorship of
Pietro A. Sasso and Joseph L. DeVitis

Also available

Neighborhood Democracy
Building Anchor Partnerships Between Colleges and Their Communities
Richard Guarasci

The Future of American Higher Education
How Today's Public Intellectuals Frame the Debate
Edited by Joseph L. DeVitis

Advance Praise for
The Future of American Higher Education

"Joseph DeVitis's *The Future of American Higher Education: How Today's Public Intellectuals Frame the Debate* is an extensive review of the myriad crises facing American higher education through the eyes of public intellectuals who have taken on the academy and society writ large. It is a compelling compilation that inspires readers and contemporary scholars to take up their own role as public intellectuals as we work to challenge and re-envision the academy toward the ever-changing public good. An array of topics includes deliberative democracy, neoliberal higher education, affirmative action, activism, consumer demand, ethics and equity, and the role of the public intellectual in their own right. This book is ideal for any course on American higher education as it takes up important topics facing the historical present through the work of public intellectuals including university presidents and highly visible scholars within and outside of the field of higher education."
—**Penny A. Pasque**, *Professor of Educational Studies and Director of Qualitative Methods at The Ohio State University*

"By focusing on public intellectuals through the lenses of a rich array of scholars in their own right, Joe DeVitis captures the complexity and struggles of modern-day higher education. Are colleges and universities headed down the rabbit's warren as they negotiate larger economic, social, and political goals and their own educational and intellectual purposes? Reasonable minds will disagree about how the academy should balance these interests. *The Future of American Higher Education: How Today's Public Intellectuals Frame the Debate* is a compelling, lively, and thought-provoking read—and it could not have come at a better time in light of the many existential pressures surrounding higher education."—**Jonathan Brand**, *President, Cornell College*

"This is a 'must-read' book for anyone concerned about the state of contemporary higher education as it relates to the broader social, economic, and political realities within which it is embedded. Cutting across many of the essays are hard-hitting critiques of persistent problems such as systemic racism and income inequality that are inadequately addressed by, and too often reproduced within, our colleges and universities. Collectively, the essays are engaging, thought-provoking, and worth broad attention, both inside and outside of the academy."—**Dorothy Leland**, *Chancellor Emerita, Professor of Information and Cognitive Sciences, University of California, Merced*

"I came to the United States for its 'superior' colleges and universities and have been working here for the past 20 years, witnessing and sharing the trials and tribulations they face. This book not only helps me better understand their struggles; it also sheds light on how we can unshackle them toward fuller imagination and creativity. The engaging minds of the public intellectuals so compellingly illumined by DeVitis and his collaborators present a promising road map for the renewal and transformation of the American academy."
—*Tian Yu, Professor and Chair, Department of Educational Leadership, Southern Illinois University Edwardsville*

THE FUTURE OF AMERICAN HIGHER EDUCATION

How Today's Public Intellectuals Frame the Debate

Edited by Joseph L. DeVitis

Foreword by Richard Guarasci

STERLING, VIRGINIA

COPYRIGHT © 2022 BY STYLUS PUBLISHING, LLC.

Published by Stylus Publishing, LLC.
22883 Quicksilver Drive
Sterling, Virginia 20166-2019

All rights reserved. No part of this book may be reprinted or reproduced in any form or by any electronic, mechanical, or other means, now known or hereafter invented, including photocopying, recording, and information storage and retrieval, without permission in writing from the publisher.

Library of Congress Cataloging-in-Publication Data
The CIP data for this title is pending.

13-digit ISBN: 978-1-64267-340-1 (cloth)
13-digit ISBN: 978-1-64267-341-8 (paperback)
13-digit ISBN: 978-1-64267-342-5 (library networkable e-edition)
13-digit ISBN: 978-1-64267-343-2 (consumer e-edition)

Printed in the United States of America

All first editions printed on acid-free paper
that meets the American National Standards Institute
Z39-48 Standard.

Bulk Purchases

Quantity discounts are available for use in workshops and for staff development.

Call 1-800-232-0223

First Edition, 2022

In Loving Memory

Linda Irwin-DeVitis (1948–2019)

CONTENTS

FOREWORD   xi
Richard Guarasci

INTRODUCTION   1
Joseph L. DeVitis

PART ONE: ON LIBERAL EDUCATION

1. SETTING THE STAGE
   The Cultural Work of Russell Jacoby   11
   Joseph L. DeVitis and Greg Seals

2. AMY GUTMANN'S ETHICS, DELIBERATIVE DEMOCRACY, AND
   CHALLENGES IN HIGHER EDUCATION   30
   Spoma Jovanovic

3. MICHAEL ROTH AND THE LIBERAL ARTS
   Transforming Society and Selves   41
   Daniel P. Liston

4. SAVING THE UNIVERSITY FROM ITSELF
   Stanley Fish and the Future of the Academy   56
   Dan Sarofian-Butin

5. THE TROUBLE WITH ELITISM
   William Deresiewicz's Critique of Neoliberal Higher Education
   in the United States   68
   J. Todd Ormsbee

PART TWO: ON LABOR AND LEARNING

6. ACCESSING THE ACADEMY
   David Kirp on Higher Education   85
   Kevin Murray

7 MICHAEL BÉRUBÉ AND THE NEOLIBERAL UNIVERSITY
  Humanities, Academic Freedom, and the Crises in
  Higher Education   97
    Deron Boyles

8 THE WAL-MARTIFICATION OF HIGHER EDUCATION
  Marc Bousquet's Critical Examination of Contingent Faculty and
  Academia's Labor Practices   106
    Dan Bauer and Marshall Martin

9 THE NEOLIBERAL TRANSFORMATION OF HIGHER EDUCATION
  Stanley Aronowitz and the Rise of the Corporate Knowledge Factory   119
    John M. Elmore

10 NEWFIELD AS A *NEW FIELD*?
   The Substance and Subjectivities of a Cross-Disciplinary
   Voice in the Public Domain   132
     Cassie L. Barnhardt

11 CONSUMER DEMAND AND THE STATUS-SEEKING SOCIETY
   David F. Labaree on the American Higher Education System   152
     Timothy Glander

PART THREE: ON EDUCATION AND SOCIAL CHANGE

12 #REALCOLLEGE
   The Work and Activism of Sara Goldrick-Rab   171
     Carrie Freie

13 LORI PATTON DAVIS
   Mapping the Landscape of African American Postsecondary Education   183
     Sabrina N. Ross

14 EQUITY AND ADVOCACY
   The Scholarship of Marybeth Gasman   197
     Pietro A. Sasso, Cheron H. Davis, and Adriel A. Hilton

15 AFFIRMATIVE ACTION IN HIGHER EDUCATION
   The Perspectives of Randall Kennedy   214
     William L. Nuckols and Dennis E. Gregory

16 PATRICIA HILL COLLINS'S *ON INTELLECTUAL ACTIVISM*
   The Expansion of Our Field of Perspective 227
   Brooke Judie and Stephanie M. McClure

17 THE FIGHT FOR THE PUBLIC
   Henry Giroux, the Neoliberal Project, and the Limits of Critical Pedagogy 238
   Dana Morrison

   ABOUT THE CONTRIBUTORS 251

   INDEX 253

FOREWORD

In an era when the essential organizing principles and structures of American democracy, its economy, and higher education all face serious interrogations, engaged publics seek useful analyses. Too often the academic disciplines work within the prism of the status quo of their intellectual frameworks and, consequently, their approaches become prisoners of long-standing orthodoxy. In contrast, the historic role of the public intellectual is the pursuit of transparency, critique, and transformative solutions. They seek to challenge well-established assumptions and approaches to public policy, the structures of authority, and the unequal distribution of opportunity. They contest established values that have led to unjust social outcomes. As such, they serve as intellectual outsiders, but they can be important voices in pursuit of substantive changes predicated on greater social inclusion, racial equity, and civic prosperity.

This impressive anthology presents the reader with an introduction to a gallery of public intellectuals through the critical eyes of a wide array of contributing writers from various academic fields. Both the latter and the public intellectuals themselves are responding to the state of American higher education. Importantly, most of them (there are a few public intellectuals in the book who cling closer to the status quo) do not separate colleges and universities from the political, economic, and social currents of American society. They attack the realities of growing social inequality, the intractable presence of institutional racism, and the recurrent reliance on the free market as the arbiter of value. Public intellectuals assess the impact of these social factors on the organization and practices of contemporary American higher education. They force the reader to consider serious challenges to the current arrangement of higher learning and, as such, they ask us to assess the efficacy of their respective perspectives. Do they present the reader with insight or idealism, pathways or dead ends? This compendium provides an abundance of ideas for higher education leaders, policymakers, faculty members, trustees, and governmental officials, as well as social theorists and graduate students interested in higher education careers.

There is much to critique. Higher education is experiencing a serious fiscal crisis. As a result of reduced governmental appropriations, public institutions have suffered dearly. They have sought to increase revenue by raising tuition. This has resulted in increasing financial burdens on students and their families. Student debt is soaring. For public institutions, which hold 80% of total undergraduate enrollment, their state legislatures have displaced the cost of education onto educational consumers instead of taxpayers. States have pressured their public universities to hold tuition steady and find savings through austerity strategies that contain costs, usually at the expense of faculty, staff, and students. Similarly, private colleges and universities have found themselves without adequate net operating income. For the first 20 years of this century, private colleges increased their tuitions at a record pace. Since then, they have experienced a serious consumer backlash to higher tuitions. They have demanded and received dramatic price offsets from spiraling financial aid packages. In short, both sectors are in deep fiscal crises that threaten their stability and, in a growing number, their own financial viability.

At a time when political and economic policies have produced the highest levels of inequality in income and wealth since the Great Depression, higher education's fiscal challenges threaten commitments for greater diversity, equity, and inclusion on college campuses. These consequences provide an abundant canvas for critiques of the mission, goals, and organization of higher education. Enter the public intellectuals and their responses.

What should be the fundamental mission of colleges and universities? Is to serve as a primary instrument for workforce development? Should it be the handmaiden to a flawed and highly unequal capitalist economy? Is it to be, first and foremost, a pathway for personal advancement? Or is it a foundational contributor in preparing knowledgeable and critically engaged citizens for a fully participatory democracy? Is higher education a necessary contributor in building a democratic culture where the arts of democracy are learned and reinforced? Should knowledge, discernment, empathy, and reciprocity be joined to active voice, mediation of differences, coalition building, and civic engagement? All of these questions and more are key questions raised by public intellectuals in higher education.

Public intellectuals do not separate higher education from society, but for some time higher education has defaulted to an insular identity. Its leaders prize institutional autonomy in pursuit of its research interests and organizational priorities. They disdain any direct political responsibilities. This position is now untenable. The forces of racial injustice, economic inequality, identity subordination, environmental and health disparities, dramatic technological advances, and significant demographic changes all demand a fundamental questioning of how higher education is organized and experienced. Most importantly, leaders of higher education must come to grips with the viability of higher learning in an era of nativist and anti-intellectual attacks on the values, institutions, and protocols of American democracy. Without acceptance of logic, reason, and evidence-based argument as the bases for knowledge acquisition and decision-making, colleges and universities have no autonomy to extol and protect. In this sense, these public intellectuals need to be heard if for no other reason than without democracy there is no higher learning as we know it. Higher education, its leaders, faculty, and campus stakeholders need to become partisans in defending democratic governance and democratic culture.

In the end, these public intellectuals are responding to the late C. Wright Mills's call for a higher learning that allows for an explanation of how "public issues and personal troubles" are entangled. They are investigating how the larger institutions function and how they produce a menu of social opportunities that sustain racial and class inequalities. They are questioning whether higher education has become complicit in this sociological map in spite of laudable intentions and a public narrative that higher learning is a pathway to prosperity and well-being. There is much value in reading their work, contesting their logic—and joining them in pursuit of a more just educational outcome.

Richard Guarasci
President Emeritus
Wagner College

INTRODUCTION

Joseph L. DeVitis

In *The Future of American Higher Education*, leading academicians from diverse disciplines (African American studies, American studies, communications, English and rhetoric, higher education, history and philosophy of education, and sociology) present their assessments of various public intellectuals' perspectives on crucial issues in postsecondary education. The book is meant to prod readers to reevaluate policies and practices currently in place. Will U.S. colleges and universities respond haphazardly to societal demands, or will they rise to the occasion with solutions of their own? The text is grounded in diverse discourses that offer grist for thought and action in answering that difficult question. It explores some of the most persistent and pressing problems facing the academy today and in the future. In particular, it will appeal to graduate students in higher education, as well as faculty, staff, and administrators who care for its continuing improvement in these tough times.

Public intellectuals seek to appeal to a wider public, unlike the vast majority of academicians who write as confined specialists. By seeking such an insular professional route—often focused on padding their curriculum vitae—they largely spurn the wider world. Instead, many public intellectuals hope to motivate broader groups of people to think about ideas for social change or conservation through more accessible, generalizing vocabularies. They aim to communicate with both reason and passion; after all, they are engaged in the arena of public issues and action. They need, however, to take care not to flaunt esoteric academic jargon or parade as elitist high priests. More effective public intellectuals reach out to urgent public interests while foregoing any attempt to mystify in language or thought. It should be noted that not all public intellectuals discussed in this text would grant all these suppositions. Many progressive intellectuals would likely accept most of them. But there are several outliers who are either guardians of the status quo—for example, David Labaree's (2019) toleration of the perennial "mess" in U.S. higher education—or a steadfast protector of academic propriety. The latter is exemplified by Stanley Fish's (2008) contention that professors should occupy a "purified academic enterprise" without any intention to affect cultural values (p. 153). Critics might reply that cloistered monks would be hard-pressed to sustain such an immaculate conception.

It is fortunate that at least some public intellectuals are intent on improving education and society more broadly instead of being overly content with professionalization. In a highly polarized body politic energized by special interests, college students themselves are challenged by difficult civic and intellectual tests:

> Students are steered away from asking the broad, disturbing questions that challenge the assumptions of the power elite. . . . The new classes of expert professionals have been trained to focus on narrow, specialized knowledge independent of social ideas or conceptions of the common good. (Donoghue, 2008, pp. 110–111)

Higher education faces innumerable questions in these dangerous days. Today's public intellectuals do not, of course, have all the answers. They do, however, care deeply about the issues surrounding higher education and society. They deserve to be heard as we wrestle with the knotty uncertainties besetting our unsettled colleges and universities. When all is said and done, I leave it to readers to foster a robust dialogue—and action—on the competing arguments. Then I hope they will assess which ones are more, or less, attractive for their own efforts to make universities better. (This volume includes only authors who have written recently and extensively on American higher education.)

Part One: On Liberal Education

Veritas liberabit vos ("Truth shall set you free") is the motto of a number of colleges, including my alma mater, Johns Hopkins University. As applied to higher education, I would modify that biblical saying by arguing that it is the *search* for truth that is most significant. Why? The journey for truth can afford robust capacity for questioning, critical analysis, comfort with ambiguity, empathic understanding, and sociocultural and political engagement. But once we believe we have discovered Truth, the prospect of rigidity to that authority can take hold. If it does, we may forego any movement toward mindfulness and openness and cling to dogmatism and fanaticism (Hoffer, 1951). Our society is already too riddled by the latter. Instead, genuine liberal education seeks to prepare students by a process of reflective development in which they are actively involved in considered discourse and decision-making. Philosopher William Hare (2002) put it well: "Do not pretend to know more than you do or assume that what you think is beyond challenge" (p. 123).

For most of human history, liberal education has been a monopoly of the privileged—the segregated gift of those who held power, wealth, and status. In medieval times, the interests of the Church provided the dominant rationale for the existence of universities; thus, its curricular offerings were painted with a large religious brush. In colonial America, preparation for the ministry sent a small slice of affluent male youths to places such as Harvard and Yale. In the 19th century, many U.S. college presidents, particularly at liberal arts schools, taught a capstone seminar in moral philosophy. (Today one might wonder whether university leaders would instead conduct classes in public relations.) We need to ask deeper questions to enliven liberal education. At its best, liberal education can prepare students for self-actualization as they wade through a largely superficial culture. It can help create a more discerning citizenry that distinguishes between fictitious and reasoned argumentation. And it *must* embrace ethical imperatives even as we inhabit twisted landscapes of artifice and surveillance.

The various public intellectuals discussed in Part One treat liberal education in both theoretical and practical ways. Russell Jacoby laments how American culture and its universities have been dangerously prone to social amnesia, thus losing history's memory and recapitulating grievous mistakes. Amy Gutmann provides a more ethical and political critique on the importance of access to liberal education for *all* social classes. Especially in a posttruth climate, she urges us to build a stronger democracy through critical thinking. Michael Roth invokes progressive and pragmatic arguments for the worth of liberal education in both the cognitive and affective realms, with a particular focus on enlarging human connectedness as we face an even wider technological future. Stanley Fish hopes to "save the university" by arguing that faculty should stick to their own disciplinary "interpretive communities" and not move into the arena of social, political, or economic justice. His is a seldom heard voice amid the changing academic and sociocultural landscapes portrayed in Part One. William Deresiewicz berates the sheep-like behavior of parents and students who look at liberal education as purely instrumental—as a proving ground for "hoop-jumping," making professional connections, and striving toward elitist social positions. The next section of the book illustrates overlapping elements in Parts One and Two.

Part Two: Learning and Labor

"Learning and Labor" is the motto of the University of Illinois, where I did my doctoral work. As a result of the federal Morrill Act of 1862, it is one of 48 original land-grant colleges. Offering preparation in agricultural and mechanical arts, they aimed to serve the needs of a fast-growing population—but solely for White citizens. The second Morrill Act (in 1890) established 19 predominantly African American colleges and 30 American Indian institutions. However, state matching funds for the latter fell far below those for the initial legislation. Despite those inequities, federal and state governments did create a ray of hope for some social mobility.

In the 20th century, that public tradition grew during the Great Depression. After World War II, the impetus for college attendance continued as the federal G.I. Bill took hold. The bill largely benefited White veterans; local and state Jim Crow laws severely limited its use for African Americans. Veterans made careers and bought homes, though gross inequities persisted: White citizens received 98% of FHA-insured loans through the 1950s (Brown, 2021). Lyndon Johnson's "Great Society" program passed the Higher Education Act (in 1965), with new federal grants and tuition waivers for lower-income students. "Equal opportunity" became a popular slogan, but not, of course, a full reality. Yet, as we debate the concept of "free tuition" today, we should note that it is not a fantastical notion at all. The University of California began such a policy in 1868; it was challenged by Governor Ronald Reagan in the mid-1960s and closed down several years later. For many decades the University of Florida maintained a "free" system, abandoning it in 1969. And the City University of New York (CUNY) had a "free" plan from 1961 to 1976. The 1970s and 1980s, particularly the Reagan administration, brought marked setbacks to the themes of access and equity. They shed doubt on the worth of college education and so-called "free rides." Once a promising policy, affirmative action became less a priority, as did federal aid for education in general.

Ironically, institutions of higher learning are running a race against the American Dream: "The tragedy is that while public policies in the past helped mitigate inequality and open the doors to college to more Americans, today they themselves pay a crucial role in segmenting our society" (Mettler, 2014, p. 4). John Covaleskie (2016) also points to the dilemmas facing those who are not wealthy or powerful:

> It is increasingly becoming a false narrative that upholds a system that creates and increasingly protects great inequality . . . while blaming the inequality on its victims, not its perpetrators or beneficiaries. In an economy in which there is a shortage of good jobs and a large percentage of young people going to college, a college education only decreasingly transmits economic opportunity, even while it becomes more expensive. Meanwhile, the benefits of college attendance accrue to graduates of the more elite schools, whose students develop networks more important than any body of knowledge, intellectual skills, or critical acumen. (p. 57)

As several contributors to this text argue, the major culprit in the drastic decline in support for public higher education can be found in the notion of neoliberalism. Indeed, every president since Reagan has been content to carry heavy neoliberal baggage. Given its significance in the scheme of things, David Harvey (2005) offers a succinct picture of it:

> Neoliberalism is . . . a theory of political economic practices that proposes that human well-being can best be advanced by liberating individual entrepreneurial freedoms and skills with an institutional framework characterized by strong property rights, free markets, and free trade. (pp. 18–19)

The upshot of neoliberal policies has been fourfold in public higher education: massive institutional budget cuts, a decades-old pattern of striking decreases in public spending, astounding hikes in tuition, and oppressive student debt (Folbre, 2010).

Part Two makes clear that neoliberalism is still powerful in higher education. Will the public academy move beyond rigid and harmful corporatist priorities and instead foster a climate more beneficial to students, staff, and faculty—especially contingent instructors who are so exploited? How will state universities, other than elite flagship campuses, withstand the economic shocks to their systems, which had been worn down even before the pandemic? Will more wealthy colleges dampen preferential legacy admissions and devote more financial resources to underrepresented students? How do they ensure more equitable access and mentoring to students of color and *all* those with less material and social capital? Can public higher education substantially educate for the elusive common civic good?

The competing interests of postsecondary education and the middle- and lower-income classes form the focus of Part Two. David Kirp bemoans campus leaders who are lax about access, retention, equity, diversity, and other democratic aspirations. According to him, they have too often given way to market mandates and crass commercialization. Michael Bérubé claims that corporate interests, so shielded by neoliberal ideology, have shunted the humanities to the sidelines. He further contends that academic freedom itself is under assault in the process: Efficiency models and hiring practices (so many adjuncts working in grossly underpaid, unprotected conditions) demean both labor and academe. Marc Bousquet sharply criticizes neoliberal policies and exposes unreasonable labor practices as affronts to academic freedom, democratic learning arrangements, research, and faculty governance. He strongly supports the formation of a united, activist faculty that can fight for both tenure- and nontenure-track scholar-teachers. Stanley Aronowitz worries about the corporatization of the academy and the diminution of higher learning in its curriculum and instruction. He views oligarchical and neoliberal power as the engine of excessive privatization, massive tuition increases, exploitation of contingent faculty, and market economies that threaten the public good. Christopher Newfield sees himself as a guardian of working-class families who face myriad college challenges. He seeks to widen societal resources among that class, aiming for a more equitable form of public higher education via an innovation economy that better serves them. Lastly, historian David F. Labaree argues that the American system of higher education has always been "a perfect mess" that allows elitist, consumerist, and populist constituencies to work out pragmatic solutions to its problems. An outlier in this book, he is basically satisfied with colleges and universities as they are.

Part Three: On Education and Social Change

American higher education has never been insulated from the wider sweep of sociocultural, political, and economic currents in the nation's life and times. The latter are always present, and they generate ideological and policy pressures in every epoch. Indeed, education, at any level, is profoundly political. Hit full force with marketing and sloganeering, the public is forced to entertain such notions as "excellence" and "world class," no matter the actuality of the educational institution in question. Thus, it is incumbent on us to rise above deceptive persuasion, sift through the glittering debris, and think critically about what is real and what is manufactured about the academy in national magazines, commercial college guidebooks, and campus viewbooks. Though public intellectuals also need to be closely scrutinized, they can be helpful in that process of discernment.

Colleges and universities have tended to be both transmitters of inherited cultural knowledge and reluctant transformers for educational and social change. They can often be seen in a time warp of cultural lag, but those times may be changing. However, make no mistake; change does not come easily.

The organization of higher education over time has embedded power asymmetries that

> impede socially just and equitable processes and outcomes. To maintain their profit share and attract financial resources, campuses have pursued prestige through research and athletics, oftentimes de-emphasizing teaching and learning and undergraduate education. (Kezar & Posselt, 2019, p. 3)

Critical theorists, in particular, have urged academicians who are willing and able to be "transformative intellectuals" who "speak out and engage" in social change (Giroux, 2007, p. 206), and not allow universities to be content to "mirror the rest of society" (Aronowitz, 2001, p. 11). Critical race theory (CRT) has provided more power as a parallel movement. They remind us, once again, of C. Wright Mills's (1959) earlier evocation of "the awareness of the relationship between personal experience and the wider society" (pp. 5, 7). And how do we right the university to ensure a better, more just world? We turn to such currents of thought and action in Part Three.

Sara Goldrick-Rab presents detailed analysis of the problems of accessibility and affordability in American higher education and how our society can find solutions for those facing financial struggle. She includes an exploration of their hardships in everyday life, including with food and housing. Lori Patton Davis establishes a large imprint on scholarship related to African Americans, including power relations, leadership, gender and identity, and diversity on campus. She creates a storytelling technique that livens her intersectional inquiry. Marybeth Gasman is a pioneer in the study of historically Black colleges and universities (HBCUs) and other minority-serving institutions (MSIs). She has been a leading mentor of underrepresented students, founding centers to facilitate their development as leaders and scholars for HBCUs and MSIs. Randall Kennedy, a prominent law professor, presents a nuanced, well-reasoned defense of affirmative action while specifically addressing its critics' claims. Abjuring arguments for meritocracy, he also deals sensitively with the stigma attached to that federal policy. Patricia Hill Collins, a noted sociologist, employs feminist theory, CRT, and the potent concept of intersectionality to shed significant light on patterns of power and structural racism. She shows how they undermine schools and society as she seeks to create more genuine human sensibilities. Henry Giroux, a founding theorist of critical pedagogy, has impacted educational thought for a half century. His intellectual interests in higher education are broad-ranging, including such topics as power elites, culture and youth studies, and a biting critique of capitalism and neoliberalism as dangerous threats to the academy, civil liberties, and democracy itself.

For most Americans, the Trump years were among the worst of times. Now, it is prime time, in John Lewis's words, for more "good trouble."

References

Aronowitz, S. (2001). *The knowledge factory: Dismantling the corporate university and creating true higher learning.* Beacon Press.

Brown, D. A. (2021). *The whiteness of wealth: How the tax system impoverishes black Americans—and how we can fix it.* Crown.

Covaleskie, J. F. (2016). Higher education: Private good? Public good? In J. L. DeVitis & P. A. Sasso (Eds.), *Higher education and society* (pp. 42–59). Peter Lang.

Donoghue, F. (2008). *The last professors: The corporate university and the fate of the humanities.* Fordham University Press.

Fish, S. (2008). *Save the world on your own time.* Oxford University Press.

Folbre, N. (2010). *Saving State U: Fixing higher education.* The New Press.

Giroux, H. A. (2007). *The university in chains: Confronting the military-industrial-academic complex.* Paradigm.

Hare, W. (2002). Teaching and the attitude of open-mindedness. *Journal of Educational Administration and Foundations, 16*(2), 103–124.

Harvey, D. (2005). *A brief history of neoliberalism.* Oxford University Press.

Hoffer, E. (1951). *The true believer.* Harper.

Kegan, A., & Posselt, J. (2019). Introduction: Call to justice and equitable administrative practice. In A. Kegan & J. Posselt (Eds.), *Higher education for social justice and equity: Critical perspectives* (pp. 1–18). Routledge.

Labaree, D. F. (2019). *A perfect mess: The unlikely ascendancy of American higher education.* University of Chicago Press.

Mettler, S. (2014). *Degrees of inequality: How the politics of higher education sabotaged the American dream.* Basic Books.

Mills, C. W. (1959). *The sociological imagination.* Oxford University Press.

PART ONE

ON LIBERAL EDUCATION

I

SETTING THE STAGE

The Cultural Work of Russell Jacoby

Joseph L. DeVitis and Greg Seals

In *The Last Intellectuals: American Culture in the Age of Academe*, Russell Jacoby (1987/2000) popularized the term *public intellectual* to characterize independent scholars and university professors who write broadly and passionately about the urgency to speak out on larger public interests. A huge irony emerges as we set the stage for this chapter. When he published his pioneering polemic in 1987, Jacoby was an independent practitioner. In 2009, he became the Moishe Gonzales folding chair of critical theory at UCLA. Throughout his career Jacoby has long been acknowledged as among the fiercest critics of academic culture. His more recent books attempt to show how identity politics puts limits on individuality and instead fosters groupthink—see *On Diversity: The Eclipse of the Individual in a Global Era* (Jacoby, 2020); how cultural illiteracy, political correctness, and commercialization have deflected attention from overriding societal issues—see *Dogmatic Wisdom* (1995); and how thinkers on the left have seemingly lost their "utopian spirit"—see *The End of Utopia: Politics and Culture in an Age of Apathy* (1999).

Indeed, these factors have led many academicians to obviate their potential role as public intellectuals. That trend has had marked consequences for the academy. The authors will treat each book by Jacoby that relates to higher education in separate pieces. We will first explore Jacoby's *The Last Intellectuals*. Though he speaks mainly of faculty issues, his biting critique has implications for students and administrators as well; unfortunately, Jacoby himself does not make adequate connections to undergraduates in his writing. This chapter will examine how his thought permits further understanding of certain aspects of higher education while treating some omissions and gaps in it. We will also point out important lessons for the theory and practice of higher learning that Jacoby does not lay out in granular terms. Yet the kernel of Jacoby's book merits close attention for all those who care deeply about the present and future of America's colleges and universities.

The Last Intellectuals' Relevant Focus: Obsessive Professionalization and Specialization

This section of the chapter spotlights those aspects of *The Last Intellectuals* that are most relevant to Jacoby's contentions about present-day higher education in America. Originally published in 1987, the book deals with those public intellectuals whom Jacoby selects from the period of the late 1940s to the 1980s. To cover its whole scope would require a separate chapter in itself. The theme of professionalization and specialization seems most central to our interest in his seminal writing. Jacoby's chief argument against extreme professionalization is that it "leads to privatization . . . , a withdrawal of intellectual energy from a larger domain to a narrower discipline" and away from cultural and public interest (Jacoby, 1987/2000, p. 147). New faculty members, gearing up for tenure and promotion, spend much of their time beefing up their vitae by publishing very specific work (mostly gleaned from their dissertations), presenting at conferences, networking in various professional associations, and appealing to those upholding the proper paradigm within their academic discipline in a transactional manner:

> The lessons for the striving professor are clear: cast a wide net, establish as many mutual relations as possible, do not isolate yourself from the mainstream. It pays not simply to footnote but to design research to mesh smoothly with the contribution of others; they refer to you as you refer to them. Everyone prospers from the saccharine scholarship. (Jacoby, 1987/2000, p. 146)

Such professional activity can undermine critical thinking and creativity, produce endless repetition throughout one's career, and lead to a deadening attitude rather than mindfulness. For example, it is not unusual for a professor to stay with the subject of her dissertation over the decades. In many cases, that practice might actually help her advancement (she will become known as an "expert" in her narrow specialty with a distinct corpus of work and a coherent scholarly agenda). According to Jacoby, she would also be skirting any meaningfulness to the society writ large. That prospect could well be, in part, why academic knowledge is often seen as so disembodied, so alien to a wider public. Indeed, the more specialized the professor's topic and language (scholarly jargon can be oppressive), the greater the chances that only a few dozen other specialists might actually read it with any care. Available mainly as technical expertise, its reach to a wider public is highly improbable. (Of course, public intellectuals can also be guilty of arcane communication and illogical use of thought.) But it is a truism that most professors speak principally to their sisters and brethren—and the articles submitted and papers presented can spiral into ever-narrowing webs of specificity and even lesser audience attention.

It is noteworthy that the two intellectual figures perhaps most prominent in his analysis of professionalization and specialization are John Dewey and C. Wright Mills. (They stand out among the heroes in *The Last Intellectuals*.) Mills's dissertation was actually devoted to the professionalization of philosophy. His study found that philosophers writing in professional journals spent much more time talking to each other rather than disseminating their ideas in the larger, more public, media (Jacoby, 1987/2000). Mills also saw that substantive philosophy was on a ghostly decline in terms of its relevance to society.

In general, Jacoby contends that independent thought has been in steep decline. He notes that post-Deweyan philosopher Richard Rorty would seek to revivify creative and critical thinking in the 1980s. Rorty peppered his arguments with a blend of pragmatism and literary allusions instead of sterile technical mechanics, as was the general method of analytic philosophers. One of Rorty's best-known students, Michael Bérubé, is included in the present volume. Bérubé wrote the introduction to Rorty's *Philosophy as Poetry* (2016). Yet higher learning has not always been so hospitable to such broadly open thought.

Jacoby (1987/2000) lauds Mills for his public advocacy of "the politics of truth" and for being a "moral conscience of his society" (pp. 117–118). He was a professor, a radical sociologist, and at his heart, a public intellectual. For Mills, that status provided his favored epitaph. He would not join the great majority of his colleagues who neglected their social responsibility by taking a safer, more aloof, professional stance. Likewise, Jacoby (1987/2000) commends Stanley Aronowitz, another theorist who appears in our text, for bringing his background as a union organizer and antipoverty worker to the academic scene—and into the public arena. In another twist of events, Aronowitz eventually became a distinguished professor at the Graduate Center of the City University of New York. His long-standing labor movement roots nourished his scholarship. Along with Dewey and Mills, Noam Chomsky also receives high marks in Jacoby's universe of public intellectuals. Jacoby refers to him as "the most energetic critic of intellectuals." Indeed, Chomsky's anarchist tendencies draw explicit plaudits from Jacoby (2000): "They distrust large institutions, the state, the university, and its functionaries. They are less vulnerable to the corruptions of title and salary because their resistance is moral, almost instinctual" (pp. 96–97).

Some Gaps and Omissions

Despite Jacoby's piercing critique, he surprisingly fails to consider a number of significant issues that would inevitably seem to flow from his analysis. Though he deals heavily with the place of faculty members in academe, he largely neglects students, except for a few references to Students for a Democratic Society (SDS), the Student Non-Violent Coordinating Committee (SNCC), and the Student Peace Union (SPU) during the stormy years of the 1960s when anti-Vietnam and civil rights protest were at their height. That is to say, the daily life of students, particularly undergraduates, is basically left untouched. (As a general rule, it is still not unusual for this sad circumstance to be played out on many campuses, particularly those labeled as "research" institutions.) One wonders why Jacoby's emphasis on independence and critical thinking does not provide him grist for the mill in a more direct discussion of liberal education. Ironically, he pays little explicit attention to the latter. It is disappointing that he does not go further because the implications of his thought would be welcome and likely quite enlightening. (Some of his work is applicable to graduate students, but only in terms of how their professors relate to them.)

In addition, for all his focus on the cultural and sociopolitical aspects of American life, Jacoby leaves the economic realm in a flattened state. He does not delve into some obviously crucial factors that influenced higher education as he was writing his book. Neither economic growth nor constriction is given much daylight in his treatise. Commercialization, status-seeking, consumerism, credentialing, and the neoliberal movement had begun to rear their heads during the Reagan years. Jacoby (1987/2000) *does* mention how the launching of Sputnik in 1957 provided colleges and universities monetary allotments that permitted expansions in their student bodies, hiring practices, and physical plants.

Yet he does not note that higher education was becoming more privatized by the mid- to late 1980s. Given his suspicion of privatization as an intellectual and practical matter, it is curious that he fails to allude to how it started to affect colleges and universities, especially in the public sector. Shrinking budgets were already pushing state institutions to tighten their priorities. Neoliberal policies were giving clear signals that public campuses could soon be seen as "state-aided" or even "state-located" instead of state-supported.

Nor does Jacoby show how increasing commercialization, consumerism, and marketing were influencing colleges, particularly those not known as "elite," into displays of glitzy overkill by branding their institutions in often inauthentic ways—for example, via glamorous viewbooks. It seemed that every college wanted to appear "distinctive," when only a thin minority actually were.

And, once again, Jacoby had largely forgotten undergraduates. With a nudge from their parents, students were coaxed to play the game of status-seeking and credentialing. College became imperative to the ethos of success. Job aspirations were making the life of the mind a tertiary concern, and liberal education was becoming prone to vocational interventions. These are all considerations that lurk between the lines of Jacoby's writing, but they are never brought to light—except in the case of faculty members. Not surprisingly, his focus on status-seeking is most germane to how professors can climb the ladder of their supposed success—and Jacoby (1987/2000) *does* make an interesting point: "In plain English, . . . studies suggest that where one went to school and whom one knows, not what one does, are critical. Not quality of work but social relations permeate academic success" (p. 145).

Though he does not treat everyday accounts of how administrators work, Jacoby takes a stand on several cases of blatant executive overreach: McCarthyism of the 1950s and the academic "lynching" of Henry Giroux (another prominent intellectual covered in this text) at Boston University in the early 1980s. As Jacoby reminds us, American universities set the stage for the weeding out of countless leftist professors. Indeed, he lays the academy's silencing methods at the altar of professionalization, which he claims "served as a refuge" that "entailed a privatization that eviscerates academic freedom." In Giroux's case, his authoritarian president, John Silber, appointed Nathan Glazer, a neoconservative sociologist at Harvard, to an ad hoc committee that reviewed Giroux's dossier—for a tenured position in Boston University's School of Education, *not* in its College of Arts and Sciences! Personal and ideological animosity by Silber and Glazer played the major role in discharging a young assistant professor with a potent academic record—but one which was both "critical" and "dissenting" from the more conventional mindsets of both his henchmen (Jacoby, 1987/2000, pp. 136–137).

Finally, Jacoby pays scant attention to public intellectuals from underrepresented groups in the first edition of *The Last Intellectuals*. In the introduction to the second edition, he mentions Henry Louis Gates, Gerald Early, Adolph Reed, Jr., Randall Kennedy, and Cornel West, but gives them only a glancing nod. In passing, Jacoby both compliments and jabs at them:

These are smart, hard-hitting and often graceful writers who weigh into public problems of race, sports, politics, law, and culture. They have been both acclaimed as successors to the New York intellectuals and criticized as publicity hounds who ignore earlier black intellectuals such as W. E. B. Dubois and C. R. James. In no way did my book anticipate their appearance. . . . Yet it seems to me that the new black intellectuals demonstrate that a literate, hungry, public still exists. What is lacking is the will and ability to address it. (Jacoby, 1987/2000, pp. xix–xx)

Finally, Jacoby allows relatively lean space to women as public intellectuals. Although he cites a number of them, he provides substantial coverage to only June Jacobs, acclaimed author of *The Death and Life of Great American Cities* (Random House, 1961) and Mary McCarthy, prominent novelist who wrote *The Group* (New American Library, 1963) who was also an antiwar activist. Intellectuals with other racial, ethnic, and gender identities are hard to find in Jacoby's seminal work. Many years later, Jacoby (2020) would focus on the issue of diversity, as this chapter will discuss.

Dogmatic Wisdom—Relevant Focus: Illiberality in Academy and Society

In *Dogmatic Wisdom: How the Culture Wars Divert Education and Distract America*, Jacoby (Doubleday, 1995) spins a tale of decline, a modernist lament. America is losing its love of education. Education is losing its sense of self. And selves are becoming concretized and shattered as mounting pressures from an intensely illiberal orientation to social life fragment and fracture civil society into a loose but contentious consumerist confederacy of cultural groups and lifestyle choices. Often these groups are narrowly conceived, sometimes doxastically authoritarian, and seldom constitutive of distinct structures of work, living, and beliefs. Although Jacoby never explicitly suggests a way out of the dire straits he describes, he does suggest criteria of adequacy for development of a general response to issues presented to education and society by social facts found at the root of the evil of illiberalism.

A society becomes illiberal when it becomes difficult to find activities considered valuable in themselves. Intrinsically valued activities become harder to find as everything, even higher education, and everyone, even students, reduce culturally to elements in a free market populated by free consumers. An education becomes illiberal to the extent invasion of market-valued vocational and (pre)professional studies drive out/diminish interest in traditional liberal arts. The 'old education,' Jacoby (1995) remarks, "aimed at 'wisdom,' the new education at power and cash" (p. 7). At a loss to reconstruct a common curriculum from nontraditional sources, colleges and universities struggle with issues of identity as college-wide curriculum collapses "under the weight of professional and practical studies" (p. 6). Warped by this burden higher education takes the shape of "the departmentalized university, offering innumerable items to student shoppers" (p. 94). Department names become trademarks that declare: "Stop. Do Not Enter. We are scientists, you need credits, degrees, and training to judge our work. It also means: We use a special vocabulary" (p. 167). Linguistic compartmentalization among departments leads from argot to general principles, a process Jacoby names "the fetish of theory" (p. 179), a cottage industry of idea generation that finds any idea a theory, assumes all theories are the same, and all are good. The result is virtually every academician speaking in generalities few others, even other academicians, acknowledge as valid. The Ivory Tower devolves into a "Tower of Babble [sic]" as academic infighting reinforces disciplinary conformity.

Although Jacoby provides no list of courses, an education becomes liberal as it provides students opportunity, time, and wherewithal to study, think, and evaluate ideas. Jacoby (1995) derides metalinguistic/metatheoretical scholarship as mistaking names for things and set obscurantism and contradiction as strict limits on creating new academic fields. However, he applauds academic work "to establish the insufficiency of everyday thinking and language" (p. 169); insists, "Education must explode racial and ethnic approaches, not simply cultivate them" (p. 149); and remains confident "educational conflicts would ebb if the instructional infrastructure were solid and secure" (p. 196). That infrastructure is weak when students engage in classes as recipients of information from instructors. Vigor returns to classrooms when students engage intellectually with classmates, professors, and their studies. On Jacoby's stated assumption that "education and society reflect each other" (p. xii), society becomes more liberal as it promotes among its populace habits of thinking, studying, and evaluating. A consumerist market culture leaves little time, except for the wealthy, to indulge/inculcate any liberal practices. Both conservatives, who look to a beloved past as guide to a better future, and liberals, who look to a better future transcendent of what has gone before, miss this point. Both "ignore the ingression of the market that makes a mockery of a return or an advance; both avoid the commercialism that constructs a liberal education, both sidestep the invidious elitism that poisons civil life" (p. 194).

Cultural supports other than consumerism bolster illiberal society/illiberal education, too. Jacoby (1995) observes, "An instrumental ethos is nourished not only by market forces but also by parallel pressures of specialization and professionalism" (p. 17). Forces of specialization/professionalization find comeuppance in industrial society, however: "The American cultures partake of a larger American industrial society; they carry its signature in their souls and wallets. Even when locked outside the main event, they bear its marks and scars, and only want to be admitted" (p. 157). Jacoby emphasizes this point, asserting, "This is not a moral judgment, but a statement about the texture of American life" (p. 158).

Consideration of social supports for illiberalism seems to make Jacoby despair. At the societal level, Jacoby (1995) keens, "The simpler truths and plainer realities are gone forever, dispatched by shifts in jobs, technologies, and scholarship" (p. 91). At the educational level he complains that "liberal education has vanished. Yet there is no going back" (p. 94). However, Jacoby also allows "complexity is not another word for fate" (p. 193), and holds open hope for a resurgence of liberal tendencies in society/education. Just because simple truths/plain realities are no longer available is no reason to give up on reality/truth altogether. Jacoby does not look around for ways out of illiberalism and into liberalism, but his analysis pioneers a path worth exploring.

Error in Jacoby's Analysis

Jacoby's analysis rests on the same error he finds in those he criticizes—"the 'law' of displacement: secondary issues displace primary ones" (Jacoby, 1995, p. xii). Markets are not social bedrock. Underneath markets, as the source of specialization and professionalization, is the Durkheimian (1893/1985) social fact of organic solidarity. In division of labor, society is held together by processes of interdependence among disparate elements rather than resemblances among members of society—what Durkheim calls *mechanical solidarity*. Although it may be granted ours is a society irrevocably exhibiting organic solidarity, markets are but one possible response to this social fact. As Jacoby points out, markets are an illiberal response to organic solidarity, a response progressively characterized by chronically unhealthful consumer competition and increasingly insidious culture wars. Less hierarchical, more horizontal, more liberal responses are possible. Jacoby does not find the academy inevitably succumbing to market forces. He catches the academy dealing badly with organic solidarity internal and external to higher education.

The sign higher education is handling internal organic solidarity badly is the inability of colleges to agree upon a common curriculum. Campuses become a microcosm of larger society, waging academic culture wars in competition for students, recognition, and funding. Better to take a horizontal approach to the issue of common curriculum to minimize hostile contact between scholars in different fields and optimize collegial contact among researchers in disparate areas. Jacoby's reconceptualization of liberal education as education involving students in studying, thinking, and evaluating ideas creates conceptual space to reconstruct common curriculum horizontally. On horizontal reconstruction of common curriculum, methodology is what students come to know in general education classes. Philosophical justification for horizontal reconstruction of common curriculum comes from pragmatists, Peirce (1877/1934) and Dewey (1938/1986), who sought to "level" logic. Pierce considered general concepts guiding principles of inference. Guiding principles of inference can be arranged in terms of breadth of scope in guiding all inquiries or only some. The arrangement need not be hierarchical. All that need be meant is what is said: Some principles must be employed in all inquiries, some in very many, some in few, and so on. Dewey hypothesized that *logic* and *methodology* are virtually synonyms. Methodologies are applications of logic and define the field of logic as they are successfully applied. These two innovations in logical theory permit redescription of academic areas in terms of methodologies rather than content. Common curriculum can be constructed around guiding principles of inquiry with which colleges wish their students to think.

Redescribing inquiries in terms of methodologies opens up shareable space in the common curriculum. Widely divergent subject matter departments that share overlapping methodologies can share the common curriculum in the sense of taking turns teaching in it or teaching in it together. Methodological culture wars are a possibility, but a common curriculum of methods of inquiry defeats subject matter parochialism by making departmental boundaries as permeable as possible via shared approaches to studies. When disputes cannot be settled at departmental levels, they may be adjudicated at classroom levels. Academic disputes incorporated into individual classes provide students opportunity to experience in class the three characteristics of Jacoby's liberal education: thinking, studying, and evaluating ideas. All we must agree upon to make this happen is that college is the place to learn the "logics" of things.

In organic solidarity students need to experience varied ranges of "logics" of cultural difference inside and outside the academy. Common curriculum with a methods spin introduces academic cosmopolitanism into general education. Courses in critical study of contemporary cultural life, how to navigate/negotiate it, add a second sense of cosmopolitanism to college study, and contribute liberality to education by engaging students in thinking, studying, and evaluating ideas. As Jacoby (1995) says, "Expanded contacts lead to a reconsideration of habits and customs" (p. 127). A cosmopolitan approach to general studies offers nondogmatic wisdom of wide knowledge/flexible knowhow.

Methodologically rendered, common curriculum becomes contentless, but that may help reconcile thinkers as divided on common curriculum as the elder and the early Jacoby. In 1995's *Dogmatic Wisdom*, Professor Jacoby mourns the loss of a common course of collegiate study. In 1964, as a first-quarter undergraduate at the University of Chicago, a young Russell Jacoby (1964) excoriated the university's Great Books common curriculum in an opinion piece published in the student-run *Chicago Maroon*, entitled "General Education Is Antistudent and Antiknowledge." The methods approach to common curriculum provides an intellectually common course of study without taking recourse to endorsement of specific subject matter knowledge.

Similar to common curriculum, organic solidarity may be worked out in society in horizontal rather than hierarchical ways. Sharing resources, rather than selling/stealing them, is an underutilized approach to organic solidarity. Things like air, land, and water are probably high on most folks' list of things better shared than marketed. Most may agree it's good to preserve necessities for life in ways that make them worth sharing. Sharing remains a realizable alternative to markets as a social response to organic solidarity. But to the extent we look first to marketization when it comes to things we want or need, sharing seems an unlikely countercultural realization in everyday life. Jacoby (1995) asks, "What sort of 'a vital left counterculture' prospers in a society without a left or a counterculture?" (p. 224, n. 41). Both a left and a counterculture may be found following a "sharing" line of thought through another Jacoby cautionary tale, *The End of Utopia* (1999).

The End of Utopia—Relevant Focus: Jacoby's Optimism

Despite the plainly pessimistic claim animating the book—"A utopian spirit—a sense that the future could transcend the present—has vanished" (Jacoby, 1999, p. xi), Jacoby sees *The End of Utopia* as a "defense of the visionary impulse" (p. xiii). He finds hope in the fact that "history outwits even its most diligent students" (p. 181) and may still afford an unforeseen utopian surprise. Jacoby sketches in outline the form a utopian surprise may take. Hidden within critique of deradicalized thought on the political left, emergence of a cultural pluralism masking economic monoculturalism, anesthetization of intellectual effort rendering the intelligentsia effete in capacity to lead beyond tribalistic status quo, and moral conversion of the world to madness for minutiae; there is perceptible the profile of a utopian world awaiting development of plans composing a detailed portrait of utopian practice.

Jacoby (1999) states the sense of *utopia* central to his discussion: "I am using *utopian* in its widest, and least threatening, meaning: a belief that the future could fundamentally surpass the present" (pp. xi–xii). Denotation of *utopia* carries connotations; and Jacoby hints at these in comments about utopia. In Jacoby's utopia "history contains possibilities of freedom and pleasure hardly tapped" (p. xii). The road to utopia is clearly marked for those with "an ability, perhaps a willingness, to use expansive concepts to see reality and its possibilities" (p. 105). The journey toward utopia sees development of increasingly "more thoughtful and graceful culture" (p. 70), characterized by increasingly "widespread affluence and freedom" (p. 159). Jacoby's utopia, relative to present-day society, is fundamentally (a) more expansive/imaginative in thinking, (b) more thoughtful in planning actions/ more graceful in carrying them out, and (c) more focused on widespread affluence, freedom, and pleasure. Taking these three as criteria to qualify as utopian society, Jacoby's criticism of leftist politics, pluralistic multiculturalism, and aesthetic nativism as antiutopian comes down to complaint that each violates a qualifying criterion for utopianism.

Leftist politics fails the first criterion by unnecessarily narrowing its scope of thinking. The left loses its backbone/vision via conversion to belief in markets as fundamental/dominant social institutions. Once inside the market mindset, liberals are reduced to suggesting tweaks to the system, rather than demanding the system be surpassed. As Jacoby (1999) observes, "The defeat of radicalism bleeds liberalism of its vitality. . . . The demise of communism eviscerates radicalism and enfeebles liberalism" (p. 8). Pluralistic multiculturalism fails Jacoby's second criterion. Multiculturalism played out as attempts to get representation/power for one's preferred group taps thoughtlessly into the ideology of the market. Cultures/lifestyles become market niches when "pluralism, the ideology of the market and the individual, becomes the bedrock principle of liberals and leftists" (p. 47). Behind a façade of cultural diversity lurks monoculturalism of markets: "After the rhetoric is stripped away, the call for power and its decayed psychological form, empowerment, suggests a converging politics, monoculturalism. Everyone wants a bigger piece of the same action" (p. 62). Jacoby argues, "Multiculturalism is not the opposite of assimilation, but its product" (p. 49), denying truth to the first premise of arguments endorsing cultural pluralism: "that numerous distinct 'cultures' constitute American society" (p. 47). Without economic pluralism, "cultural pluralism" fails meaningfully to signify. Aesthetic nativism fails Jacoby's third criterion and his first, too. Uncritical aesthetic appreciation of particular cultures *sans* universal concepts to critique them fails Jacoby's first criterion for bold thinking. Jacoby cautions,

> Over time the suspicion of universals takes its revenge. Despite a rhetoric of subversion, it leads intellectuals down the path of acquiescence. Without an emphatic idea of freedom and happiness, a better society can scarcely be envisioned, utopia withers. Those who celebrate difference and discredit universals cannot think beyond the limited possibilities tossed up by history. (pp. 136–137)

Worse, "Once writers and scholars isolate local conditions from universal categories, they lose the ability to evaluate them. They become cheerleaders, nativists, chauvinists" (p. 149). Creation of cultural chauvinism flies in the face of Jacoby's third criterion. Rather than lead toward shared affluence, freedom, and pleasure, "a particularism that scorns universals inevitably ends by celebrating blood and race" (p. 150).

Jacoby extends the optimism imbuing his book to include fairly clear description of utopian society that, although borrowing content from utopian writings of Matthew Arnold, meets all three criteria for utopianism. Jacoby (1999) rests his idea of utopia on the expansive, fundamental idea of human flourishing: "Democracy," wrote Arnold, "is trying to *affirm one's own essence*; meaning by this, to develop one's own existence fully and freely, to have ample light and air, to be neither cramped nor overshadowed" (p. 92). Personal power means the capacity to improve, in mutually satisfying ways relative to others concerned, one's own flourishing. Universal conception of human flourishing supports development of the idea of human culture, distinct from ideas of class, ethnic, race-based, or lifestyle cultures. Trotsky, Jacoby informs us, declared this a desideratum of Marxism, saying, "There is no proletarian culture and . . . there never will be and in fact there is no reason to regret this. . . . The proletariat acquires power for the purpose of doing away with class culture and to make way for human culture" (p. 200, n. 30). Jacoby paraphrases Arnold, saying, "First of all, the 'well-being of the many' must be pursued—not only for itself, but for the individual, for no one can be truly prosperous, happy or even secure amid misery" (p. 93). Jacoby adds that "Arnold believed that everyone in a democracy should be part of the elite. He rejected the private or individualist solution. Culture must be universal, or it is nothing" (p. 98).

Because "individuals by themselves lack the resources to remedy social ills" (Jacoby, 1999, p. 94), argues Arnold, "the state should take responsibility for the education of the people and, indeed, for culture in general" (p. 90). Jacoby points out Arnold "also believed in egalitarianism and objected to sharp disparities in wealth. These were not separate propositions; for Arnold, a robust public education, a solid social equality, and a vibrant culture all went together" (pp. 90–91). Jacoby gives a sense of the sorts of actions states could take to improve human flourishing by discussing failures on the part of the state to do so. For example, Jacoby discusses Arnold's arguments against the practice of "freedom of bequest," which perpetuates inequalities by limiting movement of wealth along only family lines (p. 92). Jacoby (1999) cites British socialist Raymond Williams who complained about post–World War II government throwing its weight behind capitalist reconstruction of cultural life rather than funding education programs aimed at improving the lot of the working classes. Jacoby voices dismay about failure to materialize a promised American "peace dividend" upon the collapse of the Soviet Union. Monies that might have been freed from military spending were never reallocated to fund "education, health and community needs" (p. 156).

Jacoby fulfills his third criterion by building into his vision for a better society a world of abundance. "The point is: Arnold did not defend 'sweetness and light' as abstract goods; he defended a bountiful world against a cramped life of work and money" (Jacoby, 1999, p. 96). "What mangles people," Jacoby asserts, "are bad or no jobs, decaying communities, tattered human relations and defective education" (p. 58). "An impoverished life and circumstances do not allow cultivation and growth" (p. 93). Arnold criticizes his society by pointing out its consistent success in "materialising our upper class, vulgarising our middle class, and brutalising our lower class. And this is to fail in civilization" (p. 93). There are spiritual benefits derived from utopian society. Jacoby quotes Arnold as asking, "Can it be denied that to live in a society of equals tends in general to make a man's spirits expand, and his faculties work easily and actively?" (p. 67). However, Jacoby also cites 19th-century historian Thomas Macaulay's comparative assessment of the utopias proposed by Thomas More and Francis Bacon. Bacon comes out ahead because he proposed "not the subdivision of poverty, but the creation of plenty" (p. 175). The problem remains of how to accomplish the plentifulness on which success of utopia depends.

Some Omissions: Planning for Utopia

Mattson (1999) faults Jacoby for not proposing plans for achieving utopia, citing Paul Goodman's *Utopian Essays and Practical Proposals* as more satisfying on this account. Goodman's plans include banning cars from Manhattan and beefing up mass transit to improve livability of the city, taxing mass culture outlets to fund alternative arts institutions, and using youth camps to provide meaningful work experiences to teens. Mattson (1999) throws down the gauntlet: "We must prove by experiment that direct solutions are feasible" (p. 59). Failure to lay plans for a more perfect society gives succor to those who oppose utopianism. "There is a rational kernel within the shell of anti-utopian prejudice," writes George Scialabba (1999). "It is simply this: We all want to see the plans. And there are no plans" (p. 108). What is it, asks Hoff (2000), that keeps Jacoby from delivering on describing utopian practice?

What keeps Jacoby from ponying up is mistaking secondary issues for primary ones. Jacoby confuses markets with the deeper social form of organic solidarity and stops at the level of culture, when he should continue to the deeper level of the life world as a framing concept for talking about utopia. Considering utopianism in terms of organic solidarity provides opportunity to revive utopian thinking in ways oppositional to/

surpassing of markets. Replacing parochial concepts of culture with general ideas of the life world and biographically determined situation permits discussion of utopian thinking in general terms of human culture. Organic solidarity and life world permit revival of communistic utopian thinking in a socially oriented form more immune to capitalism than failed economic communisms Jacoby discusses.

Jacoby's market fetishism prevents him from taking to heart sound advice from Georg Lukács: "The goal is not a new economic order, but freedom from an obsession with economics" (Jacoby, 1999, p. 27). In organic solidarity, sharing sits as the polar opposite of selling. Sharing surpasses selling in its promise of plenty by not putting prices on each specific piece of plentitude. In a sharing society, planners seek to find ways to share life's necessities as widely as possible. Plans will be made/executed that keep necessities (air, water, food, shelter, etc.) worth sharing. Planners will be concerned with analysis of what is easily shared, what is progressively more difficult to share, and what may be done to promote sharing across those differences. Rules for sharing may even emerge. Perhaps people in a sharing society will begin to act regularly on a communistic maxim familiar to Marxists: "From each according to his ability, to each according to his needs" (Marx, 1891/2009, p. 13).

Utopia has less to do with destabilizing existing institutions than it does with creating stable institutions supportive of sharing at scale. Creating/maintaining/enhancing sharing sets the agenda for intellectual work in utopia. Jacoby (1999) regrets that in market-oriented society "cynicism, the belief that ideas only serve power and repression, drives intellectual work" (p. 126). Utopian thought goes beyond cynicism, urging intellectuals to come up with universals that find their meaning in application across human difference and to develop theories able to telescope out to the general in human experience and, simultaneously, microscope in on the infinite difference exhibited by persons. In utopia, reimagining society for improved flourishing of all is the business of intellectuals. Schools offer instruction in order better to imagine/more consistently bring to life an ever-improving world.

The idea of "culture" is less well suited to articulation of a society focused on human flourishing than are the companion conceptions of "life world" and "biographically determined situation." These ideas, mainstays of the phenomenological sociology of Alfred Schutz, permit sharing society to reach beyond group levels to levels of individual human existence in matters of human flourishing. Schutz (1959/1971) lists three essential elements in the eidetic structure of any life world: (a) stocks of knowledge, (b) pragmatic tasks, and (c) patterns of socialization. Schutz summarizes these invariant structures of the life world as a "biographically determined situation" saying,

> I find myself at any moment of my existence within the *Lebenswelt* in a biographically determined situation. To this situation belong not only my position in space, time, and society, but also my experience that some of the elements of my *Lebenswelt* are imposed upon me, while others are either within control or capable of being brought within my control and therefore modifiable. (p. 288)

A person's biographically determined situation provides an interpretive scheme to assess experiences and anticipate/modify future ones. Sharing society aims at accurate description of the life world generally and each person's biographically determined situation specifically as exhibiting human flourishing.

Consideration of human existence in terms of life world/biographically determined situation provides a place to stand in critiquing culture as contributing more or less fully to human flourishing. The life world subsumes culture as a mutable aspect of the life world. Some cultures rely on the immiseration of persons to continue the life of the culture. These are unacceptable cultures in utopia because they stand opposed to widespread creation of human flourishing. In hierarchically arranged cultures, flourishing is meant for some, not all. The ideas of the life world/biographically determined situation provide a place to critique cultures as more or less utopian in their outlook. Jacoby (1999) favorably quotes William Paley, a British moral philosopher of the Victorian age: "The happiness of a people is made up of the happiness of single persons" (p. 177). Using "culture" as the filter for human flourishing also risks a bureaucratic approach to understanding human individuality. Seeing everyone primarily as of/in a specific culture threatens to pigeonhole persons into stereotypes. This problem does not arise when society takes interest in broader notions of human culture.

Focus on human flourishing via life world/biographically determined situation seems a good way to avoid a violent and dominating utopia based on discipline and routine in which persons are forced to abide by rules of utopian regimes rather than participate voluntarily in utopian society. A system that successfully supports human flourishing for all is likely to find adherents everywhere. This does not mean privilege must disappear from utopia. In a utopian society in which phenomenological pluralism—a recognized plurality of life worlds/biographically determined situations all in equal need of mutually enjoyed development of personal excellence—rulers are those adept at maintaining/optimizing/sharing human flourishing. This is the fundamental change in society rendered by a utopian focus on human flourishing. Leaders become the vital left counterculture in charge of societal development. There may actually come a day when things can't get any better. But that will be the day the utopian vision is realized, not the day hope for utopia has been abandoned.

On Diversity—Relevant Focus: The Individual, the Group, and Higher Education

Jacoby's (2020) main argument in his newest book, *On Diversity*, is that the issue of diversity has become too overwhelmingly exhaustive as global society has grown more homogeneous. And he blames the universities, particularly their leftist faculties, for being the prime culprits in spreading the gospel of diversity (Jacoby, 2020). His mission is to highlight the singular individual instead of the group or identity politics. As Jacoby sketches his portrait of the individual and society, he draws on a gamut of cultural artifacts, big and small: clothing, language, biology, ecology, childhood play, ideology, and selected thinkers in Western culture (both well known and lesser studied—and *almost all* are White men) to support his position.

Among the latter theorists, Jacoby banks heavily on the 17th–18th-century Swiss-French political philosopher Benjamin Constant. Significantly, Jacoby (2020) begins his epilogue with a pithy quotation from Constant: "Variety is life, uniformity, death" (p. 175). Both theorists would denounce the rugged individualism that has been so noxious in American culture. Nor are they making a plea for mere self-interest; their view of individuality is intimately connected to a fuller sense of humane and moral sentiment. Their major concern is to curb any potency in mass feeling in order to promote individual authenticity.

Premising that the group is now defining the individual and depreciating one's distinctiveness, Jacoby (2020) contends that we are creating a "monoculture of the mind" and a "Hallmark vision of the world" (pp. 44, 50). As storytelling and children's playful experimentation wanes and technological tools (especially social media) increase, American youths' creativity begins to shrink. For Jacoby, "America is 'the source of that terrible wave of uniformity' that gives everyone the same skin, fashions, books, conversation—and the same boredom" (p. 88). Presumably, that lack of inventiveness carries over to the campus. Indeed, it is American higher education, so enamored of sustaining and spreading calls for diversity, that earns Jacoby's (2020) especially pointed criticism:

> The diversity celebrants . . . love diversity, but rarely ask what it means or what its reality is in an age of massification. . . . The conservative criticism, at least of the campuses, cannot be brushed aside. Conservatives charge that group heterogeneity does not mean intellectual heterogeneity. (pp. 175–176)

Though Jacoby does not specifically address liberal education in *On Diversity*, we can readily see that he is most interested in "the life of the mind" and independent, critical thinking. That is no small, if hardly novel, contribution to liberal education, but is it fully adequate to prepare college students in today's world for their unknown futures? Would not lessons on diversity facilitate what is to come in their lives?

Some Drawbacks in Jacoby's Analysis

At base, Jacoby appears to be establishing a false dichotomy between the individual and the group. And that discussion brings us to John Dewey's *Individualism Old and New* (1931). Dewey's principal task in much of his voluminous writing comes down to merging seeming dichotomies—the individual and society, democracy and education, experience and nature, experience and education, freedom and culture. In terms of the individual and society, he takes care not to lose the individual, but he also recognizes that society—its culture, political institutions, socioeconomic structures—can shape the context and contours of individual lives. What is needed, Dewey argues, is a reorganization of societal resources to better energize democracy and social justice. That is, a new form of society would promote both individual *and* social interests more fully and meaningfully (Dewey, 1931). Contemporary public intellectuals *and* young activists in high school and college (e.g., Parkland, Florida, high school students; Black Lives Matter; and #MeToo movements) have reignited Dewey's call for public engagement. Public projects for social justice can readily be knitted with the aim of individual growth:

> An education that is multicultural can be helpful in the realization and appreciation of one's own worth, beauty, intelligence, skills, talent, compassion, and humanity. This subjective affirmation is crucial for the realization of an inclusive, democratic, and just society in which, to the extent possible, all individuals and groups feel like, can take advantage of being, and are encouraged and supported to be empowered participants. Multicultural education, then, is not just about structures, policies, and practices. It is also about individuals feeling a positive sense of their value, potential, strength, and agency. (Teitelbaum, 2020, p. 188)

But spotlighting the individual may unduly cast blame in irresponsible ways (Ryan, 1971):

> The difficulty with focusing on individuals . . . is that it is harder to see the social system in which both [oppressor and victim] are embedded; it is important to see that the social structures can produce bad consequences such as widening economic gaps, even if there is no specific wrongdoing by any of the individual players. (Kent, 2003, p. 59)

Oddly, in a book devoted to "diversity," Jacoby gives little attention to deep-seated problems related to unjust power relations, social inequities, structural racism, and hierarchical institutional practices. His solution seems to be to afford more opportunities for individuals so that they can choose, more or less, for themselves. Ultimately, he is primarily a cultural historian. Jacoby tends to appraise diversity in terms of its capacity to augment variety for the culture and species. Culture plays an important role, but it is only one component of any struggle for larger social change. It would seem that a more intersectional—structural, disciplinary, cultural, and interpersonal—analysis would offer more thorough avenues toward both individual and public solutions (Collins, 2019).

Jacoby has cautioned us to awaken from our profound cultural amnesia—a condition that affects our everyday life in the streets and the halls of academe. On the other hand, he is less attuned to systemic social forces and vastly inequitable power relations (e.g., due to race, class, gender, poverty, and disability) that interconnect and prevent our institutions, including higher education, from being more humanizing and empowering for *all* individuals, especially those less dominant and more unfortunate. For example, this reality severely hampered an estimated 15% of college students who were homeless and 38% who faced food insecurity during the pandemic, in the world's wealthiest nation (McPherson, 2020). Like so many others, they are individuals who are part of a group that do not deserve that kind of life. Divisiveness, hatred, bigotry, and authoritarianism marked the presidency of Donald J. Trump. Quite surprisingly, Jacoby does not mention Trump in a book published in 2020. He would never have wanted that kind of "variety."

References

Brociner, K. (2001). Utopianism, human nature, and the left. *Dissent, 48*, 89–92.
Collins, P. H. (2019). *Intersectionality as critical social theory*. Duke University Press.
Dewey, J. (1931). Individualism old and new. *International Journal of Ethics, 41*, 362–365.

Dewey, J. (1986). *Logic: The theory of inquiry.* In J. A. Boydston (Ed.), *John Dewey: The later works, 1925–1953* (Vol. 12). Southern Illinois University Press. https://www.jstor.org/stable/1316511 (Original work published 1938)

Durkheim, E. (1985). *The division of labor in society* (W. D. Halls, Trans.). Macmillan. (Original work published 1893)

Hoff, S. B. (2000). The end of utopia (Review of the book *The end of utopia: Politics and culture in an age of apathy*, by Russell Jacoby). *Perspectives on Political Science, 29,* 118.

Jacobs, J. (1961). *The life and death of great American cities.* Random House.

Jacoby, R. (1964, January 14). General education is antistudent and antiknowledge. *Chicago Maroon,* 6.

Jacoby, R. (1995). *Dogmatic wisdom.* Doubleday.

Jacoby, R. (1999). *The end of utopia: Politics and culture in an age of apathy.* Basic Books.

Jacoby, R. (2000). *The last intellectuals: American culture in the age of academe* (2nd ed.). Basic Books. (Original work published 1987)

Jacoby, R. (2020). *On diversity: The eclipse of the individual in a global era.* Seven Stories Press.

Kent, G. (2003, September). Blaming the victim, globally. *UN Chronicle, 40*(3), 59–60. https://international.vlex.com/vid/the-victim-globally-56566786

Marx, K. (2009). *Critique of the Gotha Programme.* Dodo Press. (Original work published 1891)

Mattson, K. (1999). The end of declarative statements. *Social Policy, 39,* 55–59.

McCarthy, M. (1963). *The group.* New American Library.

McPherson, M. P. (2020). Tackling hunger and homelessness on campus. *Forbes.* https://www.forbes.com/sites/petermcpherson/2020/11/17-tackling-hunger-and-hom

Peirce, C. S. (1934). The fixation of belief. In C. Hartshorne & P. Weiss (Eds.), *Collected papers of Charles Sanders Peirce* (Vol. 5, pp. 358–387). Harvard University Press. (Original work published 1877)

Rorty, R. (2016). *Philosophy as poetry.* University of Virginia Press.

Ryan, W. (1971). *Blaming the victim.* Vintage.

Schutz, A. (1971). Tiresias, or our knowledge of future events. In A. Brodersen (Ed.), *Alfred Schutz: Collected papers, Volume II: Studies in social theory* (pp. 277–293). Martinus Nijhoff. (Original work published 1959)

Scialabba, G. (1999). The end of utopia. *Dissent, 46,* 107–110. http://georgescialabba.net/mtgs/1999/06/the-end-of-utopia-politics-and.html

Teitelbaum, K. (2020). *Critical issues in democratic schooling: Curriculum, teaching, and socio-political realities.* Routledge.

2

AMY GUTMANN'S ETHICS, DELIBERATIVE DEMOCRACY, AND CHALLENGES IN HIGHER EDUCATION

Spoma Jovanovic

For more than 30 years, Amy Gutmann has consistently advanced her position that educators can and should underscore the importance of democratic principles as foundational to our deliberative processes to inform educational policy, pedagogical choices, and world debates. As president of the University of Pennsylvania and as a political philosopher, Gutmann (1987) is intent on igniting in others a concern for developing practical skills and knowledge-based thinking through democratic education to enact fuller democracy, self-determination, and what she calls "moral strength" (p. 289). Her ongoing project has been to bring theory and practice together in advocating for equality, access, and multiculturalism as necessary features for a pluralistic society. Gutmann does not shy away from inevitable, conflicting values but instead reasons that they can be properly addressed through innovative thinking, expansive consideration of competing interests, and application of principled judgment through deliberative means.

It is difficult to disagree with Gutmann, but scholars who do (DeCesare, 2016; Thayer-Bacon, 2018; Young, 2001) argue that, despite her good intentions, she has skirted issues of power embedded in deep, systemic barriers that, in effect, skew what deliberations can yield and what democratic education can achieve. At the most basic unit of language, "Even the most apparently apolitical utterances set speakers within institutions and power relations just by saying them" (Backer, 2017, p. 5). Gutmann disagrees and counters that, given sufficient educational resources and knowledge, all students can reach a threshold of democratic learning necessary for deliberation in which ethics and justice are contested. In the public realm, she notes that the concern for ethics puts the spotlight on the impact of our deeds, decisions, and policies that regulate the collective body. Thus, Gutmann asks how can and should we act to protect the rights and interests of all (Gutmann & Thompson, 1989).

The significance of Gutmann's work is particularly relevant in an era of declining investments and trust in higher education. With tsunami-like changes in response to a global pandemic, calls for racial justice unlike any since the civil rights movement of the 1960s, shrinking state and federal resources, and the push for greater access for all, leaders like Gutmann face radical, unprecedented challenges. Gutmann's tenure as an administrator and scholar, even admitting her shortcomings, is built on the conviction that "our colleges and universities are fundamental to the civic health of our society" (Sawyer, 2020, p. 19). The ideals of Gutmann's democratic education are worth upholding, lest we risk leaving colleges and universities further beholden to the business model of management that too often mocks critical thinking, joyful learning, and the invaluable, time-intensive processes of learning to be a citizen in a self-governing democracy. This chapter focuses on how Amy Gutmann advocates for ethical understanding that enables students to use their education in the service of building beloved communities that are essential for a true democracy. In such communities, people speak and stand up for a better, fairer world, marked by a freedom that is inclusive of our profound differences (Gutmann, 2019).

Amy Gutmann is a proud first-generation college graduate and only child of Kurt and Beatrice. Born in Brooklyn, New York, in 1949, Gutmann credits her father's courage for inspiring her own ideas and love of learning. Stories of her father's escape, with his siblings, from Nazi Germany in 1934 to India and later the United States left an indelible mark on her life. She, like him, was raised in a Jewish household and early on experienced what it was like to be an outsider in the schools and town where she was raised. She graduated from Radcliffe College (Harvard-Radcliffe) before earning a master's degree in political science from the London School of Economics and a doctorate in political science from Harvard University (Simon, 2018).

Gutmann entered full-time academic employment in 1976 as a faculty member in the Department of Politics at Princeton University. She remained there for nearly 3 decades, collecting honors and accolades for her scholarly work, eventually taking on administrative duties. She was the founding director of Princeton University's Center for Human Values, one of the country's first multidisciplinary ethics centers, and then later served as provost before leaving in 2004 to accept her current position at the University of Pennsylvania as its eighth and longest serving president. She also holds University of Pennsylvania appointments as the Christopher H. Browne distinguished professor of political science and professor of communication in the Annenberg School of Communication.

Her national profile is noteworthy. She previously served on the National Security Higher Education Advisory Board to advise the FBI, as president of the American Association of Universities, and as chair of the Obama administration's Presidential Commission for the Study of Bioethical Issues (Simon, 2018). In 2017, Gutmann brought former U.S. vice president Joe Biden to the University of Pennsylvania's Annenberg School and School of Arts and Sciences as the Benjamin Franklin presidential practice professor. He would later be instrumental in establishing the Penn Biden Center for Diplomacy and Global Engagement before taking a leave of absence in 2019 for his presidential campaign.

Gutmann's childhood experiences and early career writings continue to fuel her ideas and activities as one of America's leading higher education voices—for example, being named to the list of *Fortune*'s "World's 50 Greatest Leaders" (Fortune Editors, 2018). She regularly acknowledges the impact of her undergraduate days in shaping her life today. As a low-income, first-generation college student, Gutmann was awestruck at the abundance of differences she was exposed to in college. From that, she set her sights on forming a new, more diverse community in which she could grow—one that would catapult her to a prominence that enabled her to publish books, serve as director on myriad boards, and lead one of the top universities in the world. What happened to her in college, she says, "would become my cause, my mission, my identity" (Gutmann, 2019, 0:10:37-0:10:42).

Her "three core democratic values—liberty (personal and political), opportunity (education, health care, security), and mutual respect" frame Guttman's scholarly pursuits in ethics, education, politics, and philosophy (Sardoc, 2018, p. 245). As she sees it, higher education's distinct advantage is in offering spaces for radical difference of views, backgrounds, and values to inspire students to expand their thinking in creative and courageous ways in order to solve the world's vexing problems. Toward that end, as a university president Gutmann has advanced policies and reaffirmed strategic plans aimed at fostering inclusion to increase access to higher education, inspire innovation, and cultivate impact through deliberation, mutual respect, and deep consideration of differing cultural, political, and economic worldviews (University of Pennsylvania, Office of the President, n.d.).

To put her ideas into actions, Gutmann has in just over a decade led the University of Pennsylvania to increase financial aid 161% and enroll twice as many first-generation freshman students (Amtzenius, 2015). She has also guided the institution to attract larger numbers of students from low- and middle-income families by promoting its all-grant policy that began in 2009. At Penn students get grants and work-study options, not loans, to defray the cost of their tuition for 4 years. Though many students at Penn still graduate with some debt (e.g., to cover school costs beyond eight semesters, summer housing, and unexpected expenses), Penn's plan is the largest among 50 selective institutions with similar programs (Sadurni, 2016).

Gutmann's prowess at fundraising, including a $4.1 billion campaign concluding in 2021, is part of the reason she is among the highest paid private university presidents with a $3 million annual compensation package (Bauman et al., 2020). This point of distinction is one to which her board of trustees speaks with pride (Gross, 2020). It also stands out to her detractors for being in tension with her educational philosophy that speaks of equity: How does Gutmann justify a continuing, escalating salary while she leads a changing academic workforce that is increasingly dependent upon underpaid adjunct and temporary labor rather than tenured professors?

Higher Education as the Ethical Engine of Individual and Societal Progress

Gutmann advocates for instilling civic, communally based values in higher education while upholding the importance of individual autonomy as enacted through freedom and choice (Thayer-Bacon, 2018). She suggests that a civic education ought to begin early and "must be shared by parents, citizens, and professional educators" (Gutmann, 1987, p. 42). She fully recognizes that disagreements abound surrounding the ideals, purpose, and desired outcomes of education; she offers democratic deliberation as the means by which to reconcile those differences. In this way, Gutmann contends that discussion and decision-making, inherent to the deliberative process, serve vital functions in surfacing empirical and ethical arguments where mutual respect and reciprocity are practiced even if consensus is not always achieved (Gutmann & Thompson, 2018).

Her theoretical position draws from critical and feminist studies, but at its core is steeped in John Dewey's view of education as a tool and outcome, of and for, democratic practice. Dewey (1916) writes in *Democracy and Education*, "A democracy is more than a form of government; it is primarily a mode of associated living, of conjoint communicated experience" (p. 87). Gutmann (2015) concurs and further suggests that a university education ought to have as its primary aim not to enrich the economic comfort of its graduates, but instead to offer students the pathways to understand the world so that they can contribute to its betterment by way of democratic self-governing.

Gutmann's groundbreaking book, *Democratic Education*, was first published in 1987 and remains a seminal text on the democratic theory of education. Paying tribute to the legacy of Dewey, Gutmann understands education to be both an individual pursuit and a public-worthy enterprise. She sees community members as critical partners who, with teachers, have a responsibility to shape policy and assume shared authority for implementing state-directed education, starting with primary schooling and extending through higher education. Central to that proposition, Guttman (1987) highlights three guiding principles to educating future citizens: "nonrepression" in which "new and unorthodox ideas are judged on their intellectual merits" (p. 174); "nondiscrimination," including its application to college admissions standards and policies; and "conscious social reproduction" (p. 175) or the collective molding of society's future through democratic deliberation. Taken together, these principles within higher education aim to equalize opportunities so that students are provided the skills and capacities to address and evaluate how pluralism can best flourish in our democracy (Gutmann, 1987). This argument is further developed in many of Gutmann's 16 coauthored and edited books, as well as in articles, book chapters, invited papers, lectures, and speeches numbering in the hundreds.

According to Gutmann, maximizing the promise of both education and democracy, recognizing that each reinforces the possibilities of the other, requires that people engage in thoughtful dialogue and deliberation, pursue truth and knowledge, fulfill public obligations to better the community, and center ethics in daily actions as Socrates, Plato, and Aristotle proposed in their conceptions of the good life. Democracy provides the platform and arena in which to perform and showcase how education prepares wildly differing citizens for cooperative self-governance (Holzman, 2009).

Gutmann's work, building on a long tradition of liberal education, has progressed in the 20th and 21st centuries during a time of increasing threats to colleges and universities that had traditionally been less susceptible to undue outside influences. Among those threats, Gutmann points to markedly reduced state funding for higher education, citizen mistrust of public institutions, a decreased commitment to the value of free speech, a resurgence of intolerance toward others, and caustic partisan politics.

While state and federal lawmakers continue to laud the importance of higher education, they simultaneously take actions that eviscerate funds available through public budgets. Since 1987, state funding for higher education has dropped on average 25%, leaving students to absorb most of those cuts through higher tuition (Weber, 2018). The methodical disinvestment in higher education has continued over such a long time that it has had a numbing effect on people's perceptions (Jovanovic, 2017). In the last 10 years, according to an American Public Media survey, state funding for higher education fell $9 billion, yet two thirds of Americans believed otherwise. In fact, 27% of Americans surveyed thought government funding for public higher education increased and 34% thought that it has at least held steady (Absar & Helmstetter, 2019).

Other studies illuminate additional perils to higher education that Gutmann also cites. There is falling public trust in the value of higher education that has been well documented by both the Pew Research Center and Gallup (Jones, 2018; Parker, 2019). Questions of higher education's responsibilities surrounding the First Amendment have made headline news around the country as campuses played host to contested understandings of free speech, often focusing on the question of who should get to speak—controversial speakers or protestors who both assert the right to be heard and, in the process, silence the other (Baer, 2019). Related is the growing intolerance of "the other" and escalation of incidents reflecting extremist ideologies leading to violence, as reported by both the Anti-Defamation League and the FBI (Lowery et al., 2018). Finally, corrosive partisan politics have fueled the rise of embattled legislators and gridlock surrounding policies, budgets, and political appointments, all having adverse impacts on higher education planning and growth (Carothers & O'Donohue, 2019).

The challenge in this environment, according to Gutmann (1987), is to "provide principles that in the face of our social disagreements, help us judge (a) who should have authority to make decisions about education, and (b) what the moral boundaries of that authority are" (p. 11). These have been contested questions in higher education for quite some time, but even more so today as faculty bodies resist the neoliberal creep that has permeated virtually all aspects of academic life (Jovanovic, 2017). The university-as-business model paradigm reveres benchmark data, production numbers, job readiness, and vacuous quantitative assessments to drive teaching and learning rather than pedagogy and professor–student relationships that aspire to generate wisdom, new critical knowledge, and justice as educational goals (Jovanovic, 2014).

Gutmann convincingly asserts that it is by cultivating an educated and considerate citizenry that a democratic society can provide the civic, political, economic, and cultural freedoms we desire. Countering the many systems and rankings that seek to establish universities as elite and prominent institutions, Gutmann (1987) retorts, "A democratic society is responsible for educating not just some but all children for citizenship" (p. 13). Thus, Gutmann, though operating during her career always within the halls of elite institutions, turns her sights toward inclusion, innovation, and impact as the paths that can sustain and build democracy with informed, educated citizens.

Gutmann's Impact and Reach

Gutmann was among early supporters who sought to integrate the liberal arts with professional schools and imagined the possibilities of interdisciplinary studies. She has not wavered from her position that it is intellectual diversity that can best grapple with ethical concerns inherent in such political issues as global climate change, gross inequalities, terrorism, abortion, and bioethics, to name just a few (Gutmann, 2015). And for her, it is within the halls of higher education that critiques and innovation can emerge—protected from government intrusion—to consider novel, often uncomfortable, but always reasoned, arguments. In that way, colleges and universities provide indispensable public space for exploration:

> American colleges and universities derive their greatness by protecting the freedom of professors and students to read widely and explore topics in all their complexity, to think critically and debate issues where there are grounds for reasonable disagreement, and to imagine and express new ideas and new worlds without fear of reprisal or retribution. (Guttman, 2005, p. B13)

This kind of thinking, along with her distinguished publishing record, has bolstered Gutmann's influence far and wide, from education circles to political spheres, public health fields, the federal government, and legal environs.

As Gutmann has assumed greater responsibility in her academic and public duties, she admits that theories, including her own, may benefit from adjustments. Today, she argues that her conception of deliberative democracy must reach beyond talk and scholarly argument to be "understood as reasoning that is deployed not only to criticize power but also to exercise it" in decision-making and action (Gutmann & Thompson, 2018, p. 904). For her, as powerful an instrument of reasoning as deliberation represents, to pit it against nondeliberative forms of decision-making (e.g., voting, referendums) would miss the potential that a plurality of processes presents for people to give life to democracy.

Still, for all her discussion of democracy and the means by which people can engage with one another, Gutmann's views of deliberative democracy do not provide a full hearing to the role of dissent and disruption as necessary features of expression by communities prevented from holding the levers of power. That is, the many advances and achievements made by activists in democratic societies are not taken up sufficiently in her writings. To fufill the potential of deliberative democracy, other theorists suggest that activism needs to be uplifted as a means by which to draw attention to injustices, albeit often through less orderly ways. Deliberation on its own, they suggest, has a distinguished record of reproducing, rather than eliminating harms:

> The activist is suspicious of exhortations to deliberate because he [sic] believes that in the real world of politics, where structural inequalities influence both procedures and outcomes, democratic processes that appear to conform to norms of deliberation are usually biased toward more powerful agents. (Young, 2001, p. 671)

In other words, critical theorists find that "rationality (deliberation) is not politically neutral" (Thayer-Bacon, 2018, p. 206). The content, procedures, and timing of deliberations are often set by those in power. As Gutmann is fond of doing, a case example may best illustrate this point. Professors at the University of Pennsylvania argued that Gutmann was slow in advancing racial diversity among the higher ranks at her institution. They felt the sting of deliberations gone nowhere and thus turned to other tactics. They boycotted a university-sponsored faculty of color dinner in 2013 hosted at Gutmann's home. At the time, despite a well-funded faculty diversity plan and opportunity to replace vacated positions, Gutmann had not hired a single person of color as dean (Flaherty, 2013). This was true despite the fact that Gutmann had previously written about the need for active recruitment of historically underrepresented academics in her book *Color Conscious*. There she said,

> A color blind perspective fails to leave room for according moral relevance to the fact that we do not yet live in a land of fair equality of opportunity for all American citizens—let alone in a world of fair equality of opportunity for all persons, regardless of their nationality. (Appiah & Gutmann, 1996, p. 125)

Indeed, the faculty activists eschewed deliberation in an attempt to disrupt the status quo and to call attention to the need for change. They did not forward a reasoned argument, but instead conveyed criticism in action that proved more effective. The faculty boycott led to a positive outcome. By 2017, the university's *Faculty Inclusion Report* noted that minority representation at the rank of dean swelled to 25% with three out of 12 appointments held by people of color (Gutmann & Price, 2017).

Challenges Ahead

Increased attention to education by hegemonic business interests coupled with the rising use of technology in the classroom, assaults on academic freedom, prohibitively expensive tuition and fees, and elevated visions of neoliberalism in higher education pose monumental threats to university education "as a vital public sphere central to democracy itself" (Giroux, 2012, p. 133). These factors, when combined and without collective resistance, may prove too strong a force for Gutmann's conception of deliberative democracy to fend off (Ford, 2020). Disagreements about the values and purposes of education, as well as the direction in which it should move to attract and retain a diverse study body, are certainly fodder for deliberative forums. Yet many people remain opposed to rational deliberation and even the teaching of the skills required for deliberation on religious and other grounds (Pybas, 2004).

Gutmann's commitment to education as the bedrock of democracy deserves praise. She has modeled throughout her life, in word and deed, that progress is possible and change is necessary, with communication as the route to achieving both. She recognizes that we need to attend to the ethical dimensions of public life that pivot around systems leading to rising inequalities. At the same time, she entreats us to address those political, economic, and social challenges, now and in the future, because higher education can provide both resources and spaces to do just that.

References

Absar, K., & Helmstetter, C. (2019, February 25). *What Americans think about college: Government funding and assistance.* American Public Media Research Lab. https://static1.squarespace.com/static/5c9542c8840b163998cf4804/t/5d82409dd4a414168dd1adfd/1568817309685/1_apm-survey-report-college-funding-and-assistance-2-25-19F.pdf

Amtzenius, Linda (2015, October). Amy Gutmann. *Princeton Magazine.* http://www.princetonmagazine.com/amy-gutmann/

Appiah, K. A., & Gutmann, A. (1996). *Color conscious: The political morality of race.* Princeton University Press.

Backer, D. I. (2017). The critique of deliberative discussion. *Democracy & Education, 25*(1), 1–6. https://democracyeducationjournal.org/cgi/viewpoint.cgi?article=1300&context=home

Baer, U. (2019). *What snowflakes get right on campus: Free speech, truth, and equality on campus.* Oxford University Press.

Bauman, D., David, T., & O'Leary, B. (2020, July 17). Executive compensation at public and private colleges. *The Chronicle of Higher Education*. https://www.chronicle.com/article/executive-compensation-at-public-and-private-colleges/?cid=CDP-articlebottom#id=table_private_2017

Carothers, T., & O'Donohue, A. (2019). *Democracies divided: The global challenge of political polarization*. Brookings Institution Press.

DeCesare, T. (2016). A capabilities critiques of Amy Gutmann's democratic interpretation of equal education opportunity. *Philosophical Studies in Education, 47,* 129–139.

Dewey, J. (1916). *Democracy and education*. The Free Press.

Flaherty, C. (2013, January 31). With regrets. *Inside Higher Ed.* https://www.insidehighered.com/news/2013/01/31/minority-faculty-university-pennsylvania-question-presidents-commitment-diversity

Ford, B. (2020). Negating Amy Gutmann: Deliberative democracy, business influence and segmentation strategies in education. *Democracy & Education, 28*(1), Article 4. democracyandeducationjournal.org/home/vol.28/issI/4

Fortune Editors. (2018). The world's 50 greatest leaders. *Fortune*. https://fortune.com/longform/worlds-greatest-leaders-2018/

Giroux, H. A. (2012). *Twilight of the social: Resurgent publics in the age of disposability*. Paradigm.

Gross, H. (2020, February 19). Penn president Amy Gutmann earned $3.6 million in 2017, an 8% decrease from 2016. *The Daily Pennsylvanian*. https://www.thedp.com/article/2020/02/amy-gutmann-salary-penn-president

Gutmann, A. (1987). *Democratic education*. Princeton University Press.

Gutmann, A. (2005). Academic freedom or government intrusion. *The Chronicle of Higher Education, 52*(3), B13.

Gutmann, A. (2015). What makes a university education worthwhile? In H. Brighouse & M. McPherson (Eds.), *The aims of higher education: Problems of morality and justice* (pp. 7–25). University of Chicago Press.

Gutmann, A. (2019). *Penn President Amy Gutmann, commencement 2019* [Video]. YouTube. https://www.youtube.com/watch?v=iP-YGcJdA7I

Gutmann, A., & Price, V. (2017, March 21). Faculty inclusion report. From the president and the provost. *Almanac* [Supplement]. https://almanac.upenn.edu/uploads/media/032117-full-supplement.pdf

Gutmann, A., & Thompson, D. (1989). *Ethics and politics: Cases and comments* (2nd ed.). Nelson-Hall.

Gutmann, A., & Thompson, D. (2018). Reflections on deliberative democracy: When theory meets practice. In A. Bachtiger, J. S. Dryzek, J. Mansbridge, & M. Warren (Eds.), *Oxford handbook of deliberative democracy*. Oxford University Press.

Holzman, L. (2009). *Vygotsky at work and play*. Routledge.

Jones, J. M. (2018, October 9). *A crisis in confidence in higher education*. Gallup. https://news.gallup.com/opinion/gallup/242441/confidence-higher-education-down-2015.aspx

Jovanovic, S. (2014). The ethics of teaching communication activism. In L. R. Frey & D. L. Palmer (Eds.), *Teaching communication activism: Communication education for social justice* (pp. 105–138). Hampton Press. https://doi.org/10.1177/15327086/17706125

Jovanovic, S. (2017). Speaking back to the neoliberal agenda for higher education [Special issue]. *Cultural Studies/Critical Methodologies, 17*(4), 1–6.

Lowery, W., Kindy, K., & Tran, A. B. (2018, November 25). In the United States, right wing violence is on the rise. *The Washington Post.* https://www.washingtonpost.com/national/in-the-united-states-right-wing-violence-is-on-the-rise/2018/11/25/61f7f24a-deb4-11e8-85df-7a6b4d25cfbb_story.html

Parker, K. (2019, August 19). *The growing partisan divide in view of higher education.* Pew Research Center. https://www.pewsocialtrends.org/essay/the-growing-partisan-divide-in-views-of-higher-education/

Pybas, K. (2004). Liberalism and civic education: Unitary versus pluralist alternatives. *Perspectives on Political Science, 33*(1), 18–29.

Sadurni, L. F. (2016, February 13). "No loans" but Penn students still graduate with debt. *The Daily Pennsylvanian.* https://www.thedp.com/article/2016/02/student-debt-national-penn-analysis

Sardoc, M. (2018). *Democratic education* at 30: An interview with Dr. Amy Gutmann. *Theory and Research in Education, 16*(2), 244–252. https://doi.org/10.1177/1477878518774087

Sawyer, P. (2020). Fatal attraction: A critical analysis of the toxic love affair of the university and neoliberalism. *Philosophy, Theory, and Foundations in Education, 2*(1), 19–27.

Simon, C. (2018, April 2). How Amy Gutmann is—quietly—leading Penn through political tumult. *The Daily Pennsylvanian.* https://www.thedp.com/article/2018/04/amy-gutmann-profile-donald-trump-upenn-philadelphia-ivy-league-immigration-penn

Thayer-Bacon, B. J. (2018). Amy Gutmann and liberal, deliberative democracy: Implications for schools. In P. Smeyers (Ed.), *International handbook of philosophy of education* (pp. 199–209). Springer. https://doi.org/10.1007/978-3-319-72761-5_17

University of Pennsylvania, Office of the President. (n.d.). *Penn Compact 2022.* https://president.upenn.edu/penn-compact

Weber, D. (2018). Higher education, lower spending. *Education Next, 18*(3). https://www.educationnext.org/higher-ed-lower-spending-as-states-cut-back-where-has-money-gone/

Young, I. M. (2001). Activist challenges to deliberative democracy. *Political Theory, 29*(5), 670–690. https://doi.org/10.1177/009059170/029005004

3

MICHAEL ROTH AND THE LIBERAL ARTS

Transforming Society and Selves

Daniel P. Liston

A liberal arts education is often seen as one that immerses students in knowledge and inquiry so they better know the world and themselves. I encountered such an education at Earlham College, a small Quaker liberal arts school, years ago during a time of political and curricular turmoil (early 1970s). Back then, what constituted the core of the liberal arts approach was an intensely debated contest between traditional content and more contemporary, socially relevant material. I was quite fortunate; Earlham's version of the liberal arts offered me an invaluable educational experience.

Today we find the "liberal arts" operating in many U.S. small colleges, as well as the rationale behind the required "core" curriculum offered in many larger universities. The natural and social sciences, the humanities, and the arts comprise the core of most tertiary liberal arts experiences. Many of us hold to a broad understanding of what constitutes a liberal education, and it runs something like this: A liberal arts program utilizes distinct disciplinary modes of inquiry to explore, and further understand, ourselves as well as the natural and human worlds we inhabit. Through these inquiries, individually and with others, we come to see, create, and accept provisional understandings of who we are and the worlds of which we are a part.

But this understanding is certainly not settled. Some have argued for an immersion in distinct forms of disciplinary knowledge (e.g., Hirst, 1965). Others favor a more general emphasis on interdisciplinary "habits of mind" (e.g., Meier, 1995; Sizer, 1996).[1] Some integrate the liberal arts educational process with practical, social, and cultural projects, claiming that meaningful and worthwhile understandings are best achieved in practice with others (e.g., Sizer, 1996). Other proponents maintain a more scholastic, text-based approach.[2] Many have argued that the liberal arts curriculum pursues the essential questions for humanity and examines the answers provided by thoughtful individuals throughout the ages (e.g., Adler, 2000). In contrast to this "great books" approach, critics proclaim the liberal arts as a vestige of a significantly flawed past, one incapable of exploring a world riven by power and structural injustice (e.g., see Boler, 1999; Bowles & Gintis, 1976, for distinct critiques). Generally, liberal arts programs have been offered to the economically advantaged. However, recent efforts have shown great engagement with, and power for, disenfranchised, incarcerated populations (e.g., the Bard Prison Initiative). Various scholars have examined these and other disagreements.[3]

Today the liberal arts seem mired in conflict, and in decline. With enhanced polarization of cultural and political views, there is a growing narrowness and brittleness around communities of identity. In some settings students protest a curriculum that includes any White male authors, in favor, exclusively, of authors of color and an educational agenda of social justice advocacy.[4] Others decry these "social justice warriors" who have purportedly taken over campus discourse as leftist ideologues.[5] Examples abound of invited campus speakers whose talks were protested and subsequently allowed or disallowed to offer their points of view. We have moved from an era of strongly held and debated political stances to one mired in expressions of political absolutism, a kind of entrenched tribalism.[6] These are challenging times for the liberal arts.

And so it was with anticipation and relish that I responded to Joe DeVitis's invitation to comment on Michael Roth's (2014) *Beyond the University: Why Liberal Education Matters*.[7] For much of my academic teaching life, I have embraced something akin to the liberal arts—set within professional education. Over the last 35 years, I have encouraged prospective and practicing teachers to engage with rich, contrasting, and sometimes opposing ideas about what and how we teach. Conservative, progressive, radical, and spiritual framings abound and offer prospective and practicing teachers varied and contrasting approaches to teaching and learning. I want my future and experienced teachers to enlarge, examine, and reconsider their educational goals, desires, and practices. Lately though, some students have chafed against this request. Their irritation has rekindled my focus on the liberal arts terrain. Roth is an instructive guide here. Roth's take on liberal education, one with roots in the American pragmatist tradition (e.g., W.E.B. Du Bois, William James, Jane Addams, John Dewey, and Richard Rorty), pursues changing selves and transforming social worlds. His historical and philosophical interpretive leanings, as well as his experiences as teacher and university president, provide an outlook both expansive and partial.

Liberal Education and Pragmatism

In *Beyond the University*, Roth (2014) structures his defense of the liberal arts in four separate chapters. Toward the end of the first chapter, "From Taking in the World to Transforming the Self," he summarizes a guiding telos of liberal education:

> Our universities are supposed to have the authority and creativity to conduct research, produce knowledge, and spread it to as many people as possible. . . . But our universities are also supposed to be places that protect critical thinking—thinking that undermines belief in received wisdom. . . . The productive tension between the university as a bastion of productive research and the campus as a place for aversive thinking and personal transformation has been at the heart of liberal education since the nineteenth century. (p. 60)

With this central tension in hand, Roth moves to his second chapter where he inventories contributions of various progressives and pragmatists so as to offer greater depth and definition to our understanding of the liberal arts. Roth provides a rich reservoir from which to draw. In particular, his exploration of W.E.B. Du Bois's, Jane Addams's, and William James's educational views knits together the twin goals of a revised "critical thinking": autonomy and empathy.

Roth's elaboration of Du Bois's educational stance emphasizes that education is for human development and freedom, not skill or job training. He offers Du Bois's words to reinforce this point:

> If we make money the object of man-training, we shall develop money-makers but not necessarily men; if we make technical skill the object of education, we may possess artisans but not, in nature, men. Men we shall have only as we make manhood the object of the work of the schools—intelligence, broad sympathy, knowledge of the world that was and is, and of the relation of men to it—this is the curriculum of that Higher Education which must underlie true life. (Du Bois, quoted in Roth, 2014, p. 69)

In today's framing: We must educate all to become intelligent, sympathetic, and knowledgeable human beings.

Roth draws upon Jane Addams's rich conception of "affectionate interpretation." Having experienced the strife and violence between the rich and poor of the early 1900s, she offered a distinct perspective on justice. Justice could only come about by recognizing the legitimacy of others' points of view and interests. Roth (2014) captures this theme:

> Affectionate interpretation is the imaginative effort to see things from the point of view of others, and this is especially important when faced with major differences. It is much too easy to mount a critique of positions whose weaknesses we detect. It is more challenging and more rewarding to try to comprehend why what looks to us as a weakness might in fact make a great deal of sense from another's point of view. Education, from Addams's perspective, must not merely make us more adept at defending ourselves against those with different agendas. Education should increase our powers of empathy and our ability to act in concert with others. (p. 84)

For Addams, and for Roth, the analytical goal of critiquing distinctly different "others" must be placed in relation to an all too often missing emphasis on affectionate interpretation and engagement.[8]

William James reinforces this "affectionate turn" by underscoring people's unfortunate tendency to be blind to one another, "enclosed within their own worlds of experience, and capable only of (mis)translating the experiences of others into their own terms" (Roth, 2014, p. 89).

The antidote is to learn to be "open" to others. Roth writes:

> Although James notes that there is no recipe for achieving this openness, teachers are in a privileged position to help us recognize the ways in which we all fail to see, pay attention to, and connect with the experiences of others. (p. 91)

This attention and connection to others seems to be a central takeaway for Roth. He ends this chapter by underscoring this feature:

> James emphasized that looking for the "whole inward significance" of another's situation is a crucial dimension of any inquiry that takes us beyond the comfortable borders of our own insular groups. Teaching is neither preaching to the choir nor energizing a base of believers. In crossing borders, we don't only confront strangers when we teach; we also find people who desire acknowledgment and mutual recognition. In so doing, we can teach our students to become teachers of themselves and others beyond their university years. This path of lifelong learning is a cornerstone of American liberal education. Learning to become citizens eager to understand those around us as we understand ourselves is also a cornerstone of American democracy. (p. 94)

For Roth, a central if not *the* central tenet of a liberal education is this: learning to understand others as we understand ourselves. It is nourished and informed by the pragmatist legacies of W.E.B. Du Bois, Jane Addams, and William James.

In chapter 3, "Controversies and Critics," Roth details a number of criticisms and controversies surrounding the liberal arts in U.S. higher education over the past 200 years. In the space allotted I cannot do justice to the chapter's scope. Here I'll underscore four controversies that pertain to the themes identified thus far.

First, Roth delves into Benjamin Franklin's critique that liberal education supports academics who are out of touch and tends to serve elites. If accurate, neither tendency serves students or democracy well.

Second, Roth (2014) underscores how the *Yale Report* of 1828 defended the liberal education model against claims that it is irrelevant to the spirit and age of industrialization. In effect the *Yale Report*'s authors argued against vocational preparation in part by claiming that

> the liberal college of education provides the discipline and furniture of the mind. And it is the intellectual discipline that is more important. Liberal education provides the habits of thinking on which a lifetime of learning will be erected. "The scholar," the report emphasizes, "must form himself by his own exertions." (p. 105)

Something broader, more foundational and oriented to human development, was needed in American higher education and for an industrialized society. Liberal arts education, the defenders maintained, provided this needed foundation.

Third, what defines this "foundation," the core content and disciplines of the liberal arts, has tended, over time, to become much too diffuse and ill-defined. After World War II, Roth (2014) notes, "Liberal learning seemed to be thought of as access to a smorgasbord of specific topics, and one could add to these topics willy-nilly" (p. 138). And for some this smorgasbord beget a pernicious relativism. In particular, Allan Bloom, author of the infamous *The Closing of the American Mind* (1987), decried the relativism inherent in 20th-century liberal arts. In effect, Bloom's claim was that liberal education was undermining its own telos.

Fourth, throughout the 20th century (and as mentioned previously, in the 19th century), the liberal arts model was viewed as preparing students for their eventual work lives. However, the notion that a liberal education could provide a basis for that development was scrutinized and frequently rejected. But these days, Roth (2014) observes, "critics no longer claim to be in search of 'true liberal learning,' but instead they call for an education that simply equips people to play an appropriate role in the economy" (p. 146). Liberal education is losing the public battle and can no longer rely on the "thin reed of 'antivocationalism.'" Roth ends his third chapter with the following call: "The traditions of liberal education in the United States are much more robust than mere antivocationalism. Today we must draw on those pragmatist traditions to once again articulate what liberal education is and why it matters" (p. 161). That is the topic of Roth's fourth and final chapter.

In chapter 4, "Reshaping Ourselves and Our Societies," Roth utilizes Dewey's pragmatist educational framework to distill an emboldened and revitalized liberal arts program; comments briefly on the recent work of Rorty, Nussbaum, and Hirsch as disparate but nevertheless sympathetic supporters of liberal education; and returns to the likes of Addams and James to move forward.

Roth (2014) develops several features of Dewey's informed pragmatism—within philosophy and education—maintaining that for Dewey, "A liberal education should help us develop the intellectual and moral capacities to imagine a future that is worth striving for, and enhance our ability to create the tools for its realization" (p. 173). The central question for Dewey was

> How can we educate people so that they can continue to learn through inquiry in their private and public lives? (p. 174)

And Dewey's response, according to Roth (2014), is this:

> The development of the capacity for inquiry isn't due to the inherent properties of a set of traditional disciplines. The capacity is fostered by connecting subjects to "their humane sources and inspiration." (p. 174)

Liberal learning serves the student, in part, by integrating and fueling individual and social purposes within traditional disciplinary knowledge.

Roth underscores Rorty's contribution as one of highlighting the role of liberal education "to help students realize that they can reshape themselves—that they can rework the self-image foisted on them by their past, the self-image that makes them competent citizens, into a new self-image that they themselves have helped to create" (Rorty, quoted in Roth, 2014, p. 181).

The current problem, as Roth sees it, is that liberal education today, especially the humanities, is overwhelmed and poorly served by the focus on "critical thinking." In Roth's (2014) framing, present-day critical thinking relies almost solely on "unmasking," "debunking," and "disrupting" earlier and current intellectual contributions and contributors. Such reliance obstructs learning. "As teachers, however, we must find ways for our students to open themselves to the emotional and cognitive power of subjects that might initially rub them the wrong way. . . . Critical thinking is sterile without the capacity for empathy and comprehension that stretches the self" (p. 184).

Roth (2014) goes on to argue,

> We have been less interested in investigating with our students how we generate the values we believe in, or the norm according to which we go about our lives. In other words, we have been less interested in showing how we make a norm legitimate than in sharpening our tools for delegitimation. (p. 185)

He provides an antidote to deal with the weaknesses of the "unmasking and debunking" view of critical thinking and liberal learning. We need to connect with others and with ourselves through inquiry. There are two routes:

> For many, this would mean complementing our literary or textual work with participation in community, with what are often called "service-learning" or "community-partnership" courses. For others, it would mean approaching our object of study not with the anticipated goal of exposing weakness or mystification but with the goal of turning ourselves in such a way as to see how what we study might inform our thinking and our lives. (Roth, 2014, p. 186)

These two routes seem promising but not unproblematic. The community, service-learning pathway has been around for a while and has engaged students in community partnerships toward collaborative engagement. However, at times, service-learning's connection to disciplinary inquiry is vague at best. Inquiry, at times, seems to get lost. And too frequently these efforts operate less as an invitation to self and community reflection and more as engagement in tunnel vision and righteous collective action. I fear, as a bald proclamation inviting others to engage in community liberal arts efforts, we overlook potentially troublesome weeds. Exemplary programs exist. Others with greater experience in the service-learning domain would be able to provide much needed distinctions, practices, and directions. I hope they do.

Roth's (2014) second option, "turning ourselves . . . to see how what we study might inform our thinking and our lives" is suggestive and also needs further examination (p. 186). However, it lacks sufficient detail and direction. I've been more engaged with the self-reflective route; I'll head there.

In the remainder of this essay, I will (a) pursue Roth's suggestion that we outline a plan of study that encourages critical self-reflection and self-formation through exploring Mark Edmundson's "final narrative" proposal, (b) examine whether this pathway and Roth's call for "safe enough" classrooms provide the needed elemental guidance, and (c) reconsider whether this plan can address intolerance from both the right and left.

Final Narratives and the Liberal Arts Curriculum

Michael Roth and Mark Edmundson must know each other, at least textually. Both envision a liberal arts education that transforms self and others—one that honors and builds upon Richard Rorty's educational pragmatism. If they haven't met, now's the time. Roth calls for an education that informs and challenges our thinking and our lives, that transforms selves. And Edmundson provides a humanities pathway that tries to do just that.

In *Why Read?* (2004) Edmundson maintains that we read so as to discover ourselves, to learn the language of ourselves and others, to come to know aspects of ourselves and the world previously unrecognized.[9] Each one of us is unique *and* we experience common human refrains and themes. We learn these languages of self and other so that we might get a glimpse of who we are and what we might become. The goal, according to Edmundson, is human transformation: an education that challenges students to consider their central or ultimate values by posing critical questions about what they value and how they ought to live.

A transformative education guides us along central life questions: How should I live my life? What are my purposes? What is work that matters? How do I picture God? Why should I go to school? Should I marry? Whom should I marry? Should I have a family? What sort of parent do I want to be? It is risky and at times difficult and messy stuff. But these questions begin to get at students' core values, or what Edmundson (following Richard Rorty) calls individuals' *final narratives*.[10] Final narratives are the stories we tell ourselves when things that really matter are questioned. They are not final in the absolute sense but rather provisional attempts to address final, ultimate life questions.

A transformative liberal arts education offers alternative narratives to challenge students' received views and enlarge or redirect their circle of meaning. It does so in a manner that engages feeling and intellect, does not presuppose a particular answer, is frequently most powerful when it comes at a time one is not sure of the way, and relies on an inner eye, an inner self.

Edmundson (2004) relates that a humanistic and transformative education invites students to empathize with a reading, a character, a point of view. Students are asked to imagine what it looks and feels like to be a character or hold a particular perspective. In doing so, the classroom can become disordered and complicated—neither pristine nor analytically precise. He writes:

> The process of human growth—when it entails growth of the heart as well as of the mind—is never particularly clean or abstract. To grow it is necessary that all of our human qualities come into play, and if some of those qualities are not pretty, then so be it. But to keep them to the side so as to preserve our professional dignity—that is too much of a sacrifice. (Men and women die every day, perish in the inner life . . . for lack of what we have to offer.) (p. 67)

Developing the inner life and facilitating human growth require that we fuse mind and heart; a transformative liberal arts education recognizes this.

How does this occur? Edmundson claims that we offer our students history, philosophy, poetry, as well as novels and their characters to invite students to imagine and empathize with ourselves and other selves (see also Nussbaum, 1990, 2001). This sort of agenda adds significant flesh and bones to Roth's call for a more self-reflective turn and illustrates just how final narratives are encouraged. To illustrate this further I'll draw from my teaching life.

In a course I teach to prospective and practicing teachers, Curriculum Theories, I have assigned Edmundson's autobiography—*Teacher* (2002)—which focuses on his high school life and a significant teacher.[11] When I first read the memoir, I struggled through what seemed at the time to be an unduly long and drawn out section recollecting his life as a visually and physically challenged linebacker. When I first assigned the text many of my students slogged through the account of his struggling football achievements. But over time I came to see this portion of his text and life as depicting a particular kind of living—the Homeric-heroic struggle of bodily pain and athletic achievement. Edmundson helped me understand my family world. He captures why my oldest son took up lacrosse and put up with bruises and welts and why my youngest son just wouldn't give up his pursuit of being the best soccer goalie around despite a delayed growth spurt. For some, excellence in physical prowess and achievement is a marker of a life that is quite valued and worth living. Many of my practicing and newly arrived secondary teachers tend to scoff at the brutish and violent elements of the football playing field.[12] Their feelings tend to be quite strong—grounded as they are in their own past, and not so distant, adolescent lives. They recall the high school smells; the characters in their school; their hurts, feelings, and varied student lives. For many of them, football and much of high school athletics are seen as distractions at best—not pursuits worth valuing.

Edmundson's rendering of his high school football existence challenges so many of those received beliefs and assumptions. It points to a gangly Edmundson entangled on a field full of human sweat, mud, and machismo hype. It points to the athletic achievement that can be had from pushing one's physical edges and captures the camaraderie and emotions attached to being part of a team. Edmundson's memoir also depicts a school year and a culture that all too often dehumanizes students and teachers, portrays a male culture that demeaned girls and women, but also illustrates that physically demanding and sometimes violent sports can help some young men become more powerfully human. Edmundson's account can be a troubling text. It can and should be a text ripe for use in prospective and practicing teachers' final narrative formation. When we read it, we ask ourselves: Is this the life we want students and teachers to lead?

In class I've had former athletes, men and women, tell others just what that life of physical achievement meant to them. They frequently tell tales filled with heart, grit, attitude, and courage. A heroic image lurks underneath. And I've had teachers return to tell me that they see their athletes differently. Of course, some of the prospective and practicing teachers in class are not challenged or changed—the text or the experience simply wasn't powerful for them.

Wrestling with such challenging texts can prompt serious examinations of our worlds and ourselves. To do so, our classrooms have to be settings where students feel safe and secure enough to challenge themselves and others—to create their final narratives. With Edmundson's text, I thought I was encouraging that. I thought I was accomplishing what Roth and Edmundson envision: an education that informs and challenges our thinking and our lives, that transforms selves. For a number of years, I believe I was.

Safe Enough Classrooms?

But last year, after a 2-year absence, I was preparing to teach my Curriculum Theories class and I reread Edmundson's memoir. This time, I heard and felt particular passages in ways I hadn't quite before. Perhaps it was due to the recent Brett Kavanaugh judicial hearings and the repercussions of the #MeToo movement. With this reading I found Edmundson's depictions of gender and high school sexuality to be, at times, much more offensive.

Before meeting to discuss the memoir, I read over the short responses that students wrote after reading the book, including the following:

> *I don't think we needed to read this book.*
> *This book pissed me off.*
> *The way he talked about women was really offensive.*

At least two students (out of 24) were deeply upset by the book and, it seemed to me, felt unsettled to the point of harm.

In the first half of our class session, students discussed, in small groups, themes in the book. And for the second half of our class session, we talked about the appropriateness of assigning the book. I posed this question: If I were to teach this class again, should I assign Edmundson's *Teacher*? Two groups formed—one in favor, the other opposed. Women and men were in both groups.

Those in favor of keeping it basically said that although some of the book's depictions seemed flawed and one-sided—seriously so at times—its value outweighed the drawbacks. Edmundson, one student said, underscored much that's truthful, then and now, about the reality of schools and teaching. Those against reassigning it said the book's expressions of toxic masculinity were over the top and unnecessary. Some students said that passages in the book reeked of disdain for, and dismissal of, women. It either shouldn't be assigned or selective, nonoffensive chapters might be used.

During the discussion, I saw more clearly, and felt more directly, the harm and heartache some students experienced. A troublesome text should challenge us to think and feel—but it shouldn't inflict harm. Listening to the women in my class, to their pain and their experiences, caused me to reconsider the *Teacher* text and look to Roth's call for "safe enough" classroom spaces. At the same time, I knew prospective and practicing teachers needed to examine and confront the "toxic masculinity" in our culture and schools. Final narratives that ignore the very real cultural conditions of our lives neither fruitfully engage nor adequately prepare. The upshot was that I had to reconsider my curriculum selection and reexamine my gendered lenses. For some students I hadn't achieved the right curricular balance between feeling safe and confronting challenges. But for all students it seems as if I had created a safe enough space where they could disagree with each other and their teacher about my curriculum selections.

Roth (2019b) maintains that in this era we need to create "safe enough" classroom spaces where students can challenge and can be challenged:

> A college classroom, then, should be a "safe space" . . . where students know that, if they espouse unpopular views, they will not be attacked, that there will no reprisals. Students then feel free (safe enough) to disagree with one another and with the professor. To use the old-fashioned term, they can "unfreeze"—abandon previously held beliefs because they will not be attacked for doing so. (p. 103)

I wish Roth would have offered more analysis of these "safe enough spaces" and revisited his prior work on "knowing others." Missing here is any qualitative or felt sense of the differences among "espousing," "disagreeing," and "attacking." In much argumentative academic discourse, the participants are not striving to achieve, as Jane Addams proposed, an "imaginative effort to see things from the point of view of others . . . especially . . . when faced with major difference" (Roth, 2014, p. 84). Instead they dice and slice an opponent's points of view so as to discredit and dismiss her. It is frequently a mean and dismissive, not safe, space. A safe enough space needs to incorporate Addams's "affectionate interpretation" as Roth espoused in *Beyond the University*.

Righteous Intolerance in the Classroom

My sense is that Roth, the university instructor, knows that both separate-analytical and connected-empathetic modes of discourse need to be conjoined in classroom discussions, that ad hominem or bald ideological attacks are to be discouraged and soon thereafter disallowed. But he doesn't delineate how this is to be accomplished in *Safe Enough Spaces* (2019b). If classrooms are to be safe enough spaces, differences need to be more than tolerated; they need to be valued, explored, and honored.

What I'm seeing on campuses these days is a marked tendency for political and ideological separatism, not the formation of final narratives that value difference. In classrooms we sometimes have the "conservative defenders" and the "social justice warriors." In the more extreme cases, one side supports intolerance and dismissal, while the other side cites verbal violence and irreparable harm to themselves and others. In a recent op-ed piece entitled "Do We Kill the Liberal Arts When We Demonize People for Their Ideas?" Roth (2017) writes:

> Instead of training our students to call out as morally inferior people with whom they have intellectual differences, we must cultivate curiosity and openness. We must highlight and enhance the consideration of alternative perspectives on culture and society. We must promote vigorous debate that doesn't degenerate into personal attack. This kind of consideration and debate is increasingly rare in the public sphere, and that's why it is more important than ever to cultivate the terrain for it on our campuses. (para. 10)

In this era when intellectual, personal, and political perspectives are melded within students' cherished identities, a simple call for "curiosity and openness" won't work. These days curiosity and openness can easily constitute unwanted challenges to students' identities. A level of detachment and remove on the part of the participants has to be accomplished. Students must be willing and able to ask themselves (and others) critical and honest questions. And we, the teachers, need to ask ourselves the following questions:

> In what ways do we cultivate the discursive classroom terrain?
> How do we encourage students to examine but not demonize differences?
> How do we create settings that challenge but don't invalidate?

This is new territory for classroom discourse and considerable thought must be given to classroom interactions that enable and facilitate the formation of challenging final narratives. It's time for liberal arts supporters to address these very real concerns. Roth hasn't, Edmundson hasn't, and I haven't. At least I haven't seen those classroom practices delineated in their published work. Michael Roth and Mark Edmundson have provided much needed support for, and examination of, the liberal arts. They have, I believe, much more to offer. I hope they do.

Notes

1. Meier and Sizer focus on high school curricula. However, their "habits of mind" approach is applicable to tertiary education also.
2. See, as an example, St. Johns College (https://www.sjc.edu/academic-programs).
3. Bard Prison Initiative: https://bpi.bard.edu/; in addition to the authors cited, see Delbanco (2012), Henry (1995), Martin (1981), Nussbaum (1997), and Oakeshott (1962).
4. During my final years at the University of Colorado-Boulder's School of Education this demand was issued by some of our doctoral students.
5. And I heard these criticisms from my undergraduate students.
6. A thoughtful discussion around the uses and appropriateness of the terms *tribe* and *tribalism* can be found at the following sites: https://www.theatlantic.com/notes/2017/11/a-nation-of-tribes-and-members-of-the-tribe/544907/, https://www.theatlantic.com/notes/2017/10/on-the-many-connotations-of-tribalism/544535/, and https://www.theatlantic.com/notes/2017/11/tribalism-before-and-after-the-virginia-vote/545408/. *The Atlantic* discussion captures a debate over a current linguistic and discursive term. The debate and the term are worth serious consideration and call upon our individual judgment. I'll return to discussions of difference at the end of this piece.
7. I'll draw mainly from two books—Roth (2014) and Roth (2019b)—and am informed by three opinion pieces: Roth (2017), Roth (2019a), and Roth (2020).
8. It needs to be noted that this empathetic turn is not easily accomplished and fraught with challenges but, I would argue, worth the effort.

9. In an earlier essay I provided some of what follows (see Whitcomb et al., 2007).

10. Edmundson uses the term *final narratives* whereas Rorty employs *final vocabulary*.

11. In this essay I focus on the male athletic focus of Edmundson's memoir. That's only a small part of the book's rich challenge. Another much larger part is how one particular teacher—Franklin Lears—provided a truly challenging and enriching liberal arts curriculum to his high school students.

12. This concern over players' well-being has been intensified in the last decade with greater awareness of the physical injuries sustained in contact sports—such as chronic traumatic encephalopathy.

References

Adler, M. (2000). *How to think about the great ideas: From the Great Books of Western civilization*. Open Court Publishing.
Bloom, A. (1987). *The closing of the American mind*. Simon & Schuster.
Boler, M. (1999). *Feeling power*. Routledge.
Bowles, S., & Gintis, H. (1976). *Schooling in capitalist America*. Basic Books.
Delbanco, A. (2012). *College: What it was, is, and should be*. Princeton University Press.
Edmundson, M. (2002). *Teacher: The one who made the difference*. Random House.
Edmundson, M. (2004). *Why read?* Bloomsbury.
Henry, W., III. (1995). *In defense of elitism*. Doubleday Anchor.
Hirst, P. (1965). Liberal education and the nature of knowledge. In R. D. Archambault (Ed.), *Philosophical analysis and education* (pp. 113–138). Humanities Press.
Martin, J. R. (1981). The ideal of the educated person. *Educational Theory, 31*(2), 97–109. https://doi.org/10.1111/j.1741-5446
Meier, D. (1996). *The power of their ideas*. Beacon Press.
Nussbaum, M. (1990). *Love's knowledge: Essays on philosophy and literature*. Oxford University Press.
Nussbaum, M. (1997). *Cultivating humanity: A classical defense of reform in liberal education*. Harvard University Press.
Nussbaum, M. (2001). *Upheavals of thought*. Cambridge University Press.
Oakeshott, M. (1962). Learning and teaching. In T. Fuller (Ed.), *The voice of liberal learning* (pp. 43–62). Yale University Press.
Roth, M. (2014). *Beyond the university: Why liberal education matters*. Yale University Press.
Roth, M. (2017). Do we kill the liberal arts when we demonize people for their ideas? [Editorial]. *The Hechinger Report*. https://hechingerreport.org/opinion-kill-liberal-arts-demonize-people-ideas/
Roth, M. (2019a). Don't dismiss safe spaces. *The New York Times*. https://www.nytimes.com/2020/09/19/opinion/campus-free-speech.html

Roth, M. (2019b). *Safe enough spaces.* Yale University Press.
Roth, M. (2020). Colleges, conservatives, and kakistocracy. *The New York Times.* https://www.nytimes.com/2020/09/19/opinion/campus-free-speech.html
Sizer, T. (1996). *Horace's school.* Houghton Mifflin.
Whitcomb, J., Borko, H., & Liston, D. (2007). Why teach? *Journal of Teacher Education, 59*(1), 3–9. https://doi.org/10.1177/0022487108322199

4

SAVING THE UNIVERSITY FROM ITSELF

Stanley Fish and the Future of the Academy

Dan Sarofian-Butin

Stanley Fish is too late. He tried to save the university, but the university that he loved, dreamed of, and fought for may be long gone. Fish, for those who may not be aware, was once the *enfant terrible* of the academic world. Tired of turning the world of Milton scholarship upside down in the 1970s, and then tired again of dismantling the deep foundations of literary and critical theory in the 1980s, Fish turned his gaze inward to his own world of the academy. In "The Unbearable Ugliness of Volvos," Fish (1994) described faculty as reveling in self-abasement, preferring ugly cars and all that went with it, such as bad offices and no power. A few years later, he castigated academics trying to shape their students into good citizens. "You can't make them into good people," Fish (2008) intoned, "and you shouldn't try" (p. 59). To be clear, Fish is not some out-of-touch academic. While dean of the College of Liberal Arts and Sciences at the University of Illinois at Chicago, he described faculty as if they were caught in a kind of Stockholm syndrome: faculty "who have been long-time inhabitants of a place and who have spent many years being disappointed, being underpaid, being under-noticed, will have entered into a strange relationship with that unhappy situation. To put it simply, they've learned not only to tolerate it but to love it" (Williams, 2001, pp. 115–116).

So why, you may be asking yourself, should I care what this seemingly haughty and puerile octogenarian—who at 83 is now the Floersheimer distinguished visiting professor of law at Yeshiva University—has to say? What does he have to offer our understanding of the university?

Is it enough that several of his books—*There's No Such Thing as Free Speech* (1994), *Is There a Text in This Class?* (1982), and *The Trouble With Principle* (1999)—are go-to classics of pragmatist and antifoundational thought? That one theorist called his book on Milton *Surprised by Sin* (1967) "an atom bomb" (MacFarquhar, 2001, p. 1)? That he has been called "America's most famous professor" (Borné, 2011)? That Russell Jacoby (2013) did a hatchet job on him in the pages of *The New Republic*: "[Fish represents] the postmodern academic life: its self-satisfaction, its self-promotion, its glibness. If the humanities are in trouble today, humanists like Fish are one of the reasons" (p. 1)? That there are 157 boxes and four oversize folders (equaling 54.6 linear feet) of his writings archived at the University of California Irvine? That he was once the chicagoan of the Year for culture? That he inspired the character of Morris Zapp in David Lodge's series of campus novels? That he published a weekly opinion blog at *The New York Times* from 2006 to 2013, which, on any given day, received hundreds of comments, most of which claimed Fish was just dead wrong about whatever it is he was writing about?

No, dear reader. Those things don't matter. What matters is that Stanley Fish has your back. He has defended you and what you do for half a century, and he's going to keep doing it until his dying breath. Or at least he will if you are a professor who searches for truth as their true calling, who leaves their politics at the door, who demands that destabilization (and not certainty) is the calling card of teaching, who believes (as Fish writes in an elegy to Harold Bloom) that higher education "is for itself, and any bending of it to an external purpose will not simply harm it, but destroy it" (Fish, 2019, p. 4).

Which is why, as I said, he is too late. Higher education may be many things, a "perfect mess" of historical serendipity and organizational mashups (Labaree, 2017), but it can certainly no longer claim to be an ivory tower of disinterested and dispassionate scholasticism. From the rise of the "new majority" of nontraditional students to the systematic defunding of public institutions to the marginalization and disappearance of tenure-stream faculty to the current "zoomification" of teaching, anyone and everyone has a position on whether a college education "is worth it" and how to make it more relevant and valuable for our current historical moment and generation of students. No one wants to claim that such a conversation is irrelevant; no one wants to suggest that higher education, "like poetry . . . makes no claim to efficacy beyond the confines of its performance" (Fish, 2008, p. 52). No one, that is, except Stanley Fish.

Look, let's be real. Fish, of course, knows the worth and value of higher education. That's why he's fought so hard for it for so long. But he would never, ever get caught in the trap of instrumentalism, trying to substantiate its value. That's just not how one of the smartest antifoundationalist thinkers out there does his job. And yet, I would argue that his job is actually more relevant and more important now than ever. It is not an anomaly nor a coincidence that higher education has become "weaponized" in the ever-expanding political battlefield of values, ideologies, free speech, and social justice. Headlines (and legislators) demand to know (and thus potentially change) the ideological positioning of what we teach our students and what we stand for (Ellis, 2021; Mitchell, 2021; Pettit, 2021).

Which leaves it up to me to explain Fish's job of trying to save the university from itself. I therefore, in the rest of this chapter, lay out Fish's vision of the university, sketch out his conceptual assumptions and foundations, and offer some parting words of both warning and hope for those of us who believe (yes, with Fish) that education is truly a process of transformation.

At first glance, Fish's vision of the university may not seem worth saving. Fish (2008) says,

> The view I am offering of higher education is properly called deflationary; it takes the air out of some inflated balloons. It denies to teaching the moral and philosophical pretensions that lead practitioners to envision themselves as agents of change or as designers of a "transformative experience," a phrase I intensely dislike. . . . Teaching is a job, and what it requires is not a superior sensibility or a purity of heart and intention . . . but mastery of a craft. (p. 53)

"Do your job," says Fish, in his always-pithy and crisp way, "don't do somebody else's job and don't let someone else do your job" (p. 8).

Colleges and universities, Fish claims, have vastly and inappropriately overreached in what they claim to do and be. Higher education should not be in the business of enhancing or expanding students' moral, civic, or social characters; nor to inveigh on current social, cultural, and political issues such as war, poverty, or racism; nor to revitalize, transform, or collaborate with local and regional communities. "I want an academy inflected by no one's politics," Fish (2008) argues, "but by the nitty-gritty obligations of teaching and research" (p. 16).

Fish is, of course, aware that there is no such thing as a space without politics, and that any claim to the contrary is itself a political move. As he wrote in a brutal and typical pragmatist takedown of both the political left and right regarding the mirage of neutral principles, "it's politics all the way down" (Fish, 1999, p. 3). Rather, the politics of the higher education classroom revolves around the debates, discussions, and (yes) political infighting of our respective academic disciplines about what to teach and research.

This is what Fish (1982) would describe as an "interpretive community" (yet another conceptual bombshell of reader-response theorizing he developed) and all the normal stuff that occurs within it. Our job as academics, Fish suggests (in one of his few less-than-elegant phrases), is to "academicize" any and every issue in front of us.

On this, Fish is a one-trick pony. "Rather than being a vocation or holy calling," Fish (2014) argues in a book on academic freedom, "higher education is a service that offers knowledge and skills to students who wish to receive them" (p. 10). In his most sustained exposition on this, Fish (2008) couldn't be clearer:

> College and university teachers can (legitimately) do two things: (1) introduce students to bodies of knowledge and traditions of inquiry that had not previously been part of their experience; and (2) equip those same students with the analytical sills—of argument, statistical modeling, laboratory procedures—that will enable them to move confidently within those traditions and to engage in independent research after a course is over. (pp. 12–13)

Everything else—all those lofty things in your institution's mission statement, all those social justice events on your campus, all those passions you have inside of you that your students should know about—"are contingent effects, and as contingent effects they cannot be designed and shouldn't be aimed at" (p. 13).

Fish is not blind to the importance of the world around us and all that is happening in it. But even though "a passion for justice is of course a good thing," Fish (2014) intones. "It's just not an academic good thing" (p. 17). This is why, to jump ahead just a bit, Fish (2014) neatly and crisply (yet again!) defines *academic freedom* as simply and solely the freedom to be an academic in your own subspecialty, pursuing such knowledge and then disseminating it to whomever has the interest in reading your work or is forced to sit in a classroom and listen to it.

> Academic freedom, correctly and (modestly) understood, is not a challenge to the imperative always to academicize; it is the name of that imperative; it is the freedom to be an academic, which is, by definition, not the freedom to be anything and everything else. (p. 80)

Yes, you can just hear the air going out of that balloon.

The question, of course, is why? Why would Fish force such a "deflationary" position on the vision and mission of higher education? Because he wants to save the university from itself.

One must first, Fish (2008) writes, "define academic work precisely and narrowly" (p. 17). Higher education, and the faculty teaching and researching within it, has a very specific function: knowledge production and dissemination. There are, of course, intended and unintended byproducts to these actions, and there are, of course, cocurricular and extracurricular functions to which higher education increasingly attends to; and the university is, of course, a part of a larger web of social, cultural, economic, and political interconnections. But ultimately, for Fish, "the pursuit of truth is the cardinal value of the academy" (p. 119). And this pursuit of truth—wherever it may lead, without end, without undue external encumbrance, done diligently and carefully within the bounds of academic practice—is what drives Fish's arguments.

It is thus job enough—and a hard one at that—to get your students to understand the content one is teaching:

> You can reasonably set out to put your students in possession of a set of materials and equip them with a set of skills (interpretive, computational, laboratory, archival), and even perhaps (although this one is really iffy) install in them the same love of the subject that inspires your pedagogical efforts . . . [but] you have little chance . . . of determining what they will make of what you have offered them once the room is unlocked for the last time and they escape first into the space of someone else's obsession and then into the space of the wide, wide world. And you have no chance at all (short of a discipleship that is itself suspect and dangerous) of determining what their behavior and values will be in those aspects of their lives that are not, in the strict sense of the word, academic. You might just make them into good researchers. You can't make them into good people, and you shouldn't try. (Fish, 2008, pp. 58–59)

This line of argument may seem pedestrian and technocratic: doing one's job as a faculty member is hard enough already. Don't, as such, Fish intones, pile up other tangential responsibilities, no matter how high-sounding or politically expedient. Faculty are "responsible for the selection of texts, the preparation of a syllabus, the sequence of assignments and exams, the framing and grading of a term paper, and so on" (p. 57). To go beyond that—to, in his words, not stick to one's job—undermines one's contractual agreement to be a good pedagogue.

And Fish is deeply concerned about the power of pedagogy. Fish wants, implores, demands, that faculty teach, and teach well. But he's not doing this because he cares about your students. He doesn't. He cares about the university. "Distinctiveness," says Fish (2008), "is a prerequisite both of our survival and of our flourishing. Without it we haven't got a prayer" (p. 100). By distinctiveness, Fish means your job.

When I walk into a classroom, all that matters is the pursuit of truth, as defined by my particular discipline's academic standards, protocols, histories, and lines of inquiry. My job as the instructor is to teach the truth as I best surmise it within the context of my specific course. I do not have to "teach the controversy" or balance my reading list to fit the desires of intelligent design advocates, conservative commentators, or anyone else attempting to influence what or how I teach. That's why I got a PhD. That's why I keep up on my literature and research. That's why I was hired. That's my job. (And not someone else's.) So back off.

The classroom thus becomes one of the few spaces where we put aside the distracting and tangential issues of, for example, political affiliations, gender identity, or whatever is on everyone's social media feed to create a "classroom full of passion and commitment" (Fish, 2008, p. 39) to whatever is on today's syllabus. We academics have a job to do, and we must do it well, because we don't want to get caught doing something we are not trained to do and open ourselves up to being told by someone else how supposedly to do our job. Fish's (2003b) point that we should "save the world on our own time" is but another way of reminding us that the academy is a highly specialized institution with highly specialized functions. It cannot be and do everything for everyone. For if we don't attend to what we do best—which is developing, testing, critiquing, transforming, and transmitting knowledge—we open ourselves up to the critique of dealing with issues for which we are not equipped or trained.

What Fish has done is attempt to safeguard the mission and practice of higher education by placing the criteria of success internal to the workings of the mission and practice of higher education. In so doing, he is attempting to dismantle external threats of imposition or intrusion into classroom practice. My status, success, and legitimacy as an academic is fully and solely dependent on, and convergent with, what I do as an academic: teach and research. And if I do this well, I am not bound by political pressure, students' desire for "balance," or even Stanley Fish's own prognostications about how I should teach my course. I am simply and solely bound to the pursuit of truth as I best see fit within my own academic and interpretive community.

I don't know about you, but I find this to be incredibly liberating. It is liberating because it allows me the opportunity to figure out what truly matters for my students—whether that's the "hidden curriculum" in my Foundations of Education class; systemic racism in my Diversity, Social Justice & Ethics class; community organizing in my Theories of Organizational Change class—and teach these as the truths (and issues) that they are. It is liberating because if I "academicize" it, I can examine anything! Which is why, by the way, one of my scholarly soapboxes (Butin, 2006, 2010; Sarofian-Butin, 2017a) has long been the "disciplining" of service-learning; if I can academicize it, I can, like any other discipline, defend it as an intellectual movement rather than a social movement (see Butin, 2008; Frickell & Gross, 2005). It is liberating because what I do matters and can actually change the world.

Which, really, is exactly Fish's point.

Fish (1994) says it this way about the impact feminism has had: "The true power of a form of inquiry or thought [is] when the assumptions encoded in the vocabulary of a form of thought become inescapable in the larger society" (p. 294). And Fish (Williams, 2001) says it this way about public scholarship: "Criticism is participating in this self-conscious rejection of a firm boundary line between the academic and the non-academic, in, let's say, gay studies courses or Latina studies courses or third-world literature courses" (p. 121).

So let me try and unpack this. For Fish will never, ever try to defend the university on instrumentalist foundations because, well, there are no foundations (see Fish, 1982). And he will never, ever try to defend the university on ethical or intellectual principles because, well, principles have no consequences (see Fish, 2003c). All Fish can do is fight as hard as he can for what he believes in with whatever tools are at his disposal. This is his strategy in regard to arguments about so-called neutral principles, and, I would suggest, in defending the university:

> I might then attack the [neutral-principle] rhetoric as part of my attack on what it was used to do. But I might turn around tomorrow and use the same rhetoric in the service of a cause I believed in. Nor would there be anything inconsistent or hypocritical about such behavior. The grounding consideration in both instances (whether I was attacking neutral-principles rhetoric or employing it) would be my convictions and commitments. (Fish, 1999, p. 8)

The key is to realize that Fish's perspective on higher education can be read as the public culmination of an academic endeavor begun more than 30 years ago in his groundbreaking analysis of John Milton, specifically, and literary theory more generally (Fish, 1967, 1972, 1982, 1999). (It is far beyond the scope of this chapter to offer a deep archeology of Fish's position; I hope it is thus sufficient to offer a few broad brushstrokes, and to note parenthetically that Fish's position aligns easily and elegantly with an entire scholarship of poststructuralist and antifoundational arguments—Biesta, 1998; Ellsworth, 1998; Kelly, 2012; Sarofian-Butin, 2017b.) Three key and interrelated themes return again and again through Stanley Fish's half century of scholarship and writings and ultimately manifest in his vision and defense of the university: the role and importance of constraints in the service of freedom—"There's no such thing as free speech, and it's a good thing too" his pragmatist stance of antifoundationalism—"why hate speech cannot be defined"; and his subsequent insistence that all we thus have is "politics all the way down" within our own "interpretive communities." These three themes serve as the basis for understanding Fish's full-throated and contrarian defense of the university and his insistence for the value and power of "doing our job" to save the academy.

For what Fish deeply and fervently wants is that the university be the *doppelganger* to his first (and still continuing) love: Milton's *Paradise Lost*. Namely, Fish (1967) discovered and was finally able to explain why Satan was seemingly more likable than God in Milton's tale; for the reader had to fall, to be seduced, to be jolted into recognizing their seeming allegiance to the Prince of Darkness, to be "surprised by sin," in order to ultimately find her way to heaven. This is how Fish (1972) derived his fundamental leitmotif of "self-consuming texts," which destabilize our sense of the normal and help us internalize a "state of doubt" as our default mode of understanding of the world.

Literature such as Milton's, Fish (1972) argues, functions as "self-consuming texts" that "do not allow a reader the security of his normal patterns of thought and belief" (p. 409). The point of such texts is exactly to avoid having the reader come to a final point: "Coming to the [final] point fulfills a need that most literature deliberately frustrates (if we open ourselves to it), the need to simplify and close" (p. 410).

This, dear reader, is why Fish wants to save the university. Because what we do, or should be doing, is "the seeking of truth, [which] must always be defended" (Fish, 2008, p. 38). For Fish, this truth-seeking is always to be understood as a verb, as a restless and never-ending encounter with the unknown, as an object of inquiry rather than an endpoint of pedagogy. This, for Fish, is the only job worth doing. So let me try to weave these threads together.

We begin with the realization that there is no such thing as freedom or truth or objectivity just floating out there in space waiting to be discovered. This is not relativism; it is how our world is constructed, as there is no neutral, objective, or God's-eye view by which to demand certainty (Rorty, 1989). Once we realize this, it becomes clear that we are free (and constrained) to build our own world. Fish (2018) phrases it this way in dismantling the statistical claims of the digital humanities:

> Everyone who preaches digital liberation should be required to read Wordsworth's "Nuns Fret Not at Their Convent's Narrow Room" once a day, and take note especially of these lines: "In truth, the prison, unto which

> we doom/Ourselves, no prison is." Wordsworth means two things: first, that the very confines of the room—be it prison, study, library, or classroom—are what makes movements of a precise kind possible; boundaries do not stifle creativity, but give it definition; and second, that the choice is not between a confined and artificial space—a prison—and freedom, but between alternative prisons. (p. 349)

These "alternative prisons" are, in fact, what give definition and meaning to what we do and how we do it. These are the interpretive communities that we build and sustain and which, in turn, build and sustain what we do. To be just a tad cliché (and yet gladly and willingly to try and follow Fish's lead): You can't have free speech without censorship; in fact, censorship must precede free speech; no censorship, no free speech (see Fish, 1994). And you can't have tolerance without intolerance; in fact, intolerance must precede tolerance; no intolerance, no tolerance (see Fish, 1999). And you can't have heaven without hell; in fact, hell must precede heaven; no hell, no heaven (see Fish, 1967).

And so, finally (thank you for waiting for it), you can't have public scholarship without scholarship.

What Stanley Fish dreads most is that academics and the academy think they can try to be "relevant" or substantiate their worth as their starting condition. But this would be like saying you can have freedom without constraints, creativity without boundaries, a heaven without a hell. That's just not the way the world (or the academy) works. To put it bluntly, our scholarship—the books we write, the conferences we attend, the department meetings we run, the syllabi we teach from—is our hell, our boundaries, our constraints, our prison. And it is only when we start there, and live there, and create our "alternative prisons," that we can be—like feminism and gay studies and (my soapbox of) academic programs in community engagement—as free as we want to be.

So let me end where Stanley Fish began. "Self-consuming texts," Fish (1972) explained, "do not allow a reader the security of his normal patterns of thought and belief" (p. 409). Rather, they undermine our sense of the normal to foster a positionality of doubt such that one can never be sure of a firm foundation, which, in turn, allows us to truly explore and engage with the text. This is, to my ear, a perfect antifoundationalist argument. One need only consider Dewey's (1910) conception of thinking as a "forked road" situation whereby the individual had to "endure suspense and to undergo the trouble of searching . . . to sustain and protract [a] state of doubt" (pp. 14, 16), which, in turn, creates a public, and, ultimately, a democracy, or Rorty's (1991) argument that the novel is "most closely associated with the struggle for freedom and equality" as it forces us to "alter our self-image" (p. 68), which, in turn, ultimately fosters a more democratic society. "A good liberal arts course is good," Fish (2008) argues, "because it introduces questions you did not know how to ask and provides you with the skills necessary to answer them, at least provisionally" (p. 52).

So there, dear reader, you have it. Do your job. Do it well. Our goals of research and teaching must be modest exactly because the job is so complex. Education is an opening into the unknown, and careful, deliberate, and powerful research and teaching is extremely difficult to do well. It really isn't our job to save the world. Rather, if we instead come to embrace the seemingly modest vision of doing our job in the academy, we might actually end up saving the world. And, if we're lucky, we might just help Fish save the future of the academy as well.

References

Biesta, G. (1998). Say you want a revolution . . . : Suggestions for the impossible future of critical pedagogy. *Educational Theory*, *48*(4). http://doi.org/10.1111/j.1741-5446.1998.00499.x

Borné, E. (2011, January). *Stanley Fish: The miracle of sentences* [Interview]. BookPage. https://bookpage.com/interviews/8659-stanley-fish-arts-culture#.YG3H-2p1KiUk

Butin, D. (2006). Disciplining service learning: Institutionalization and the case for community studies. *International Journal of Teaching and Learning in Higher Education*, *18*(1), 57–64. https://scholarworks.merrimack.edu/cgi/viewcontent.cgi?referer=https://www.google.com/&httpsredir=1&article=1017&context=soe_facpub

Butin, D. (2008). Saving the university on his own time: Stanley Fish, service-learning, and knowledge legitimation in the Academy. *Michigan Journal of Community Service Learning*, *15*(1), 62–69.

Butin, D. (2010). *Service-learning in theory and practice: The future of community engagement in higher education*. Palgrave.

Dewey, J. (1910). *How we think*. Heath.

Ellis, L. (2021, February 19). A Georgia lawmaker asked how colleges teach "privilege" and "oppression." Here's how they responded. *The Chronicle of Higher Education*. https://www.chronicle.com/article/a-georgia-lawmaker-asked-how-colleges-teach-privilege-and-oppression-heres-how-they-responded

Ellsworth, E. (1989). Why doesn't this feel empowering? Working through the repressive myths of critical pedagogy. *Harvard Educational Review*, *59*(3), 297–325. https://doi.org/10.17763/haer.59.3.058342114K266250

Fish, S. E. (1967). *Surprised by sin: The reader in* Paradise Lost. Harvard University Press. https://doi.org/10.5399/uo/hsda.3.3196

Fish, S. E. (1972). *Self-consuming artifacts: The experience of seventeenth-century literature*. University of California Press.

Fish, S. E. (1982). *Is there a text in this class? The authority of interpretive communities*. Harvard University Press.

Fish, S. E. (1994). *There's no such thing as free speech: And it's a good thing, too*. Oxford University Press.

Fish, S. E. (1999). *The trouble with principle*. Harvard University Press.

Fish, S. E. (2003a, May 16). Aim low. *The Chronicle of Higher Education*. https://www.chronicle.com/article/aim-low-45210/

Fish, S. E. (2003b, January 3). Save the world on your own time. *The Chronicle of Higher Education*. https://www.chronicle.com/article/save-the-world-on-your-own-time/

Fish, S. (2003c). Truth but no consequences: Why philosophy doesn't matter. *Critical Inquiry, 29*(3), 389–417.

Fish, S. (2008). *Save the world on your own time*. Oxford University Press.

Fish, S. (2014). *Versions of academic freedom: From professionalism to revolution*. University of Chicago Press.

Fish, S. (2018). If you count it, they will come. *NYUJL & Liberty, 12*, 333–351.

Fish, S. (2019, October 19). Harold Bloom's warning to the world. *The Atlantic*. https://www.theatlantic.com/ideas/archive/2019/10/question-one-should-never-ask-about-work-art/600337/

Frickel, S., & Gross, N. (2005). A general theory of scientific/intellectual movements. *American Sociological Review, 70*(2), 204–232. https://doi.org/10.117/00031224050/000202

Jacoby, R. (2013, August 21). Stanley Fish turned careerism into a philosophy. *The New Republic*. https://newrepublic.com/article/114224/stanley-fish-careerism

Kelly, C. (2012). Derrida in the university, or the liberal arts in deconstruction. *Canadian Journal of Higher Education, 42*(2), 49–66.

Labaree, D. F. (2017). *A perfect mess: The unlikely ascendancy of American higher education*. University of Chicago Press.

Macfarquhar, L. (2001). The Dean's List. *New Yorker, 11*, 62–72. https://www.newyorker.com/magazine/2001/06/11/the-deans-list

Mitchell, M. (2021, April 2). *The death of God and the death of higher education*. Real Clear Education. https://www.realcleareducation.com/articles/2021/04/02/the_death_of_god_and_the_death_of_higher_education_110561.html

Pettit, E. (2021, April 5). "Anti-American," pushing "Marxism," and more: Do your college here? *The Chronicle of Higher Education*. https://www.chronicle.com/article/anti-american-pushing-marxism-and-more-do-you-recognize-your-college-here

Rorty, R. (1989). *Contingency, irony, and solidarity*. Cambridge University Press.

Rorty, R. (1991). *Essays on Heidegger and others: Vol. 2. Philosophical papers*. Cambridge University Press.

Sarofian-Butin, D. (2017a). Me and the devil was walkin' side-by-side: Demythologizing (and reviewing) the *Cambridge Handbook of Service Learning and Community Engagement*. *Michigan Journal of Community Service Learning, 24*(1). https://quod.lib.umich.edu/cgi/p/pod/dod-idx/review-essay-the-cambridge-handbook-of-service-learning.pdf?c=mjcsloa;idno=3239521.0024.115;format=pdf

Sarofian-Butin, D. (2017b). Democracy dies in dualisms: A response to Atkinson's "Dewey and Democracy." *Democracy & Education, 25*(2), Article 7. https://opinionator.blogs.nytimes.com/2007/07/22/democracy-and-education/

Williams, J. J. (2001). Stanley *agonistes*: An interview with Stanley Fish. *Minnesota Review, 52*(1), 115–126.

5

THE TROUBLE WITH ELITISM

William Deresiewicz's Critique of Neoliberal Higher Education in the United States

J. Todd Ormsbee

During 2020, U.S. higher education was on the precipice of a crisis. The COVID-19 pandemic had ravaged the ill-prepared and feckless United States. The pandemic in less than a year had pushed states to slash budgets, lay off faculty and staff, transform pedagogy into "online content delivery," and streamline organizational structures within universities and colleges across the country (see Taylor, 2020). Such "emergency measures" were taken straight from neoliberalism's toolkit. Thus, the pandemic merely served as the most recent context for the ongoing and troubled restructuring of higher education in the United States over the past 50 years, as neoliberalism's values and structures have gradually remade U.S. universities in its image. The term *neoliberalism* can be used narrowly in its economic sense to indicate the structures of late 20th-century capitalism, including post-Fordist production in the developed world. But neoliberalism's impact on higher education warrants a more expansive usage that encompasses its values, perceptions, structures of feeling, and the social habits of everyday people that continually (often unwittingly) reproduce it (see Brown, 2019). In the United States in early 2021, we are in many ways witnessing a reckoning of neoliberal orthodoxy on both the right and left. None of this indicates, however, a reversal or even reduction in neoliberalism's reach and power in the United States or the world, least of all in higher education.

Among those who have been pointing out the weaknesses and problems of American higher education, William Deresiewicz has written from the perspective of the elite universities, the Ivies and highly selective liberal arts colleges. He penned a brief piece for *The American Scholar* (2008) enumerating the ways that an "elite" education might actually be bad for students. A few years later, Deresiewicz expanded his analysis into a book-length argument, *Excellent Sheep: The Miseducation of American Elite and the Way to a Meaningful Life* (2015a). And he has continued to write and speak out about higher education over the past 5 years in shorter essays, YouTube videos, and public speaking engagements. In the final chapter of *Excellent Sheep* as well as in the clarifying article "The Neoliberal Arts," Deresiewicz (2015c) connects his critique of elite higher education to the dominating values and practices of neoliberalism. His is not a systematic analysis, but more a defense of a traditional liberal arts, humanistic education from the perspective of a former Yale professor.

Reckoning with Deresiewicz's criticism of American higher education can open up some of the foundational, student-, and pedagogy-level transformations that neoliberalism has wrought in the American university. Throughout his writings and talks, Deresiewicz espouses a somewhat traditional theory of education (and by extension, *mis*education) that reaches broadly to a theory of learning, a defense of the humanities, and a resuscitation of older ideas of liberal arts education. His critiques of higher education rest upon these value propositions, but he often leaves them largely decontextualized and unexamined.

Deresiewicz focuses his critique of elite university education on an analysis of meritocracy and its relationship to larger structures and inequalities within elite education. His critique of meritocracy in education is thin; nonetheless, it focuses on the elite students who by and large already benefit from the cultural and social capital of their parents and will move into parallel social positions after graduation. Deresiewicz examines parents and their high-achieving (or "hoop-jumping," as he calls them) children who attend elite universities. His case rests largely on an unexamined presumption of individual agency within larger socioeconomic systems. Finally, he critiques neoliberalism's impact on higher education writ large, without the kinds of details and system-level analysis that would lend credence to his position. Taken as a whole, Deresiewicz's argument offers little more than surface-level analysis and unexplored assumptions about the current systems, while also proposing what might still be a useful value proposition for higher education. The strengths in Deresiewicz's argument remind us of what might still be valuable in American higher education, and his shortcomings suggest some fruitful ways to more accurately see how we got to this point in the first place and where we should focus our attention for redressing the problems and, perhaps, a full-scale remaking of the American university.

A Return to a Liberal Arts Theory of (Mis)Education

In *A Jane Austen Education*, Deresiewicz (2012) uses his interpretation of Austen's novels, particularly *Northanger Abbey*, to build a theory of education. In *Excellent Sheep,* Deresiewicz (2015a) further developed this theory into a normative recommendation for students (and their parents)—a way out of the brutal competition of the meritocracy, toward a truer, deeper education:

> There is an intense hunger among today's students, my travels in the last few years have shown me, for what college ought to be providing but is not: for a larger sense of purpose and direction; for an experience at school that speaks to them as human beings, not bundles of aptitudes; for guidance in addressing the important questions of life; for simple permission to think about these things and a vocabulary with which to do so. (p. 73)

Most recently, Deresiewicz (2017b) has defined *liberal arts education* as "inquiry into the fundamental human questions, undertaken through rational discourse" (para. 33) and argues that the current university resists the liberal arts because they challenge both "political correctness" (the university's own moral certainty) and neoliberalism's underlying market rationales.

The ideal university, for Deresiewicz, should offer a "liberal arts education, centered on the humanities, conducted in small classrooms by dedicated teachers" (p. 149). College should be four years of "slow, painstaking work" to learn the arguments of others and formulate your own (2015b, p. 150). The *humanities-focused* education is one that brings us to a "knowledge of ourselves," he argues (p. 160). "'That's me!'" is the essential experience of art. Universities should be "places of free, frank, and fearless inquiry" (2017b, para. 43). And liberal education should liberate us from doxa, while making us comfortable with doubt by giving us an interval of time to think and be free (see 2012, pp. 80–81). Deresiewicz's entire theory of higher education rests on his presumption of the cultivation of the self. His constant focus on the self-focused *experience* of humanities education is barely brought back from the brink of complete solipsism by a corollary argument that the humanities in turn invite us to experience the world as the Other, thereby decentering the self. Yet the argument he makes to students is that education is for their selves, for finding their vocation, their purpose, what they believe, and how they feel as individuals.

In his 2008 article, Deresiewicz argues that the contemporary university fails to teach students "how to think" and instead teaches them the rhetorical skills necessary for law, business, and medicine (see also 2015b). In other words, for Deresiewicz, the university as it is offers quite the opposite of a liberal education, having become the "corporate university," offering specialties that are lucrative, not scholarly or intellectual. This is the core of his theory of miseducation: the tension between professionalization and educating "the whole man." Since the defunding of public higher education that began in the 1970s, universities have needed students as revenue centers, and so treat them as consumers. Nonlucrative research is not valued; teaching is only valued inasmuch as it pleases students and delivers the credentials they are paying for; new buildings rather than first-rate teaching and broad exploration of the world through scholarship are the "selling points" (2015b, p. 69).

Deresiewicz's (2015a) solutions, however, are anemic: "[B]ring back teaching to the center of the mission" and double the number of professors (p. 188) is all he has to offer. I do not wish here to dismiss out of hand his theory of teaching as a craft (see 2012). For Deresiewicz, the good teacher awakens and inspires, practices pedagogy as a craft aimed at mentoring others in the practice of thinking. He argues that in his experience, students really want teachers who challenge them and care about them (2015b), but that the university institution "brackets" good teaching, relegating it to a secondary (at best) part of a professor's work. He goes so far to argue that bad teaching is actually rewarded in research universities. Unfortunately, this critique of the professoriate all but ignores the neoliberal context he claims to be addressing. To wit, he only cursorily analyzes higher education's reliance on contingent and adjunct faculty (only one page), whereas such part-time instructors routinely teach over 65% of courses on a given campus, especially at public institutions. Contingent faculty are more dependent on the consumer relationship they have with students than permanent faculty, as their continued employment often depends on student evaluations of their teaching effectiveness.

If he is right that miseducation derives from the perverse incentives of the corporate university (and I think he is right), then solving that basic problem will take more than simply doubling the number of professors (although that might begin to address the ever-growing academic labor injustice that he ignores). The education problem Deresiewicz has observed demands fundamental reorganizations based on values antithetical to the value-driven atomized individualism of neoliberalism. Left alone, the structure of the neoliberal university will simply continue to reproduce the miseducative values Deresiewicz deplores unless and until those structures are addressed, no matter how many professors there are or how central teaching is to retention, tenure, and promotion.

Although Deresiewicz makes very clear that the current state of higher education is in opposition to liberal arts and humanities traditions, it is less clear whether American education ever did actually provide a liberal arts education approaching his ideal. His appeals to history notwithstanding, it more often seems that Deresiewicz doesn't know how deeply divided Americans have been from the beginning about the relationship between the economic *utility* of education and its democratic, intellectual, or spiritual value. American universities were shifting toward the professionalization he decries by the 1880s at the latest; Harvard of yore was notoriously *not* student-centered, experiential, or humanistic (Thoreau's descriptions of the rigid, rote learning of his Harvard education in the early 19th century come to mind; see Walls, 2018). The elite of the early republic were suspicious of educating the masses, and it took nearly 100 years for the United States to develop anything one could reasonably call "public education." Education within a large modern society is institutionalized and structured by law, and flows of money and power (be they small or great) are determined by the values of legislators, board members, parents, and students rather than ideals of a liberal arts education. This makes the values that drive the institutions and judgments about miseducation far more complicated than Deresiewicz's analysis of education allows. What would *liberal arts* and *humanities* mean either within or against neoliberal institutionalization?

In the end, Deresiewicz's ideal humanities education is compelling and resonates with the like-minded (and has been explored much better and more thoroughly by many others), but in the context of a critique of elitism, meritocracy, ruling classes, and neoliberalism, it comes off as tone deaf. What do such things mean to a student coming from poverty or from an immigrant family or a rural, working class, non-"high-achieving" student? Opposing neoliberalism and its concomitant values requires far more than an "alternative perspective" and individual choice for "elite" students. Value arguments (or normative arguments, or idealist arguments, if you prefer) are among the most difficult and fraught kinds of arguments to make, as any good ethical philosopher can tell you. And yet they must be made.

Deresiewicz's argument for a deep, self-reflective, humanities-focused, liberal arts education with mentor-guides as teachers is not only orthogonal to neoliberal higher education, but it is indeed directly oppositional to it. That means a more thorough, sound, and detailed argument against the larger social structure that surrounds and shapes the 21st-century U.S. culture of education is required. This flaw is not unique to Deresiewicz and can be found even in some of the best defenses of liberal arts education (see, e.g., Nussbaum, 1998). In other words, "humanities" and "liberal arts" are value propositions that must be made within and in contradistinction to the neoliberalism that has remade the old (false) promise of meritocracy into its central ideology. Neoliberalism's values are constantly being made concrete in the real world and embodied by professors and students, administrators, and support staff. Only a complete reorganization of the university and the states (or donors) that fund them could produce anything other than what we currently have. No amount of hiring of professors will fix this.

Meritocracy and the Elite

Emerging from both his own elite education and his experience as a professor at Yale University, Deresiewicz defines *elite* in a straightforward way as the class of people who run the economy and government. The elite universities, by which he means for all intents and purposes the Ivies and selective liberal arts colleges, are then the organs of class reproduction. Indeed, Deresiewicz argues that class reproduction and self-continuation are the twin motivations of elite higher education in the United States. Education at the elite end today, Deresiewicz (2015a) argues, is a production line that begins in competitive preschools and spits out elite students from elite high schools at the other. From the parent perspective, college prep tutors and test prep comprise the cost of transforming their offspring into elite university students. From the university's perspective, the system produces those who "merit" an elite education in order to reproduce their own social power and economic base. After all, "meritocrats *are* future donors, as long as you select and train them right" (p. 72).

Deresiewicz (2015b) illustrates this with his time serving on Yale's admissions committee and the "resume arms race," where he saw firsthand how the shift to a meritocratic admissions process has produced twin problems. On one hand, the egalitarianism and opportunity that meritocracy claims to create are nothing more than veneers over a system of privilege, and on the other hand, it has transformed the entire process of educating the ruling class, so that "diversity of sex and race is a cover, even an alibi, for increasing economic resegregation" (p. 213). Once a student (statistically the vast majority of whom are from the professional classes and above) is accepted, she is praised for her "merit" in everything from recruiting documents to speeches to the ways she is treated by professors. For Deresiewicz, the university is now a context of stroking student egos, as they will be the future donors and reproducers of the system that produced them. Deresiewicz also makes a moral diagnosis of this meritocracy, that having "merited" admission to an elite university, students are then enculturated into seeing their own excellence as superiority, part of a "big sort" that segregates Americans by mindset and status (p. 214).

Deresiewicz's narrow focus on elite universities undermines his larger claims, as he largely ignores or misapprehends the full social context in which the "elite" students who "merit" admission live. In a book-length argument about higher education, he barely begins to scratch the surface of the real economic and ethnic diversity of American university students nationwide. It takes more than 100 pages for *Excellent Sheep* to boil down "non-elite" students into the children of immigrants and those lacking economic access to the training pipeline, an oversimplification to say the least. His focus on the elite leads him to produce some problematic propositions. For instance, he advises the children of immigrants to dare to go against parental wishes and poor students to choose majors based on their search for purpose and deep learning, not their economic betterment. When he talks about poverty and social injustice (among the primary concerns for the majority of my students at a public comprehensive university, regardless of their majors) he does so only in the context of pleading with graduates of elite universities to consider "social entrepreneurship" as valid occupations after graduation.

The problem with U.S. higher education is most assuredly not whether or not a Columbia graduate will choose a career as a social worker. Rather, the problem is that popular education theory tends to imagine U.S. students and schools as outside or exempt from the consequences of the nation's social problems, sidelining the pervasive issues of unequal access to social and educational goods and resources, including high-quality liberal arts classrooms. For the majority of American university students, these social inequalities are the realities of their day-to-day worlds and their experience as students. The problem isn't so much that Deresiewicz focuses on elite universities, but that he doesn't carry his own contextual critiques far or deep enough and so ends up reproducing the very elitism he purports to critique while remaining largely irrelevant to higher education as a whole.

Deresiewicz connects neoliberalism to his compelling, but ultimately underdeveloped, theory of the "elite" within meritocracy by the lightest of threads. Although he understands that he's talking about the replication of the ruling class, by focusing on the ruling class and not the system as a whole, he ultimately does little or nothing to disrupt that replication. For example, he acknowledges that university education can reproduce or grant cultural capital, but with little understanding of what cultural capital is and how it functions in the larger neoliberal order. Deresiewicz mistakenly boils cultural capital down to the 19th-century idea of "high culture," an error that could be avoided with the most cursory look at social scientific theory from the past 20 years. By having such a narrow understanding of cultural capital, he wipes from view the larger problems of cultural capital, which is the ability to function in particular social settings where power and wealth are traded upon (see, e.g., McNamee, 2018). He argues rather wanly, then, that liberal arts education should be for everyone, not just the elite, noting that "kids who really are from lower-income families" have obstacles to overcome, but that "if you grow up with less, you are much better able to deal with having less" (2015a, p. 120). In "The Neoliberal Arts" Deresiewicz (2015c) attempts to broaden his focus by acknowledging what the vast majority of U.S. professors already know—that "the most important problems are everywhere at every level: small regional colleges and large state universities, etc. . . . They are everywhere because neoliberalism is everywhere" (para. 23).

Deresiewicz's critique of elite institutions as engines of a broken meritocracy pulls against the ways that these institutions are tied into larger neoliberal systems, not merely by their values, but in their very structures. It is not, then, that elite students are victims of neoliberalism's values in their education, but rather that they are participating in, and beneficiaries of, the reproduction of neoliberalism's power through one of the primary sources of neoliberal cultural capital: elite universities. This deeper structural imbrication points us beyond the dynamics of the admissions committees, campus boosterism, and self-congratulatory meritocrats toward the American higher education system, class system, and economy as a whole. A critique of meritocracy that rests narrowly on the assembly line of "high-achieving students" at elite universities and selective colleges cannot see the forest for the trees.

Ruling Class Parents, Their "Hoop-Jumping" Offspring, and the Illusion of Individual Choice

By focusing on what parents and students are doing wrong rather than on the institutions and systems, Deresiewicz fails to fully critique the connections among elite higher education, neoliberalism, and the ruling class. Deresiewicz eschews the systemic changes necessary to resist or reverse neoliberalism's ongoing remaking of higher education and instead presents individualist choices as the pathway to a high-quality education—not a neoliberal education—that they, the ruling elite parents and students, so deserve. To put this more bluntly, Deresiewicz seeks not to solve the problems of neoliberal higher education but to reassure the individualist conceits of the meritocractic elite, by reinforcing their agency, real or imagined, to receive the education they do indeed merit. Deresiewicz understands that neoliberal meritocracy itself produces the helicopter parents and hyperprescriptive education he deplores; he also understands that students arrive at university having already been formed by those systems. Thus interpellated, students and their parents become education consumers, wanting assurances that they are purchasing an education that is "worth it." Meanwhile, universities want their money (i.e., alumni donations).

Reminiscent of C. Wright Mills's (1951/2002) mid-20th-century critique of the white-collar class who exchange their freedom of thought and autonomous meaningful work for status, neoliberalized students emerge from a meritocratic system risk-averse and status-focused. Reminiscent of consumerism's core value of predictability (Ritzer, 2018), they want a predictable educational experience with no unknowns and clear ways to "succeed" in the future (Deresiewicz, 2015a). This ultimately leads to college students who are careerist, ambitious without real direction or purpose, risk-averse, accustomed to and expecting "Hobbesian competition," and who are ultimately deeply cynical toward education in general (p. 56). But neoliberal values and structures have also reshaped the majority of American university students who are not part of the elite, in similar but not identical ways.

There is an overlap and contrast of elite students versus nonelite students at public universities and community colleges that remains unexplored or unspoken in Deresiewicz, which lessens his accuracy and declaws his argument. For elite students and their parents, higher education is a purely instrumental transaction leading to a guaranteed position in the class hierarchy on the other side. Deresiewicz (2015c) illustrates with the ways that students now interact with professors transactionally, rather than "to talk about ideas in an open-ended way" (para. 36). From my experience at a state comprehensive university, I suspect that nonelite students also instrumentalize their educations, another hallmark of neoliberal values, but this remains unexplored or merely implied in Deresiewicz.

Despite his insistence on the relationship between the neoliberal system and the personalities of students, Deresiewicz relies on the individual choices of students to solve the problem, telling them how to get a real education despite the system that brought them to this point. Individualism in the form of consumer choice is a bedrock of neoliberal cultural values (see Brown, 2017). The choices necessary for a true education, as spelled out in Deresiewicz's book, would require going against parents, social convention, and a student's own training—in other words, the deeply embedded culture of neoliberalism.

Both the *Stanford Crimson* and the *New Yorker* read Deresiewicz's call to make different educational choices as blaming students (and their parents) for their own miseducation, reiterating the life-long competition and pressure on high-achieving "elite" students (Ahamed, 2014a, 2014b; Heller, 2014). They both note the pressures and stresses of achievement that elite students endure. Indeed, much contemporary research has shown that the professional classes work extraordinarily hard to reproduce themselves in this new meritocracy (see Markovits, 2019). But this critique of Deresiewicz tends to swing to the mirror image of the same problem, where the critics end up excusing or justifying the behavior and choices of elite students because of their neoliberal context, which then denies the degree to which elite students do, in fact, have agency within the system and the possibility of resisting it. So far, neither Deresiewicz nor his critics have teased out the relationship between the individual and (neoliberal) society, between large impersonal social forces and the ways and means individual actors have of acting within that system, either to reproduce it or to resist it. And none in this elite milieu have done anything to address the inequalities reproduced by the elite higher education system, ultimately choosing to cling to the neoliberal meritocracy that grants them their status in American society.

This is a basic mistake of sociological imagination (1959/2000). Mills argues that what is needed is an adequate understanding of the interrelationship between individual agency and social structure generally, and for us today, specifically within neoliberalism. In "The Neoliberal Arts," Deresiewicz (2015c) acknowledges his critics, but continues to misunderstand the problem with his argument. "[M]uch of the negative response to my suggestion that students ought to worry less about pursuing wealth and more about constructing a sense of purpose for themselves presumes that young people are the passive objects of economic forces" (para. 45). That is also Heller's and Ahamed's respective critiques. But it is not the actual problem. Although students' options are perhaps broader than they may understand, the problems of neoliberalization of education begins in kindergarten; poor and disadvantaged students from lower to middling high schools are taught that if they play the neoliberal game—checking off boxes on rubrics, they will succeed by getting into a state college and getting a degree. This degree is for most of them still an overall income increase over that of their parents.

For example, in his discussion of risk-aversion among today's university students, Deresiewicz fails to account for how, as I mentioned previously, predictability (and certainty) are larger values of the neoliberal consumer order (see Ritzer, 2018). Predictability is neither a free-floating value nor a matter of individual choice on the part of any of the individuals in the relations of educational exchange; rather, it is part of the cultural air they breathe. Overcoming student aversion to risk involves far more than simply begging students to "let go" and "take a leap" (although to be fair, it is often all that professors have in their power to do).

For those concerned with the transformation of universities into glorified job training camps and status confirmers, a deeper critique of neoliberalism must see clearly the interconnections between student values and behaviors while accounting for the larger context that constrains individual choices.

I do not mean to imply here that students do not have some degree of agency. Rather, I would insist that the problem is much greater and deeper than individual choice allows; any solution that rests simply on the notion that (elite) students should make different choices is utterly inadequate. The conversation doesn't need to be about, as Deresiewicz says (2015c), modernity as both a gift and burden of freedom, (see paras. 19–21) but about how post-Fordist economic, social, and political structures have conspired to remove or constrain freedom and limit choice to market utility and human beings to being capital resources. In fact, those structures are massive and out of most of our control; democracy itself has been compromised thoroughly (at least in the United States) to the point that significant percentages of young people today think that democracy (freedom, self-government, choice) doesn't even matter anymore (Guilford, 2016).

Neoliberalism works to reduce humanity completely to market instrumentality, beyond and outside educational institutions. Neoliberalism, like all dominant ideologies, shapes perceptions to such an extent that the words Deresiewicz uses to explain the value of education lose their meaning completely. This is not new to the post-Fordist world, however. C. Wright Mills (1951/2002) described the "happy robots" of the middle class who *knew* that they were doing soulless, mindless, meaningless work, but they were doing so in exchange for their *social status*. In Mills's terms, the miseducation that Deresiewicz describes is the educational corollary to the middle-class dilemma he described in *White Collar*. Getting a real education is not, in these circumstances, merely a *choice* that students can make on their own. The entire social structure is conspiring against real education at this point; and the entire system would be destabilized if students questioned the values that push them to succeed within neoliberal meritocracy.

Neoliberalism *needs* the uniformly producible commodity—in this case, the labor value of students—to function at peak efficiency. Everything from formulaic TV shows, to chain motels, to pseudocustomizable automobiles and fashion are mass produced according to this rationale. This kind of predictability in institutional "product" is generated through assessment regimes, where learning and education are reduced to rubrics and checklists and pseudomeasures of quantifiability in order to demonstrate to funders (donors or state legislators, as well as tuition-payers) that the "product" they are paying for is predictable and of sound market value. The problem, then, is not that Deresiewicz blames students and urges them to make different choices; the problem is that prescribing individual choice as the solution to the problems of neoliberal education is like prescribing consumer choice as the solution to global warming or labor exploitation.

Higher Education, Neoliberalism, and Justice?

In *Excellent Sheep*, there's little direct reference to neoliberal social conditions as such, although he does correctly identify some of its most egregious consequences in higher education (2015a). "The Neoliberal Arts" takes some steps in the right direction, acknowledging that the problems, which he had myopically ascribed to the high-achieving students of the Ivy League, are in fact symptoms of broader social ills (2015c). "Call it Reaganism or Thatcherism, economism or market fundamentalism, neoliberalism is an ideology that reduces all values to money values. . . . Neoliberalism tells you that you are valuable exclusively in terms of your activity in the marketplace" (para. 9). Here, Deresiewicz correctly identifies the problems that neoliberalism per se has created for education, particularly the idea that learning could be prized as anything other than a market value. He notes correctly, across his three primary works on higher education, that the most popular majors are professional, managerial, and market-driven.

As I have argued previously, the overall problem of Deresiewicz's argument lies in his undertheorization of neoliberalism, which leads to an underestimation of how and to what extent neoliberalism is driving the institutions he decries and the student behavior that disappoints him so, which leads him to faulty and short-sighted remedies. At this point, the scholarship responding to educational neoliberalism is deep and broad; it was already largely developed when Deresiewicz wrote his 2008 article. David Harvey (1991) published his detailed description of the transformations of culture under post-Fordist production 17 years earlier. Lisa Duggan's (2003/2014) *The Twilight of Equality*, for example, laid out the ways that neoliberalism seeks to flatten culture and eliminate risk for the market by transforming cultural diversity and difference into manageable personal "flair" expressed through consumerism. And the same year that Deresiewicz published *Excellent Sheep*, Henry Giroux (2014) published *Neoliberalism's War on Higher Education*.

Bemoaning the loss of traditional liberal arts, focusing on elite students, and proposing individual choice as a solution to the whole affair simply cannot even begin to adequately account for the conditions of neoliberalism, the kinds of subjectivities it produces, the institutional instantiation and reproduction of neoliberal values, or the role education plays in that reproduction. In the end, the reduction of higher education to market efficiencies simply demands much stronger solutions than Deresiewicz has given. One could argue that at the level of the individual student (and perhaps their families), Deresiewicz's argument can help them make different, perhaps braver choices. This may be true. But the attitudes, perceptions, and values that Deresiewicz bemoans in parents, students, administrators, and professors are a result of decades of ideological work to restructure the U.S. economy (and by extension global markets) through political alliances and laws and flows of money and power. The concomitant shift in values is the cultural support network of these larger social systems, including higher education. One wonders, then, how we might actually intervene into and disrupt these systems. Surely, begging high-achieving hoop-jumping elite students to stop worrying about success, major in the humanities or social work, and go to a state university or a selective liberal arts college amounts to almost nothing. It certainly does zero to alleviate the pressures on my students, the decidedly nonelite—that is, the vast majority of American university students. Ultimately, Deresiewicz's critique of elite higher education and neoliberal education is motivated by specific cultural outcomes he doesn't like or that grate on his own sensibilities, rather than on any larger sense of injustice, inequality, or higher learning for American students. Ideal notions of what college *should* be must never be detached and therefore ignorant of, or naïve about, the flows of social, economic, and political power that are shaping, limiting, and constraining the behavior of the individuals who live within it. Any useful and productive critique of education must be a thoroughgoing interplay between what *is* and what one would like it to be.

References

Ahamed, N. (2014a, October 30). Revisiting Deresiewicz, Part I: Addressing criticisms of "Excellent Sheep" author. *The Stanford Daily*. https://www.stanforddaily.com/2014/10/29/revisiting-Deresiewicz-part-i-addressing-criticisms-of-excellent-sheep-author/

Ahamed, N. (2014b, October 31). Revisiting Deresiewicz, Part II: Toward a productive conversation. *The Stanford Daily*. https://www.stanforddaily.com/2014/10/30/revisiting-Deresiewicz-toward-a-productive-conversation/

Brown, W. (2017). *Undoing the demos: Neoliberalism's stealth revolution*. Zone Books.

Brown, W. (2019). *In the ruins of neoliberalism: The rise of antidemocratic politics in the West*. Columbia University Press.

Deresiewicz, W. (2008, June 1). The disadvantages of an elite education. *The American Scholar*. https://theamericanscholar.org/the-disadvantages-of-an-elite-education/

Deresiewicz, W. (2012). *A Jane Austen education: How six novels taught me about love, friendship, and the things that really matter*. Penguin Books.

Deresiewicz, W. (2014, December 28). The death of the artist—And the birth of the creative entrepreneur. *The American Scholar*. https://www.theatlantic.com/magazine/archive/2015/01/the-death-of-the-artist-and-the-birth-of-the-creative-entrepreneur/383497/

Deresiewicz, W. (2015a). *Excellent sheep: The miseducation of the American elite and the way to a meaningful life*. The Free Press.
Deresiewicz, W. (2015b, February 8). The academic dilemma. *Columbia Daily Spectator*. https://columbiaspectator.com/2012/02/21/academic-dilemma/
Deresiewicz, W. (2015c, September 1). The neoliberal arts: How college sold its soul to the market. *Harper's Magazine*. https://harpers.org/archive/2015/09/the-neoliberal-arts/
Deresiewicz, W. (2017, March 6). On political correctness: Power, class, and the new campus religion. https://theamericanscholar.org/on-political-correctness/#.X2fK-59ZlDUJ
Duggan, L. (2014). *The twilight of equality? Neoliberalism, cultural politics, and the attack on democracy*. Beacon Press. (Original work published 2003)
Giroux, H. A. (2014). *Higher education after neoliberalism*. Haymarket Books.
Guilford, G. (2016, November 30). Harvard research suggests that an entire global generation has lost faith in democracy. *Quartz*. https://qz.com/848031/harvard-research-suggests-that-an-entire-global-generation-has-lost-faith-in-democracy/
Harvey, D. (1991). *The condition of postmodernity: An enquiry into the origins of cultural change*. Wiley-Blackwell.
Heller, N. (2014, August 25). Poison ivy: Are élite colleges bad for the soul? *New Yorker*. https://www.newyorker.com/magazine/2014/09/01/poison-ivy
Markovits, D. (2019). *The meritocracy trap: How America's foundational myth feeds inequality, dismantles the middle class, and devours the elite*. Penguin Press.
McNamee, S. J. (2018). *The meritocracy myth* (4th ed.). Rowman & Littlefield.
Mills, C. W. (2000). *The sociological imagination* (40th anniversary ed.). Oxford University Press.
Mills, C. W. (2002). *White collar: The American middle classes* (50th anniversary ed.). Oxford University Press.
Nussbaum, M. C. (1998). *Cultivating humanity: A classical defense of reform in liberal education* (rev. ed.). Harvard University Press.
Ritzer, G. (2018). *The McDonaldization of society: Into the digital age* (9th ed.). SAGE.
Taylor, A. (2020, September 8). The end of the university: The pandemic should force America to remake higher education. *The New Republic*. https://newrepublic.com/article/159233/coronavirus-pandemic-collapse-college-universities
Walls, L. D. (2018). *Henry David Thoreau: A life*. University of Chicago Press.

PART TWO

ON LABOR AND LEARNING

6

ACCESSING THE ACADEMY

David Kirp on Higher Education

Kevin Murray

David Kirp is emeritus professor of public policy at the University of California at Berkeley. In a host of books and articles, scholarly and popular, Kirp has written extensively on social problems and public policy (see, e.g., Kirp, 2000; Kirp et al., 1986, 1997). His work has focused, in particular, on American education, including early childhood education (Kirp, 2007, 2011) and higher education (Kirp, 2003, 2019).

In this chapter, I delineate and evaluate what Kirp has had to say about higher education during his career as an academic, policy consultant, and public intellectual. I focus on two of Kirp's books: *The College Dropout Scandal* (2019) and *Shakespeare, Einstein, and the Bottom Line: The Marketing of Higher Education* (2003). My main contention will be that accessibility—to higher education and to scholarly work about higher education alike—is the central value that motivates and threads together Kirp's work on higher education. Kirp himself, however, rarely provides explicit articulations of this and other animating values and how they support and are promoted by his various educational proposals. At the end of the chapter, I develop a framework, rooted in the civic republican political tradition (see, especially, Pettit, 1997, 2012, 2014) that can be used to interpret Kirp's work and situate it within a broader educational and political context.

Higher Education's "Dirty Little Secret"

In *The College Dropout Scandal*, Kirp (2019) documents, evaluates, and proposes strategies to address the alarming dropout rate in higher education. He deems the dropout problem "higher education's dirty little secret, a dereliction of duty that has gotten too little public attention" (p. 4). Kirp details the severity of the dropout problem in the United States: 34 million Americans over the age of 25 have entered higher education and earned college credits but left before earning a degree; fewer than 60% of 1st-year students graduate in 6 years; fewer than 40% of community college students graduate or transfer to a university within 6 years; fewer than 50% of students at public universities graduate. Leaving higher education has destructive consequences for students, especially for low-income, minority, and first-generation students—a group that Kirp calls "new-gen students" (p. 3). Those 34 million Americans leave higher education with student debt but an inability to secure high-paying jobs, and they are more likely than college graduates to be unemployed and to default on their student loans. The 40% of 1st-year students who do not graduate are often denied the intellectual and social capital required for social mobility, and they are left on the bottom of an increasingly consequential education gap—one associated with home ownership, geographic mobility, life expectancy, and health status.

Kirp (2019) identifies six tools that can be used to confront and remedy the dropout problem, which he takes to be especially promising because "they don't cost a fortune and they don't require a genius to make them work" (p. 7). Students, especially talented students from low-income families, need (a) *information* about the higher education landscape. College staff can use text messages and other outreach to (b) *nudge* students to begin and persist in college. The institution can use (c) *data analytics* to identify 1st-year students who will likely need additional support and to provide that support "before their problems ripen into crises" (p. 7). Institutions can develop and provide (d) *experiences* that cultivate a sense of belonging and a growth mindset in students. Departments can (e) *revamp make-or-break classes*, such as remedial math, reading, and writing, in order to reduce failing grades and alleviate their negative consequences. Community colleges and universities can (f) *build connections* that generate smoother pathways to a bachelor's degree. Drawing together the research demonstrating the link between student success and engagement in the campus community, Kirp maintains that these tools work because they promote belonging. They allow students to feel "that they are full-fledged members of a community that takes them seriously, as individuals, rather than members of an impersonal bureaucracy that batch-processes them like Perdue chickens" (p. 8). Kirp proceeds through a series of case studies that demonstrate a range of institutions—including Valencia College, the City University of New York, and Georgia State University—that employ these tools to enhance retention and graduation.

Though Kirp does not discuss accessibility at length, a robust commitment to it appears to animate and undergird his endeavor to challenge the morally and economically troubling dropout rate. Promoting accessibility—in the sense of robust access to higher education, that is, having a genuine opportunity to succeed and graduate—is the central aim of the text. We ought to object to and challenge the high dropout rate because it undermines the opportunity of students—especially new-gen students—to access and graduate from college and to reap the considerable associated benefits. Further, in denying access, the dropout rate gives the lie to the narrative that higher education is a central source of social mobility.

Accessibility in the sense of widening access to scholarly work about higher education seems another foundational principle. Kirp avoids the academic temptation to develop and indulge in obscurant jargon. Instead, he writes clearly and directly, guiding us through the student success terrain and his six proposed solutions to the dropout problem with a series of engaging case studies. Kirp's (2019) stated aim is prodding "institutions with scandalous track records into action" (p. 11)—an aim doubtless furthered by his transparent articulation of our best knowledge about student success. A related aim—not discussed by Kirp, but one that he might well endorse—is the democratic requirement of a "contestatory" citizenry capable of guarding "against majoritarian oppression of minorities, the exploitation of public office for the electoral or other advantage of incumbents, and in particular the usurpation of state power for the purposes of advancing the special interests of the rich and powerful" (Pettit, 2014, p. 204). Drawing on Adam Ferguson, an 18th-century Scottish thinker, Phillip Pettit calls this contestatory disposition "the 'refractory and turbulent zeal' of any people fortunate enough to live under a government they could shape. He [Ferguson] thought such zeal was required to ensure the eternal vigilance that . . . was reckoned to be the price of liberty" (p. 132). To fulfill that contestatory role in contemporary deliberation about higher education and how it ought to be structured and distributed, citizens need the accessible articulation of scholarly work on student success that Kirp provides.

The Marketplace and the Academy Collide

In *Shakespeare, Einstein, and the Bottom Line*, Kirp (2003) examines and evaluates the collision of the market and higher education. He takes what may well be seen as an unusually moderate approach to this terrain, at least in education research, where many analyses of the state of education in contemporary capitalism—often deemed "neoliberal capitalism"—take a bleaker and more structural form (see, e.g., Blacker, 2013; Lipman, 2011). Notably, the book was published in 2003, before the Great Recession of 2007 to 2009, which may explain some part of Kirp's approach. Kirp's (2003) general view, drawn from the economist Arthur Okun, is that "there is place for the market . . . but the market must be kept in its place. . . . Market forces lead some schools to forget that they are not simply businesses while turning others into stronger, better places" (p. 7). That said, he does see fundamental tension between higher education, properly understood, and the direction the considerable power of market forces and principles tend to push:

> Embedded in the very idea of the university—not the storybook idea, but the university at its truest and best—are values that the market does not honor: the belief in a community of scholars and not a confederacy of self-seekers; in the idea of openness and not ownership; in the professor as a pursuer of truth and not an entrepreneur; in the student as an acolyte whose preferences are to be formed, not a consumer whose preferences are to be satisfied. (p. 7)

In the "contest between the market and the commons," we risk losing much of what we should most value in higher education:

> The commitment to test, not just replicate, the prevailing wisdoms of the day; the pride of place given to need and merit, rather than ability to pay . . . the contention that universities should be places for discovering, sharing, and passing on knowledge rather than companies for hoarding and selling it. (pp. 260–261)

It is when the market cuts against these valued principles and practices—and we have very good reason to suspect that it will continue to do so—that we ought to become suspicious and resist the market's destructive consequences. Methodologically, Kirp proceeds through a series of case studies, "tales that signify beyond their particulars, to make sense of this new world" (p. 7). He ranges widely, examining the intensification of market practices and rhetoric at institutions as diverse as the University of Chicago and DeVry University.

As with his examination of the college dropout rate, Kirp's evaluation of the collision of the market and higher education appears to be motivated by a deep concern with accessibility. He is suspicious of marketplace values and techniques, in part, because they jeopardize robust access to higher education. For example, Kirp (2003) tells us that "in the past decade or so, there have been dramatic changes in the way schools calculate how much of a 'discount' from the tuition 'sticker price' to offer, and to whom" (p. 20). He worries, in particular, about the fact that higher education has moved from a need-based model to a strategic (in terms of the market) but "ethically problematic" (p. 22) model for distributing financial aid. He writes: "Financial aid has traditionally been based on a student's need. Promising scholars, the argument goes, should not be prevented from going to school because they can't afford to pay the bills" (p. 20). But now the market has come to campus, and the admissions office has become a "profit center," expected to "raise as much revenue as possible from tuition" (p. 21) and to "help their school move up in the *U.S. News* sweepstakes" (p. 21), resulting in the morally dubious administration of financial aid. This suspect distribution of financial aid results in reduced access to higher education for a wide swath of students and also incentivizes blameworthy practices (e.g., reducing the aid offered to early decision students and students who have come to campus for an interview, on the grounds that those students are likely to enroll regardless of the aid offer they receive). Though he does not appear to articulate the principle as such, Kirp seems to endorse the general argument that the consequences of the market in higher education ought to be resisted when they undermine access to higher education.

Kirp also appears to be animated once more by a desire to broaden access to scholarly work about higher education. As in *The College Dropout Scandal*, he is clear and direct throughout the text, and he proceeds through a series of illuminating case studies. Perhaps conspicuously, Kirp does not use the concept *neoliberalism*. It is safe to assume that he did not avoid the term because he was unfamiliar with it. Much scholarly work on neoliberalism had already been produced when Kirp published *Shakespeare, Einstein, and the Bottom Line* in 2003, and much more was in progress (see, e.g., Apple, 2000; Chomsky, 1999; Giroux, 2002; Harvey, 2005; Strickland, 2002). When used clearly, neoliberalism can add explanatory power to analyses of contemporary or historical social, political, economic, and educational arrangements and institutions; their structural features and forces; and the various ills and harms they spawn (see, e.g., Mirowski & Plehwe, 2009; Stedman Jones, 2012). But it is not always used clearly, leading to confusion; neoliberalism might be dubiously taken to be coextensive with capitalism, for example, seen as an inexorable behemoth that can explain most anything, or embedded in a tangled web of similarly fuzzy terms. It is often "used with lazy imprecision in both popular debate and academic scholarship. The outlines of the term's history are widely assumed, although usually without a clear understanding of what is meant by the label" (Stedman Jones, 2012, p. 10).

In avoiding *neoliberalism* and instead employing the more specific concept *the market*, Kirp may lose some potential explanatory and critical power (e.g., a broader political-economic explanation of why the market and higher education collided when they did) but he avoids the pitfalls described previously. Most important, the accessible book that results provides citizens some portion of the knowledge needed to play the "contestatory" role described previously and to participate effectively in deliberation about the intensified role of marketplace values in higher education.

Interpretation and Evaluation: A Civic Republican Framework

At least in his work on higher education, Kirp only rarely provides extended and explicit articulations of the values—accessibility chief among them—that motivate and ground his educational proposals. In *The College Dropout Scandal*, Kirp (2019) develops a moral and economic rationale for why we ought to care about and reduce the rate at which students leave higher education without a degree—for why we should view the troubling dropout rate as "higher education's dirty little secret" (p. 4). Higher education fails morally when it bills itself—or allows itself to be billed as—the engine of social mobility, "the ticket to admission to America's middle class," but fails decisively to live up that billing for at least the "34 million Americans over twenty-five . . . who have some college credits but dropped out before receiving a diploma" (p. 3). Kirp expresses higher education's moral failure in economic terms. As documented previously, students who leave higher education are often unable to secure high-paying jobs; they are more likely than graduates to be unemployed; they are more likely to default on their student loans; they are less likely to achieve social mobility; they are left on the bottom of the consequential education gap. In summary, the alarming dropout rate, and the slow response of higher education to it, are taken by Kirp to be morally blameworthy and to leave destructive economic consequences in their wake.

In *Shakespeare, Einstein, and the Bottom Line*, Kirp (2003) provides an open-minded evaluation of the entrance of business strategies, tools, and rhetoric into the domain of higher education—the development of "academic capitalism" and the "enterprise university," and the consequent reframing of the department as a "revenue center," the student a "customer," and the professor an "entrepreneur" (pp. 4–5). Kirp articulates two sets of values that guide his examination of the collision of higher education and the marketplace. The first is the set of values rooted in the university at its "truest and best," which the market does not honor and cannot be trusted to maintain. As described previously, these values include "the belief in a community of scholars and not a community of self-seekers" and "in the student as an acolyte whose preferences are to be formed, not a consumer whose preferences are to be satisfied" (p. 7). When the market and associated tools and languages push the university to run afoul of these values, we ought to be suspicious. The second set of values, overlapping with the first, is rooted in the civic and public mission of the university—namely, promoting "the interest of the commonwealth, the *public* good, by molding students into citizens of the republic" (p. 258) and fulfilling "the promise that higher education can function as an engine of mobility" (p. 261). In summary, we should resist the consequences of the market on higher education when those consequences violate the values of the university at its "truest and best" and when they undermine the ability of the university to fulfill its civic and public mission.

In each case, Kirp points briefly at the social, political, economic, and educational values and visions that motivate and undergird his prescriptions: The alarming dropout rate in higher education ought to be addressed because it thoroughly dashes the ability of colleges and universities to live up to their promise of social mobility; and the changes wrought by the collision of the market and higher education ought to be resisted when they threaten the civic, public, and epistemic values and missions of the university. But in neither case does he provide a thorough delineation of those values and visions. We might wonder: What broader conceptions of social, political, economic, and educational justice motivate Kirp and his educational proposals? What visions of the good and the good society is he out to achieve through enhancing higher education? Are we right to think that improving higher education—boosting graduation rates, or carefully harnessing the power of the market while avoiding its pitfalls—is a feasible pathway to that conception of the good society?

Kirp should not be faulted, and indeed deserves commendation, for not having developed in these two books a nuanced framework to ground and illuminate his proposals for higher education. Such a framework does not appear to fall within the scope of what seems his prime endeavor: advancing accessible and strategic arguments that can play some role in achieving more thoroughly accessible higher education and the social, political, and economic goods that would flow from such higher education. Providing fellow citizens with transparent argument and evidence that can be used in democratic deliberation about higher education is a clear good. A complex theoretical framework of the kind that academics are wont to develop may well undermine that good.

Nonetheless, a framework for interpreting Kirp's work on higher education can be useful for understanding, evaluating, and even working to implement his various educational proposals. Whether or not some educational proposal is morally or practically desirable will be clearer in light of a broader educational and social vision. With such a vision in hand, we will be able to evaluate whether the prescription moves us toward the desired educational and social arrangement, and whether it promotes a broader set of values we have endorsed and seek to realize. To that end, I close the chapter by developing a framework rooted in the civic republican political tradition, which can be used to interpret and evaluate Kirp's work on higher education.

Many—and many competing—frames could be brought to bear on Kirp's educational prescriptions. I develop a civic republican framework, in particular, because the civic republican tradition appears to align well with Kirp's values, as articulated previously, and because it provides a powerful and, in my view, powerfully attractive vision of the kind of educational, social, political, and economic order we ought to work to achieve.

I draw primarily on Phillip Pettit's delineation and development of civic republicanism (see especially Pettit, 1997, 2012, 2014), but many political philosophers, intellectual historians, and others have contributed to the endeavor to recover and rework the tradition (see, e.g., Halldenius, 2015; Laborde & Maynor, 2009; Maynor, 2003). Though contemporary civic republican political thought has evolved substantially from its historical origins, it is rooted in the Roman republic, the medieval independent cities of northern Italy, the English republic of 1649 to 1660, and the American War of Independence (Pettit, 2014; see also Skinner, 1998). The central and most distinctive feature of the civic republican tradition is a unique conception of freedom, which clashes with the view of freedom nested in the liberal tradition.

On the republican view, and against the standard liberal account of freedom as "noninterference," freedom should be understood as "nondomination." Pettit (2014) used the image of a horse being given "free rein" to explain the republican conception of freedom:

> When a rider lets the reins hang loose, the horse enjoys free rein: it can go in whatever direction it wishes. . . . When I give a horse free rein, I do not use the reins to direct it, nor do I let the reins hang loose because the horse happens to be going in the direction I prefer; not having any preference in the matter of direction, I let the horse go as it will. (p. 1)

At first glance, we might think that the horse given free rein counts as properly free. After all, the horse is not being interfered with—it can proceed this or that way as it desires. But the horse remains saddled, and the rider remains in the saddle, "ready to pull on the reins should my wishes change. I do not exercise operative control over the horse, then, but I do enjoy potential or reserve control" (p. 2). Though the rider does not control (interfere with) the horse given free rein, that temporary freedom may be revoked whenever the rider sees fit. The rider does not leave or remove the saddle, and the horse remains in a condition of domination, under the reserve control of the rider.

Pettit's (2014) metaphor reveals the central thrust of the republican conception of freedom: A citizen cannot count as free when some other citizen or set of citizens has the power to interfere with her in the domain of her basic or fundamental liberties, even when that citizen or set of citizens opts not to exercise that power. These fundamental liberties have been taken to include "choices over what religion to practice, what party to espouse, what associations to join, as well as where to reside, [and] how to earn your living" (p. 3). The very existence of the power to interfere undermines her freedom. She will not be free when others possess that reserve control because she will be dependent on them, unable to interact with them—to look them in the eyes and to talk straight with them without deference and without fear of interference—on terms of equality. To be properly free is to be in the position of nondomination, that is, "the position of the independent person who has no master or *dominus* in their life" and who thereby has the capacity to make their "choices without any need to seek another's permission" (p. 3). On the republican view, an individual is free as far as she is free from actual and potential interference in the range of basic liberties. To test for republican freedom, Pettit develops what he calls "the eyeball test," which

> requires that people should be so resourced and protected in the basic choices of life—for short, the basic liberties—that they can look others in the eye without reason for fear or deference of the kind that a power of interference might inspire. When you enjoy social, medical, and judicial security, and benefit from a suitable legal and economic order, you do not depend for your security on the indulgence and condescension of others. You can walk tall and assume the status of an equal with the most powerful in the land. (p. xxvi)

When we fail the eyeball test, we cannot be said to be free from nondomination; we remain at risk of being forced to speak in "the mealymouthed tones of the servant" in order to avoid interference (p. xxvii).

How can the civic republican conception of freedom as nondomination help us to interpret and evaluate Kirp's work on higher education? It provides us with the broader social, political, economic, and educational vision needed to appraise the range of Kirp's educational prescriptions. If we endorse the republican construal of freedom, we can ask of each of Kirp's prescriptions: Does this proposal move us toward or away from the kind of society in which citizens are entitled to freedom from domination, from arbitrary interference? Does it move us toward or away from the "social, medical, and judicial security" and the "suitable legal and economic order" required for nondomination (Pettit, 2014, p. xxvi)? These questions form a rough sketch of a civic republican test of the normative acceptability of an educational policy. I suggest that Kirp's work on higher education in *The College Dropout Scandal* and *Shakespeare, Einstein, and the Bottom Line* passes this civic republican test.

It will be uncontroversial to contend that contemporary American society has not achieved the conditions required for citizens to enjoy freedom as nondomination. A small set of especially socially, politically, and economically powerful citizens may experience something akin to republican freedom, but the vast majority of us are not suitably "resourced and protected in the basic choices of life" to avoid fear and deference in a range of interactions with our fellow citizens. For example, we have failed to enshrine a set of economic rights—as in, for instance, the "second" or "economic" bill of rights proposed by Franklin D. Roosevelt in 1944. We have thereby failed to ensure citizens freedom from actual and potential interference in the domain of the fundamental liberties. We are not protected from the need to cower from and defer to employers in authoritarian workplaces. Many of the economic rights articulated in the economic bill of rights—housing, clothing, food, sufficient leisure, medical care, and so on—are instead dependent on educational attainment, itself not taken as a basic right. In this way, education and, in particular, higher education serve as "gateway" goods to the economic goods described previously (for a thorough articulation of this argument, see Marsh, 2011). It is through educational attainment that we can hope to secure these economic goods, and so too it is through educational attainment that we can hope to secure some measure of freedom as nondomination. Though they provide no guarantee, educational goods help to make citizens free in the republican sense.

Given this imperfect state of affairs, the civic republican will endorse Kirp's work on higher education, and especially his thoroughgoing commitment to access to higher education and to access to scholarly work about higher education. In both books examined in this chapter, Kirp advocates for widened access to higher education—one of the central goods in the endeavor to attain some degree of freedom from domination and arbitrary interference. The civic republican can straightforwardly endorse Kirp's mission to reduce the troubling college dropout rate, especially because, as described previously, the dropout rate and the resulting education gap are especially destructive to low-income, minority, and first-generation students, undermining access to the various resources needed to enjoy nondomination. The larger the education gap, the less are citizens able to pass the eyeball test—the less are they able to interact with one another on equal terms without condescension or groveling. Similarly, the civic republican can endorse Kirp's examination of the intensification of market forces and values in higher education. When left unchecked by educators and their fellow citizens, the main consequence of marketplace language and tools will be to reshape higher education in its own image, eroding the principles and practices of the university at its "truest and best," and to restrict access even to that debased educational experience. Finally, the civic republican

can endorse Kirp's accessible presentation of scholarly work on the dropout problem and the collision of the marketplace and the academy, which is vital for citizens to play the "contestatory" role described previously and to advocate for the educational and other conditions needed for republican freedom. Again, I contend that Kirp's work on higher education passes the civic republican test: He makes a valuable and, above all, accessible contribution to the endeavor to push toward freer and more just institutions, on the republican construal of those terms.

References

Apple, M. W. (2000). Between neoliberalism and neoconservatism: Education and conservatism in a global context. In N. C. Burbules & C. A. Torres (Eds.), *Globalization and education: Critical perspectives* (pp. 57–78). Routledge.

Blacker, D. (2013). *The falling rate of learning and the neoliberal endgame*. Zero Books.

Chomsky, N. (1999). *Profit over people: Neoliberalism and global order*. Seven Stories Press.

Giroux, H. A. (2002). Neoliberalism, corporate culture, and the promise of higher education: The university as a democratic public sphere. *Harvard Educational Review, 72*(4), 425–463.

Halldenius, L. (2015). *Mary Wollstonecraft and feminist republicanism: Independence, rights, and the experience of unfreedom*. Routledge.

Harvey, D. (2005). *A brief history of neoliberalism*. Oxford University Press.

Kirp, D. L. (2000). *Almost home: America's love-hate relationship with community*. Princeton University Press.

Kirp, D. L. (2003). *Shakespeare, Einstein, and the bottom line: The marketing of higher education*. Harvard University Press.

Kirp, D. L. (2007). *The sandbox investment: The preschool movement and kids-first politics*. Harvard University Press.

Kirp, D. L. (2011). *Kids first: Five big ideas for transforming children's lives and America's future*. Public Affairs.

Kirp, D. L. (2019). *The college dropout scandal*. Oxford University Press.

Kirp, D. L., Dwyer, J. P., & Rosenthal, L. A. (1997). *Our town: Race, housing, and the soul of suburbia*. Rutgers University Press.

Kirp, D. L., Yoduf, M. G., & Strong Franks, M. (1986). *Gender justice*. University of Chicago Press.

Laborde, C., & Maynor, J. W. (Eds.). (2009). *Republicanism and political theory*. Blackwell.

Lipman, P. (2011). *The new political economic of urban education: Neoliberalism, race, and the right to the city*. Routledge.

Marsh, J. (2011). *Class dismissed: Why we cannot teach or learn our way out of inequality*. Monthly Review Press.

Maynor, J. W. (2003). *Republicanism in the modern world*. Polity Press.

Mirowski, P., & Plehwe, D. (Eds.). (2009). *The road from Mont Pelerin: The making of the neoliberal thought collective*. Harvard University Press.
Pettit, P. (1997). *Republicanism: A theory of freedom and government*. Clarendon Press.
Pettit, P. (2012). *On the people's terms: A republican theory and model of democracy*. Cambridge University Press.
Pettit, P. (2014). *Just freedom: A moral compass for a complex world*. W.W. Norton.
Skinner, Q. (1998). *Liberty before liberalism*. Cambridge University Press.
Stedman Jones, D. (2012). *Masters of the universe: Hayek, Friedman, and the birth of neoliberal politics*. Princeton University Press.
Strickland, R. (Ed.). (2002). *Growing up postmodern: Neoliberalism and the war on the young*. Rowman & Littlefield.

7

MICHAEL BÉRUBÉ AND THE NEOLIBERAL UNIVERSITY

Humanities, Academic Freedom, and the Crises in Higher Education

Deron Boyles

During a 2014 "State of the State" event at Penn State University, Michael Bérubé (2014) chronicled the substantial decline in public funding for public universities in Pennsylvania, as well as nationally. He cited a person from Colorado who believed that three quarters of the cost of higher education should be funded by families (rather than the historical one third it used to cost). Otherwise, so the person reasoned, a trucker would be subsidizing someone earning a BA in medieval literature. This logic, like much of the logic of neoliberalism, sets up an "us versus them" rationality and represents reductionism and an odd hegemonic jealousy (Heller, 2016; Mirowski & Plehwe, 2009). A degree in medieval literature, like degrees in art history, philosophy, and cultural studies, represents esoteric fluff whereas truck driving, plumbing, carpentry, or auto mechanics represent "real" work. In using these two characterizations, Bérubé was not furthering the bifurcation. He was using it to show the error in logic. Keeping some people from advanced study because other people consider it superfluous, even though advanced study benefits more than just those engaged in the study, risks divisive hierarchies that need not exist. Weaving economic rationality and a defense of the liberal arts, Bérubé maintains that the choice between practical job skills and a degree in the humanities is a false dualism. It also distracts from one of the central problems facing contemporary higher education: reduction in financial support for public colleges and universities.

As Bérubé's Penn State talk indicates, his interests in defending the humanities are not separate from the precipitous decline in public investment in U.S. higher education. Concomitantly, he is interested in academic freedom and the role the American Association of University Professors (AAUP) might play in defending tenure while challenging traditional understandings of the professoriate. Taking each topic in turn, while noting the overlapping elements necessarily joining them, this chapter focuses on three main themes in Bérubé's work: the humanities, public funding for higher education, and tenure and academic freedom. Before exploring these areas, I offer a brief, professional background of the man.

Michael Bérubé is Edwin Erle Sparks professor of literature and a past chair of the University Faculty Senate at Pennsylvania State University. He is the author of 10 books, including *Public Access: Literary Theory and American Cultural Politics* (Verso, 1994); *The Humanities, Higher Education, and Academic Freedom: Three Necessary Arguments* (coauthored with Jennifer Ruth; Palgrave Macmillan, 2015); and *What's Liberal About the Liberal Arts? Classroom Politics and "Bias" in Higher Education* (W. W. Norton, 2006). He served three terms on the AAUP's Committee A on Academic Freedom and Tenure from 2009 to 2018, two terms on the AAUP National Council from 2005 to 2011, and two terms on the International Advisory Board of the Consortium of Humanities Centers and Institutes from 2011 to 2017. In 2012, he was president of the Modern Language Association. From 2010 to 2017, he served as the director of Penn State's Institute for the Arts and Humanities.

Strongly influenced by Stuart Hall, Richard Rorty, and Ellen Willis, Bérubé's (2009) work interrogates equity and justice from a critical vantage point that is also informed by empiricism. His defense of the humanities, for example, hinges largely on a rereading of the data. In most articles in the popular press, there has been a repetitive narrative about the "decline of the humanities." In these articles, year after year, readers are told that there has not only been a precipitous decline in the number of humanities majors (English majors feature prominently here) but that there has been a marked emigration from the humanities to business and technology. In this narrative, the humanities are increasingly irrelevant in a neoliberal global marketplace. In the aftermath of the Great Recession, more articles were published that questioned the value of humanities study and, at the same time, appeared to reinforce a long-standing assumption: Elite colleges and universities still had thriving liberal arts programs, but public and research universities were justifiably more focused on funded research, business majors, and the technology sector. Bérubé reveals the misuse or misunderstanding of the data that serve as the foundation for the claims about the humanities. More importantly, he argues that the repeated narratives about the humanities are less about enrollment numbers, majors, and graduates, but about political and intellectual values. In short, the numbers don't tell us what some people are telling us they tell us. Instead, the constant drumbeat lamenting the decline of the humanities is a cover for an attack on what the humanities have grown to include. Instead of "knowledge for the sake of knowledge" in the Great Books tradition or other canonical approaches, critical studies in race, gender, and sexuality become code for extending culture wars.

The data used to lament the decline of the humanities are primarily based on a blip increase in the number of English, history, and philosophy majors around 1970. Prior to and after 1970, the numbers are not only relatively constant, there have been increases. Between 1940 and 1970, for example, the number of English majors increased from 17,000 to 64,000. Between 1970 and the mid-1980s, the number of English majors dropped to 34,000. From the mid-1980s to the 2000s, those reporting on the continued decline in the number of English majors noted that only 3.9% of undergraduate degrees were awarded in English in 2004 (Bauerlein, 2013; Chase, 2009). That percentage, however, represents 54,000 graduates. A supportive interpretation of these data would be to applaud a 60% increase in English graduates from roughly 1985 to 2005 (Bérubé & Ruth, 2015). Gaming the numbers to ridicule intellectual inquiry is only part of the point, however. Denigrating the humanities by repeating caricatures and tropes about art history or queer theory advances the narrative that such majors will not help graduates get a job. Such an emphasis on neoliberalism advances the narrow view that education should be about training and universities should be run like businesses. Bérubé (2014) notes, perhaps to the surprise of many, that liberal arts majors make more money than professional degree majors. He also notes, and this is important, that the criticism of the liberal arts as a haven for radical faculty pursuing worthless inquiries into poetry and poststructuralism has had little effect on the number of students interested in those inquiries.

Although attacks on the humanities are not new, and they may not negatively influence student interest in them, they have nonetheless reinforced the idea that public institutions only squander money on superfluous scholarly flights of fancy. Studying the theme song from *Jaws* to gauge people's fear of sharks, putting goldfish on treadmills, and using holograms of a deceased stand-up comic for performance art are among the list of examples that conservatives exasperatedly tout as ridiculous (Americans for Prosperity, 2018). The examples *may be* ridiculous, in truth, but the purpose of the screeds against such projects is to advance the idea that only those studies that will generate money are worthy of exploration and financial support.

Adopting a perversion of this sort of business reasoning, specifically "return on investment" (ROI) thinking, colleges and universities increasingly operate like private enterprises (Busch, 2017). Such privatization is partially due to the significant decrease in public funding for higher education (Heller, 2016). The Great Recession of 2008 and the pandemic of 2020 are significant benchmarks to highlight the crises of higher education, but they only magnify and provide easy rationales for the push toward privatization that had existed long before 2008. Science, technology, engineering, and mathematics (STEM) initiatives have long diverted money to administrator initiatives to better "market" their schools. The fetish for *U.S. News and World Reports* rankings has become an industry unto itself. A grants culture privileges the sciences (and social sciences that really wish they were hard sciences) to the detriment of fields with limited grant opportunities—setting up a self-defeating cycle of desiring more and more grants that make graduate student assistantships more and more contingent and temporal (Bérubé, 2006).

Taken together, these initiatives *are* an attack on the humanities, if for no other reason than they force the humanities into a defensive position requiring a ceaseless demonstration of relevance. The humanities must justify themselves in corporate terms. Business schools win while history departments suffer. It is arguably worse when the humanities take an offensive position toward entrepreneurialism that sees philosophy departments advertising themselves as a career path for future lawyers. Ensnared in the trap of neoliberalism, faculty are forced into narratives requiring "impact factors" and "evidence of effectiveness," as though these are things different from poetic license or arbitrary administrator values. But how are faculty forced into such narratives? Accreditation paperwork, program reviews, "strategic planning" meetings, and "student learning outcomes assessment portal" reports in triplicate (SLOAP reports) are all redundant attempts requiring faculty time and energy to comply with externally imposed neoliberal reportage (Baez & Boyles, 2009; Brown, 2015). Another significant way faculty are forced into corporate compliance is the struggle over academic freedom and tenure and promotion. Bérubé has much to say about these topics, but I will focus on one of his more unique proposals and one that cannot be divorced from the current context of hiring in higher education.

Regarding tenure and academic freedom, Bérubé, along with scholars such as Cary Nelson, Henry Reichman, and Joan Scott, is an AAUP expert. Bérubé (2006) explores dilemmas facing academic freedom and tenure and offers a strategy to mitigate a stark reality: Almost 75% of all faculty lines are *non*-tenure-track (NTT) (Flaherty, 2018). Given COVID-19, many universities have cut staffing, including part-time instructors (PTIs) and adjuncts, but also NTT faculty. This may have an unintended consequence of revealing fissures between tenured/tenure-track faculty and nontenure-track faculty. Variously called "clinical" faculty, "professors of the practice," "instructors," "senior lecturers," and the like, NTT faculty constitute most of the professoriate. There are at least three significant problems that follow from NTT faculty holding so many positions in the academy: (a) exploitation, (b) public concern, and (c) implications for the professoriate in general.

For (a), NTT faculty are, according to Bérubé and Ruth (2015), often working for wages that put them at or near the poverty line. They scrape together course-by-course work that sometimes has them teaching classes at multiple institutions to subsist. With an average salary of around $4,000 per course, no health insurance, and semester-to-semester contracts, many NTT faculty qualify for food stamps and, if their contingent contracts are not renewed, are not eligible for unemployment. Bérubé and Ruth point out that overpaid central administrators are partly to blame, but there is enough blame to go around. With the decrease in public funding for higher education, tuition has risen significantly in the past 2 decades. Increased tuition costs advance neoliberal rationalizations on the part of parents and students: ROI recurs and is a direct link to the public's concern about the cost of attending college and the logic of derision for tenured faculty.

For (b), consider this extended quote from Bérubé and Ruth (2015), where they ask whether the general public should care about the exploitation of NTT faculty:

> If you read any online essay about contingent faculty in *Inside Higher Education* or the *Chronicle of Higher Education*, you will quickly find, in the comment section, that (a) the higher-ed press is read avidly by people who hate professors, and (b) relatedly, there is not a great deal of sympathy out there for adjuncts making $20,000–$25,000 a year. Especially since the near-meltdown of 2008, things have been, as the phrase has it, tough all over. It is accordingly harder than most exploitatively underpaid college professors might think to tell people that many college professors are exploitatively underpaid. (p. 21)

The "sell" is even more difficult given the COVID-19 pandemic. But Bérubé and Ruth offer an analogy that raises questions about professionalism. They suggest that parents and the public ask themselves whether, if they need a good lawyer, they would be satisfied to be sent to an associate without an office. "Or," they write, "think of it in terms of what a college promises and what it practices. Is it telling students that a college degree is a pathway to the middle class, while *paying its own instructors, with post-graduate degrees, food-stamp wages?*" (p. 21, italics in original).

For (c), Bérubé and Ruth (2015) offer a riskier "sell": job security. What makes this point risky, or problematic, is that

> it amounts to telling parents, students, administrators, and legislators that they have to fight for the right of professors to challenge their students intellectually, free from the fear that they will be fired the moment they say something unfamiliar or upsetting about sexuality or evolution or American history or the Middle East. (p. 22)

This defense is part of the justification for tenure, and tenure has been under attack for decades. What Bérubé and Ruth suggest, however, is a different approach to addressing the large number of NTT faculty. They point out the complexity of NTT faculty issues, including reduced tenure-track lines, but also the nonstandardized categories that constitute NTT faculty as a group. As mentioned earlier, there is a wide variance in the terms and titles used to identify NTT faculty: adjunct, instructor, lecturer, professor of the practice (and the various assistant, associate, and full or I, II, and III designations within and among these wide-ranging titles). Bérubé and Ruth (2015) also highlight complications with shared governance. I summarize four important points they make:

- NTT faculty participate in "shared governance," but at the expense of tenure-track lines. This happens when, for instance, repeated "budget crises" are announced. It is easier to cancel a search for an unknown future colleague than to cut an already existing NTT faculty member.
- Conflicts of interest are evident when NTT faculty contribute to considering what areas need increased staffing/hiring.
- Increased NTT faculty participation in committee work or program coordination increases the pressure to allow course releases.
- In turn, those course releases mean hiring more PTIs or adjuncts and not hiring tenure-track faculty.
- NTT faculty voting rights means a department with a large representation of NTT faculty will determine leadership, as with department chair searches. (pp. 99–100)

Taken together, these issues represent an attack on academic freedom because, without tenure, there is no academic freedom. Without tenure, all professors become "for hire" or "contract" employees who will abdicate academic freedom to save their employment. Well-intentioned efforts by those in support of adjuncts and NTT faculty rely on "democratic" arguments to assert rights for NTT faculty. Yet, as Bérubé and Ruth (2015) ask,

> Is there any paradox of contemporary university politics filled with a more poignant irony than the discrepancy between (a) the efforts of well-meaning idealists who insist on the universal right of academic freedom and (b) the precarious situation of the rightless adjuncts themselves? Documents like an "Instructor Bill of Rights" do not go to the source of the problem—which is that economics and expediency have driven us to erect a second and third tier of faculty without the protocols and protections of tenure. (p. 103)

The solution is to set up a tenure line for NTT faculty, but one that is not the same as tenure-track faculty. The difference is largely between tenured teaching faculty and tenured research faculty, but the peer-review requirements are strenuous and the result is a faculty substantially strengthened by academic freedom. Realistically, such a shift would cause enormous anxiety because current NTT faculty would have to apply for the new position and be considered as part of a national or regional search. Whether NTT faculty think the risk is worth the reward is unclear, at best, because we do a terrible job of explaining and showing the importance of academic freedom and tenure. Indeed, I am unconvinced that many *tenured* faculty understand the link between tenure and academic freedom and may balk at the perception that tenure is being "weakened" by expanding it to the numbers represented by the NTT faculty. Such expansion is the point, however, if faculties wish to reclaim their right to academic freedom in a meaningful way.

Problems with such a shift set aside, the result would be a substantial reduction in the percentage of faculty in U.S. colleges and universities who are denied academic freedom because they do not have tenure. On this point, Bérubé is correct. Even granting such a result, however, there is no guarantee that faculty who had been acculturated to NTT expectations will move away from them and into a robust form of academic freedom and faculty governance once they earn tenure. In fact, there are plenty of examples of *already tenured* faculty members reifying corporate logic and undermining academic freedom and faculty governance. Said differently, just because there is a university senate does not mean the senate will act in ways contrary to administrative fiat. If tenured faculty fail to challenge the neoliberalism of contemporary university politics, why should we expect recent NTT faculty to be any different once they have gone through the arduous process of earning tenure? I am not, to be clear, suggesting the project of moving NTT faculty to tenure-track is unworthy or ignoble. My concern is that neoliberalism has codified faculty *being* to such a degree that critical responses to it are so difficult and, thus, so rare as to be almost pointless.

Regardless, Bérubé offers multiple approaches to reconsidering the value and importance of academic freedom and tenure. He also provides insight relating to what academic freedom looks like in classroom practice. In *What's Liberal About the Liberal Arts*, Bérubé (2006) narrates his interactions with students and texts in ways that weave intellect and awareness, critique and caution. All the while, he is commenting on postmodernism, the debt Jean Baudrillard owes to Guy Debord (via Samuel Beckett), and the significance of incommensurability of various belief systems. In his narrations, the points are important and interesting, but *that he is making the points at all* is the debt he is paying to the very academic freedom he champions. From the Republican student caught up in Jean-François Lyotard's terror of agreement to the Mormon student caught in Martha Nussbaum's cosmopolitanism, Bérubé explores the ramifications of teaching controversial material. Insightfully, he also nuances the meanings of texts and ideas *in situ*. Students who are otherwise quick to group-think (and apparently in agreement with both Lyotard and Nussbaum) are challenged by Bérubé to think more carefully and more thoroughly about topics that are too easily cast as "left" or "right."

The skill required to engage in controversial topics, as Bérubé does, is significant and, potentially, too risky for nontenured or newly tenured faculty to contemplate. After all, their contingent status for x or y years has already reinforced an ethos of what teaching means. Too often, this ethos is characterized by rubrics, complicated grade ranges, standardized syllabi, and teaching evaluations. Fear of offending students, fear of courses "not making," and fear of not knowing enough about the content of the course they are teaching are long-standing worries that newly tenured teaching faculty may carry with them into their new role. What will be needed, in addition to expanding tenure, is a shift in understanding the purpose of the professoriate and the role that academic freedom and tenure play in that purpose. Perhaps the AAUP might initiate a national campaign where site visits include seminars in which the history of academic freedom, the history of higher education, and the history of the neoliberal takeover of higher education would be explored at length. Without understanding academic freedom and tenure, the terms are reduced to a refrigerator magnet or coffee mug. They become a bumper sticker on an office door. Academic freedom devolves into cliché.

This chapter focused on only a small number of issues within Bérubé's oeuvre. The chapter should provide an entry to those who may not yet be familiar with his work, however. He has, for example, carefully explored the politics of "bias" in college classrooms, taken David Horowitz to task in many debates, and is an advocate for disability studies. On this last point, his insights regarding his son, Jamie, are notable and profound (Bérubé, 1998, 2017). Although there was not room in this chapter to explore these and other works, Bérubé's numerous publications are worthy of further inquiry. His call is, in many ways, a call to action for those of us who take academic freedom and tenure for granted, misunderstand the challenge of too many NTT faculty, and remain uncertain about what we might do to defend and champion the role of the humanities in higher education.

References

Americans for Prosperity. (2018). *Five outrageous ways the federal government has wasted your money (Part II)*. https://americansforprosperity.org/five-outrageous-ways-the-federal-government-has-wasted-your-money-pt-ii/

Baez, B., & Boyles, D. (2009). *The politics of inquiry: Education research and the "culture of science."* SUNY Press.

Bauerlein, M. (2013, June 1). English's self-inflicted wound. *The Chronicle of Higher Education*. https://world.edu/englishs-self-inflicted-wound

Bérubé, M. (1998). *Life as we know it: A father, a family, and an exceptional child*. Vintage.

Bérubé, M. (2006). *What's liberal about the liberal arts? Classroom politics and "bias" in higher education*. W.W. Norton.

Bérubé, M. (2009). *The left at war*. New York University Press.

Bérubé, M. (2014). *State of the state* [Video]. YouTube. https://www.youtube.com/watch?v=oDYoPtvPapM

Bérubé, M. (2017). *Life as Jamie knows it: An exceptional child grows up*. Beacon Press.

Bérubé, M., & Ruth, J. (2015). *The humanities, higher education, and academic freedom: Three necessary arguments*. Palgrave Macmillan.

Brown, W. (2015). *Undoing the demos: Neoliberalism's stealth revolution*. Zone Books.

Busch, L. (2017). *Knowledge for sale: The neoliberal takeover of higher education*. MIT Press.

Chase, W. M. (2009). The decline of the English department. *American Scholar*, 78(4), 32–42.

Flaherty, C. (2018). A non-tenure track profession? *Inside Higher Ed*. https://www.insidehighered.com/news/2018/10/12/about-three-quarters-all-faculty-positions-are-tenure-track-according-new-aaup

Heller, H. (2016). *The capitalist university: The transformation of higher education in the United States since 1945*. Pluto Press.

Mirowski, P., & Plehwe, D. (2009). *The road from Mont Pèlerin: The making of the neoliberal thought collective*. Harvard University Press.

8

THE WAL-MARTIFICATION OF HIGHER EDUCATION

Marc Bousquet's Critical Examination of Contingent Faculty and Academia's Labor Practices

Dan Bauer and Marshall Martin

At no time in the history of higher education could this chapter be more timely or appropriate, given the visible dramatic divides in American culture's resounding splintering in the age of COVID and in the ever-emerging exposure of uncontrolled corruption, greed, and other predatory forces in government, corporate America, and elsewhere. In this regard, Marc Bousquet's works are prophetic and essential in analyzing and understanding root causes of such divides within academia; now, years later after their publication, his works serve as a study in miniature of the depressing larger and accelerating cultural caste system that threatens the highest ideals of our country and also higher education's foundational relationship to democracy, access to opportunity, and social mobility within the American landscape at large.

This chapter's foundation for the analysis that follows comes from several of Bousquet's works, including his three books: *How The University Works: Higher Education and the Low-Wage Nation* (Bousquet, 2008a), *The Politics of Information: The Electronic Mediation of Social Change*, a collection of 28 essays, edited with Katherine Wills and available fully online from Alt-X Press (Bousquet & Wills, 2004), and *Tenured Bosses and Disposable Teachers: Writing Work in the Managed University*, a collection of 24 essays, edited with Tony Scott and Leo Parascondola (Bousquet et al., 2004). In addition, we pay close attention to one of his many articles: "The Figure of Writing and the Future of English Studies" (Bousquet, 2009). A complete list of his publications, with useful hotlinks to all his works (including recorded media), may be found at https://marcbousquet.net/publications-htm/.

Bousquet's seminal works and arguments have influenced the academic labor movement and inspired a new class of scholars to critique higher education's proliferating move toward ever-increasing use of contingent labor. We endorse Bousquet's work and agree with his alarm regarding exploitive labor practices in higher education, and we hope for better options and possibilities for early-career scholars who optimistically see a future in the academy. As we work toward elaboration of those themes, this chapter organizes Bousquet's work into four central areas of inquiry: (a) labor, (b) the academic job market, (c) the neoliberal university, and (d) teaching of composition, particularly first-year writing. Of course, these areas converge and diverge, so our analysis will be similarly intersectional. But we take away from Bousquet's scholarship an emphatic concern about imbalance, inequity, and a desperate need for new understanding, fresh vantage points, and a mindset grounded in an ever-changing material and ideological reality, particularly for higher education.

Labor

Certainly, language normalizes and makes possible social arrangements. Indeed, Dan Bauer has often posited that adolescents and young adults are often "bored" because their vocabulary lacks abundant options for other possible mindsets. Without the ability to "name" other nuanced attitudes, boredom becomes the default for all things not "good." Similarly, understanding one's place within hegemonic workplaces is correspondingly determined, to a large extent, by the terms that name and thereby create boundaries or liberation—and all outlooks between and beyond. Beginning in the wake of the personal computer, a number of theorists including Soshana Zuboff have traced how we "think" ourselves (through language, often uncritically) into particular relationships—not always beneficial to our own happiness or well-being. This concept is best expressed in her landmark book *In the Age of the Smart Machine* (Basic, 1989), whose analysis of labor and corporate power is now complemented with her similarly incisive recent book *The Age of Surveillance Capitalism: The Fight for a Human Future at the New Frontier of Power* (Public Affairs, 2019).

Although Bousquet and Wills's (2004) *The Politics of Information: The Electronic Mediation of Social Change* has similarly examined catalysts for both social change and further subjectification, it does not explicitly focus primarily on labor relations the way his other work does. But its implications clearly have urgent relevance for a greater understanding of labor because issues of *control* and language are central to this analysis. In fact, he begins his introduction to the collection by consideration of the rhetorical justifications used for George W. Bush's post-9/11 U.S. invasion of Iraq: "The new language is a kind of freemason's handshake: strangers using the language of the Iraq invasion are able to recognize each other as persons who share the worldview, aims, and values of that invasion" (p. v). From Machiavelli and beyond (think "axis of evil" or countless other phrases of domination and classification), we have learned that one's words are essential tools of gaining and increasing power, and as we see in Bousquet's Iraq analysis, highly effective managers are masters of language as a vehicle for forging community where shared metaphors, relationships, and semantics are quickly and readily accepted without question or extended critical dialogue.

Bousquet and Wills (2004) is keenly aware of the mediation of information as essential to power and regulation as well as possible disruption of particular social arrangements. They write of both the hope and hopelessness of this mediation:

> In the early 1990s, technological optimists represented the World Wide Web as an actual or potential public sphere or, alternatively, as an anarcho-subcultural new frontier, a place of self-fashioning where the liberal dream of autonomy and self-determination could be performed and realized. (p. vi)

Unfortunately, as we will see in further analysis of Bousquet's work, liberation and solidarity of the masses in academia has not come to fruition; instead, an increasing bleakness has mostly resulted, despite the hope of the internet.

Bousquet's analysis of academia suggests that all disciplines have become subservient to colleges of business, and if one compares their increasingly inequitable salaries, workloads, or other perks (such as endless "consulting" that is clearly a monetary loyalty away from serving the needs of students or programs) the well-being and sustainability of institutions are all the more difficult, particularly in this COVID-age of austerity. In fact, Bousquet (2009) posits,

> One could easily argue that increasingly the management curriculum is "the" undergraduate curriculum, except for the vocational workforces and those of science, technology, engineering, and mathematics (STEM), while the liberal arts generally have been redefined as, effectively, extracurricular. (Or at best peripherally preprofessional for such fields such as communications, law, and teaching.) (p. 118)

With such shifts in English departments away from traditional literature and toward courses in "professional writing," this move is Darwinian survival as the humanities reinvent themselves to attract students in order to better prepare them for the privilege and perks of joining the class of managers and entrepreneurs, where at least some likely hope to become the new robber barons of the 21st century. Ironically, some within and beyond the humanities are offering Bousquet-like critiques of this shift. Former Disney executive now turned humanitarian Adam Leipzig represents well this critical analysis of the "costs" of such academic reorientation. In a personal story of his return to his 25th Yale class reunion, Leipzig (2013) says of his classmates,

> Eighty percent of them were unhappy with their lives; [speaking in their voices, he continues] "I feel as though I've wasted my life and I'm halfway through it; I don't know what my life is all about." . . . Who was happy, the twenty percent? Well, we had studied literature and renaissance rhetoric and we were the theatre people and the history geeks. We had studied classes for the joy of learning, not because we thought they were going to direct us to a specific job (1:12–2:08)

He then outlines his vantage point of a five-part journey toward happiness, unspokenly parallel to his own life's path, and contrary to the class hierarchy based in inequitable labor practices reinforced by much of today's output in higher education. His examples strengthen the affirmative power of connections and democratic community, consistent with the critique of English departments and higher education provided by Bousquet.

The Academic Job Market

Bousquet's primary attention is upon large research institutions (the kind where he has held faculty positions) and their unashamed exploitation where doctoral students are graduated but not into a market of stable tenure-track employment. Even beyond the doctoral institutions, a parallel abusive and inequitable practice also exists where low-paid contingent faculty members (particularly in the humanities) are merely substituted for doctoral students on assistantship, and their salaries are often half, or less, of tenure-track faculty members. In the wake of COVID and the rapid faculty downsizing that has resulted, as well as the proliferation of for-profit or online degree mills staffed almost entirely by contingent faculty members, we know that tenure-track faculty positions have become even more rare, as claims that the current national average for the use of contingent faculty is 51.4% (CollegeFactual.com, n.d., para. 5). As a result, those contingent positions, often without benefits or retirement plans, can be near permanent for graduates of doctoral programs. Indeed, we should remember that Bousquet wrote the following in the relatively "good" years for academia; in the nearly fifteen years since, conditions have only gotten far, far worse:

> What needs to be quite clear is that this is not a "system out of control," a machine with a thrown rod or gasket. Quite the contrary: it's a smoothly functioning new system with its own easily apprehensible logic, premised entirely on the continuous replacement of degree holders with nondegreed labor (or persons with degrees willing to work on unfavorable terms). (Bousquet, 2008a, p. 24)

A recent *Inside Higher Ed* column (Winter, 2021) concurs and affirms the worsening conditions:

> The economics of higher education preclude universities from ever returning to the model of full-time tenure-track/tenured faculty that dominated campuses during the mid-to-late 20th century. In today's campus economy, and into the foreseeable future, contingent faculty positions in the humanities—adjunct appointments and short-term contractual jobs—will be the norm. (para. 4)

Quite simply, doctoral programs are producing far more graduates than will ever find work in tenure-track positions with stable retirement plans. Indeed, when Bauer first entered the job market in composition and rhetoric in 1995, he was well qualified for about 60 tenure-track jobs that existed in rhetoric and composition, and a pool of some 200 candidates sought those positions, suggesting an employment rate of approximately 30%. Job prospects in literature, philosophy, history, or the languages were worse, even in the late 1990s! According to Bousquet's (2008b) YouTube channel, "40 percent of language PhDs will not have tenure-track job anywhere" (2:08–2:35), but as stressed previously, that dismal number is seemingly much lower at the present time. We know that tenure-track searches in the humanities regularly involve hundreds of applicants for a single position, so now, the trend of placement within tenure-track positions is likely only 10% or less of what it once was. Quite simply, the end of a PhD program is usually not the beginning of a long and wonderful teaching career, but for many, the end.

Unfortunately, those of us in academia know well that even tenure is often not job protection in the austerity coinciding with COVID and declining enrollments. In a commentary from a self-described "outspoken" Centenary University (in Hacketstown, New Jersey) professor of history and

American Association of University Professors (AAUP) leader who was one of four tenured faculty members who recently lost their jobs at that institution. This particular faculty member lost his job of 19 years during finals week of 2019—one of 168 such cases tracked at 11 different institutions, which is summarized by the term "adjunctification of the professoriate" (Zahneis, 2020a, para. 58). Whether called retrenchments, program prioritization, or layoffs, the losses are severe. "Colleges and universities employed 337,000 fewer people in August compared to February [2020], with adjuncts and staff members working in housing and dining taking the biggest hit" (Kelchen, 2020, para. 1), but we know of institutions like Ithaca College or the University of Akron, which will cut up to 25% of their tenure-track faculty, or other institutions like Green Mountain College, Southern Vermont College, or others who have simply closed completely. As we approach the coming crater of fewer high school graduates between 2025 and 2030, the academic job market looks to worsen even further. Strategic planning for the future for institutions often includes further proliferation of "professional programs," with investment of new (or redirected) resources, as cuts in the humanities conversely increase.

Significant research still needs to be done in this area of inquiry regarding labor issues. For us, along with many other critical scholars analyzing the field such as David Downing, Bruce Horner, Eileen E. Schell, and Donna Strickland, the difference between rhetoric/composition (often called "rhet/comp") and other subfields of English involves the specific position that rhet/comp has within the division and its quite severe separation of labor. Possibly the most important point is that individuals holding PhDs in rhet/comp will often expect to assume the role of manager in one way or another, often over contingent faculty. Obviously pathways for employment of rhet/comp scholars will be varied, but as one of the best early career scholars has noted, most rhet/comp PhDs will be required at some point in their academic career to administer a writing program, which oversees the labor of others and performs other such managerial tasks. This term of overseer has intentional historic connotations, as both the overseen graduate students and the contingent labor who teach composition (or on occasion, other courses as well) are completely disposable and often treated as such, rather than as colleagues. More on this divide will follow in our final, fourth section.

The Neoliberal University

At the center of Bousquet's critique of higher education is the global shift to neoliberalism at academic institutions. Neoliberal ideals are difficult to define—in the context of their relation to higher education, they are often discussed alongside the spread of free market capitalism and globalism, which have increased the "need" for efficiency in labor and the maximization of profits. The neoliberal university is thus a corporatized version of the institutions that paved the intellectual future of the mid-to-late 20th century. Rather than being seen as the future of labor and intellectualism in the United States, university students began to be framed as consumers who were obtaining a service or a good in exchange for their time and capital.

Productivity and efficiency have become the norm for all stakeholders of higher education: students, faculty, staff, administrators, and so on. In a rapid decline beginning in the 1970s and 80s, the prestige of degrees in the humanities was replaced by degrees in business. Indeed, Bousquet (2008a) parallels his analysis of the university especially with the employment of women at the beginning of the 20th century; he writes of women faculty, in particular, who often fill the low-wage contingent positions within the university. Indeed, he says,

> A chief component of [this] oppression is the very idea that this arrangement is fair or rational, the inevitable—and impersonal—consequence of some such guarantor of the public good as a "market" in the wages of women (and the men who do such "women's work" as writing instruction in higher education). (p. 91)

He launches a strident critique (ever-more appropriate, given recent developments), using such terms as "the dominative totality of higher ed marketization" and "the flexible dictatorship of university administration" (p. 46). He assigns a pseudonym to a lecturer teaching at a research university in the East, whose commentary he sees as highly representative of her peers: "Teaching here is like being in a bad marriage that looks good to outsiders. I'm the wife whose husband slaps her around but who, nonetheless, smiles gamely, maintaining the relationship 'for the sake of the kids'" (p. 90). Those faculty with privilege who could resist this kind of arrangement do not escape his notice:

> Tenured faculty, even unionized tenured faculty, accept the managerial accounts of "necessity" in the exploitation of part-time faculty, graduate students, and the outsourcing of staff. Through managerial ideology, itself supported by a vast ensemble of reactionary social movements in the 1980s and 1990s, faculty no longer question the claims of "fiscal crisis" while the campus pays millions to basketball coaches but sub Wal-Mart wages to mathematics faculty and custodians. The knowledge has taken hold everywhere that "markets" are real but "rights" are insubstantial, as if "market-driven" indicated imperatives beyond the human and political, of necessity itself, rather than the lovingly-crafted and tirelessly maintained best-case scenario for the quite specific minority interest of wealth. (p. 93)

Indeed, as a senior administrator, Bauer knows this inequality all too well as he is ordered to make cuts to faculty while the highest level of administration simultaneously adds more high-paid administrative positions, seemingly without any serious resistance from the faculty union. This move toward "market" practices constitutes a massive shift of power within the disciplines of the university, but this shift is not the only one primary in Bousquet's focus.

Within the personnel functions of the university, Bousquet adds his strong critique of administration, management, and contingency explicitly. His analysis relates to the larger idea of the neoliberal university because of the increased significance placed on productivity and efficiency that is central to this "corporatization" of the university. To ensure efficiency from the faculty and staff of universities, new management and administrative positions were created to hold those employees accountable and to measure the quality of the services they were providing. With the creation of new management and administrative roles came a shift to a labor force that *could be* managed. Contingent labor can be cycled out easily and paid very little compared to the traditional model of the more autonomous tenured professor, and these contingent faculty have a higher propensity for following management due to their precarity as temporary instructors. The neoliberal university is an extension of the global economic trends we've witnessed over the last 20 years—increased productivity, maximization of profit, managers concerned superficially with quality—criteria rarely measured by deep learning or qualitative methods that analyze the metacognitive growth of individual students. Rather, as in corporate America, "quality" is often measured by the absence of student complaints and instead the building of a "brand," no matter how superficial and how tied to athletics or other ancillaries—that creates a favorable knee-jerk impression for the larger university free from serious evidence.

In fact, a kind of "bigotry" and entitlement pervade departments of English, where a majority of tenured faculty members actively seek *not* to teach composition as a "perk" of seniority. Even in independent departments of writing, who have often broken away from more traditional departments of English because of oppressive ideologies held by senior faculty in literature, this mindset is pervasive. And Bousquet's well-known critique of neoliberal institutions of higher education is deeply situated within his own positionality as a writing studies scholar. Within such writing programs, a writing program administrator (WPA) exists to create and implement the curriculum, to hire and supervise first-year writing faculty, and to oversee the program as a whole—often as a department within a department. Not only is Bousquet critical of the exploitation of cheap labor in writing programs, but he also focuses his critique on the WPAs who essentially function as upper management. The WPA gets paid significantly more than the instructors who teach the courses in the program (and WPAs often teach upper-level or graduate courses, but ironically and often *not any* of the first-year writing courses that constitute the very program over which they have power); these WPAs are often supported by a handful of graduate assistants and assistant or junior writing program administrators. The WPA constitutes and oversees the work that takes place within the program, which can include teaching, writing, reading, and thinking. The type of labor relations between faculty, staff, and students is drastically influenced by the WPA, who often is hired merely to maintain the status quo. Writing programs that look like this, and there are *some* that don't (typically at non-Research 1 schools), serve as productive examples of the problems with neoliberal institutions examined by Bousquet.

Administrators who manage a department or program are often paid a generous salary, while the individuals in upper administration (deans, provosts, etc.) obviously get paid even more, all while many departments and programs have shifted to an overutilization of cheap labor and elimination of tenure-track jobs. This shift in higher education is neoliberal in the sense that positions of management have become more popular and powerful (and thus corporatized). Neoliberal institutions embrace the ideas of competition and data; writing programs and the scholarship that is often considered to be a part of this discipline have become undoubtedly more competitive and data-driven, as has the pedagogy. Writing programs, according to Bousquet's assessments, epitomized the neoliberal shift in higher education and served as a useful entry point in his critiques, which we have seen become only more pertinent over the past several years. And although terms like *progressive* are common within English departments and writing programs, as Chris Gallagher (2002) has written so wisely,

> [although] *traditional* is often unreflectively used—in Composition and Rhetoric and elsewhere—as a term of derogation, it is equally true that the word *progressive* is often used unreflectively as a term of approbation. These two terms—one denoting a move backward, into the past, and the other suggesting a move forward, into the future—exist in a binary that disparages the past and assumes we are on that grand march toward a far better future. . . . One of the aims of this book is to show that a wealth of contradictory reforms and pedagogies have been proposed under the banner of progressivism. (pp. xii–xiv)

Indeed, Gallagher complements Bousquet in exposing the deeply hidden self-delusion that often lurks in academia and within English departments themselves, including within those who see themselves as liberatory, radical, or even "in solidarity" with the poor while turning a blind eye to the inequity in their midst.

The kind of critique raised by Bousquet may be increasingly dangerous to careers—some administrators do not like their motives, their decisions, or their methods questioned or made public, and then they retaliate. Take the example of the firing of Ole Miss fourth-year Assistant Professor Garrett Felber for his antiracism activism and scholarly work within the Department of History. It's yet another divide, yet another challenge for shared governance, and yet another sign of instability and negative transformation in the humanities (Zahneis, 2020b). Fill a department with adjuncts or part-timers, and one has generally reduced questions of governance because one has suppressed the number of "votes," as seldom do such temporary faculty members get a "vote," including in union states—in the Pennsylvania State System of Higher Education (PASSHE), for example, one must be a "regular full-time faculty member" in order to vote on hiring decisions or on most other matters.

The Teaching of Composition

As suggested previously, since the 1980s (or before), English departments have become increasingly divided between those traditionalists whose primary focus is teaching and scholarship within literary studies versus those whose expertise lies in the ever-emerging fields of composition and rhetoric. Indeed, Peter North (1987) and others have identified this dramatic shift; North identifies it wisely as "composition" becoming "Composition" (p. 9). Bousquet's position in academia has certainly been enriched and enabled by this recent trend in the profession. Epistemological and theory-driven pursuit is threatened and diminished by contingent labor often not trained in or fluent in the praxis that should drive a first-rate writing program. Unfortunately, many contingent faculty hold their degrees in literature (and they are forever pursuing "promotion" to teaching within their field and beyond composition) or creative writing (another field in English studies whose production of graduates far outpaces the positions available), and their students often suffer because their full and primary loyalty is not to the disciplinary best practices. This divide continues in nearly all departments, sometimes unspoken or sometimes with great angst (and all classifications in between), but it's worth noting for thorough understanding of the world that Bousquet explores.

A final contradiction also exists as we consider this specialized and urgent field of composition, where students often come to college without particular high regard for English or for the relevance of first-year writing. The very best in the field are often quite transformative in the impact they have upon students, upon their awareness and their ability to analyze and understand, and upon their embrace of ambitious literate practices. But if one further considers the wake of out-of-touch managers and administrators (a favorite title within the *Tenured Bosses and Disposable Teachers* collection is "I Was an Adjunct Administrator," which magnifies the hegemony that Bousquet so intensely critiques), particularly when one also considers the giant egos that often populate higher education, we see a vexing contradiction: the aspiring and noble ideals of an institution versus the practices of an executive or a small group of administrators, a large number of whom have never taught remedial students, have never considered how to construct pedagogical practices to transform the diverse lives of students, or who have never sought to discern how to inspire the most meritorious faculty members as exemplars for their peers. Indeed, for too many administrators, one "teaches," as if all disciplines were interchangeable and ubiquitous. And many of these administrators during their interviews often point to their "teaching" to bolster their standing among faculty, but that interaction with students has merely involved an honors class or some graduate course. Rarely does it include years of heavy grading or work within composition where "access" to opportunity for underprepared students and those from low socioeconomic backgrounds is often determined.

The work of Bousquet (and others working in composition and rhetoric) leaves a stark lesson. With the long-term decline in the cultural capital of literature and a steep decline in tenure-track hires in literary studies, some faculty within English are rethinking their relationship to writing (and others resistant to change should do the same). As interest in digital media grows, and as the overwhelming majority of funding for English departments comes from tuition dollars generated from students enrolled in first-year and other writing courses, at what point does the traditional model of hegemonic literary studies as a focus of power become unsustainable? Together with rising enrollment in courses in creative, civic, and professional composition, can the figure of writing provide a sense of disciplinary coherence within the field of English? What will it take for literature faculty to agree that they, too, are interested in writers, the emergence of rhetorical studies as our dominant field of shared inquiry, and the teaching of writing as a dignified and urgent pursuit for all, not just for contingent faculty?

Conclusion

Marc Bousquet exposes a delicate divide in the humanities and within higher education, not unlike the stark economic dissonance that divides the United States politically, materially, and ideologically. Although public institutions often advertise their commitment to "access," Bousquet's work reminds us of the vast hypocrisy lurking there (and the pandemic and the most recent presidential election further remind us of the always-already systematic hypocrisy on which American political parties are likewise built). Indeed, within public higher education or even state budgets, mere lip service is paid to opportunity for all and "shared governance," but an unresolvable contradiction pervades higher education: "access" versus the traditional "gates" that are exclusionary, to keep out the undesirables. Sadly, we still "rank" institutions based on their exclusiveness, in full contradiction to democracy and opportunity. As marginalized citizens continue to fight for "liberty and justice for all," so English departments and all of us must choose our allegiance to a waning past or an alternative vision that's more inclusive, current, transformative, and responsive to the world(s) in which we actually live.

References

Bousquet, M. (2008a). *How the university works: Higher education and the low-wage nation.* New York University Press.

Bousquet, M. (2008b) *Play Ph.D. Casino: Interview with Monica Jacobe* [Video]. https://www.youtube.com/user/MarcBousquet

Bousquet, M. (2009, Fall). The figure of writing and the future of English studies [10th anniversary special issue]. *Pedagogy, 10*(1), 117–129.

Bousquet, M., Scott, T., & Parascondola, L. (Eds.). (2004). *Tenured bosses and disposable teachers: Writing work in the managed university.* Southern Illinois University Press.

Bousquet, M., & Wills, K. (Eds.). (2004). *The politics of information: The electronic mediation of social change.* Alt-X Press. https://marcbousquet.net/pubs/Politics_Information.pdf

CollegeFactual.com. (n.d.). *American University student to faculty ratio & faculty composition.* https://www.collegefactual.com/colleges/american-university/academic-life/faculty-composition/

Gallagher, C. (2002). *Radical departures: Composition and progressive pedagogy.* National Council of Teachers of English.

Kelchen, R. (2020, October 15). Permanent budget cuts are coming: The outlook for higher education was dim even before the pandemic. *The Chronicle of Higher Education.* https://www.chronicle.com/article/permanent-budget-cuts-are-coming

Leipzig, A. (2013). *How to know your life purpose in five minutes* [Video]. TEDx-Malibu. Youtube. https://www.youtube.com/watch?v=vVsXO9brK7M

North, P. (1987). *The making of knowledge in composition: Portrait of an emerging field.* Heinemann.

Winter, F. (2021, February 9). Plus c'est la même chose: The new reality for humanities Ph.D.s is a transformation, not a crisis of the moment. *Inside Higher Ed.* https://www.insidehighered.com/advice/2021/02/09/new-reality-humanities-phds-transformation-not-crisis-moment-opinion

Zahneis, M. (2020a, February 16). The latest assault on tenure. *The Chronicle of Higher Education.* https://www.chronicle.com/article/The-Latest-Assault-on-Tenure/248058?cid=wcontentlist

Zahneis, M. (2020b, December 17). The university celebrated his success. Then it fired him. *The Chronicle of Higher Education.* https://www.chronicle.com/article/his-university-celebrated-his-success-then-it-fired-him

9

THE NEOLIBERAL TRANSFORMATION OF HIGHER EDUCATION

Stanley Aronowitz and the Rise of the Corporate Knowledge Factory

John M. Elmore

It is a well-documented fact that higher education in the United States has undergone a significant transformation over the past 50 years. The bound critiques of those transformations could undoubtedly fill a small library, and they are anything but singular in their ideological orientations. Countless critiques on the right sound dire warnings of a not-so-secret den of communist vampires on our college campuses, who drain the logic of the free market from the veins of our innocent youth (Ellis, 2020; Horowitz, 2006, 2009; Shapiro, 2010; Treadgold, 2018). Liberals and pragmatic moderates have focused on a perceived loss of access and the "mysterious" rising cost of tuition and its less acknowledged partners in crime—campus housing and fees.

This "save-the-baby-and-the-bath" perspective consistently seems to argue that there is nothing fundamentally wrong with our universities; we just need to fine-tune their functions—modernize them—and make them more equally accessible (Crow & Dabars, 2015, Fitzpatrick, 2019; Selingo, 2013). On the left, including the communist vampires themselves, there is the claim that higher education (and education in general) has been fully given over to the project of neoliberal capitalism, in which a dumbed-down and vocationalized curriculum seeks to privatize the mind and commodify the bodies of our students, now labeled "customers" (Busch, 2017; Giroux,

2014; Tuchman, 2009). One of the more prominently accused vampires, Stanley Aronowitz, has been sounding that alarm, to anyone who would listen, since the early 1990s. Specifically, *The Knowledge Factory: Dismantling the Corporate University and Creating True Higher Learning* (Aronowitz, 2000), and his follow-up, a collection of essays entitled *What Is It All For? Against Schooling in the Corporate University* (2008), clearly lay out his concerns. In reviewing these various positions, there is often more than a little interplay, places where left, right, and center agree on a particular problem—constraints on free thought and expression, for example—but disagree wildly on either the resulting injury or the underlying cause. One thing is clear: The political zeitgeist of recent years demands serious questions be leveled at American higher education and the dramatic disappearance of what Aronowitz terms "higher learning."

In this chapter I intend to give credit where credit is so clearly due. The vast majority of concerns raised by Aronowitz have indeed been proven to be every bit as insidious and pernicious as he argued. I can't say, however, that I'm confident that short of an outright revolution on our college campuses, anything could have been done to stop the creep of anti-intellectual, antidemocratic, vocationalized training eclipsing any real "higher learning" on our campuses. But that does not change the fact that Aronowitz was certainly not crying wolf; the wolf is definitely here and it's sporting a full belly.

I will consider the specific concerns about the corporatization of higher education raised by Aronowitz and discuss the nature of their continued existence today, such as (a) the impact on the faculty and, specifically, their control over the curriculum and pedagogy of the institution; (b) the impact on students and, specifically, their restricted opportunities for actual learning and the prospect of criticality; and (c) the ultimate social, political, and hegemonic aims of the neoliberal, corporate model of higher education. In conclusion, I will argue that there are what I believe to be some limitations—or blind spots—in Aronowitz's proposed antidote to these circumstances. To be as fair as possible, these critiques come from the privileged perch of 20/20 hindsight. But if higher education, especially of the public variety, is ever to be reclaimed for its potential as an antihegemonic tool and proving ground for a more democratic and just society, it is important we consider the base motivation of this corporate transformation of higher education.

Stanley Aronowitz

For almost 40 years, Aronowitz has taught at the Graduate Center of the City University of New York, where he is now distinguished professor of sociology and urban education. In his unique and varied background, he has been a schoolteacher, a labor organizer, and a proud two-time college dropout. His background is decidedly working class and he has devoted much of his teaching and writing to exposing the inherent hegemony that is the beating heart of the capitalist system. Among his many books are *False Promises* (Duke University Press, 1991), *Crisis in Historical Materialism* (University of Minnesota Press, 1990), *The Jobless Future* (University of Minnesota Press, 1995), *Science as Power: The Death and Rebirth of American Radicalism* (University of Minnesota Press, 1988), and *Left Turn: Forging a New Political Future* (Routledge, 2006).

Aronowitz has sought to shine a klieg light on the realities of oligarchy, even when cloaked in noble words like *freedom* and *democracy*. Much like one of his personal heroes, C. Wright Mills, whom he writes about in the book *Taking It Big* (Aronowitz, 2012), he is always dialectic in his analysis, digging beneath the surface of issues to their undergirding, the current forces of power. Also like Mills, Aronowitz has been proven correct in many of his predictions, certainly, as I hope to demonstrate, in regard to the ruin of higher education.

Although I've never had the opportunity to meet Aronowitz in person, like many critical pedagogues in my age group, his work has been so highly insightful, motivating, and personal for me that I feel as though we've been comrades for years. As I too have followed a rather unique path to my current position, I very much feel, like Aronowitz (2000), that "although I am *in* the academy . . . I am not *of* the academy" (p. ix). Although, in many ways, my educational journey couldn't have been more different than the one Aronowitz describes in the preface to *The Knowledge Factory*—his start was in the city schools of Brooklyn, New York, whereas mine was in the K–12 school of Bennington, Kansas (population: 561)—in other ways they seem mirrored. Aronowitz and I clearly share a more than healthy wariness of authority and a general unwillingness to play the games of submission that authoritarian structures so often demand. Such characteristics and dispositions can certainly make for a bumpy ride in compulsory, mass schooling and often require the finding of alternative routes and creative solutions to move within and around the system. In this regard we share a great many commonalities. Certainly, when Aronowitz (2000) describes his early educational experiences, I can picture many of my own:

> I was a bright but disruptive child who used my skills of persuasion to lead many less talented students away from the beaten path. Consequently my friends and I spent large chunks of time in the principal's office for disruptive behavior, and my mother was hauled into school on more than one occasion to answer for my indiscretions. (p. x)

I must admit, I am always skeptical of educational critics whose schooling experience was comfortable and their procession up the academic ladder unfettered. Clearly, his perspective on education that has guided his critiques for decades was born out of the early experiences that he describes in the preface to *The Knowledge Factory*. Again, I can relate—as I often say to my students, far more of my critiques of education were born out of earning my GED than my PhD. However, I think where I somewhat depart from Aronowitz in our critiques and remedies of and for higher education may also be rooted in the differences of our experiences.

Aronowitz (2000) describes his teenage years in the Young Progressives and his attendance at the Jefferson School of Social Science where he "learned everything from Drama to Marxist orthodoxy" (p. xi). By 16, he was enrolled in the Marxist Institute,

> which among other subjects exposed me to philosophy. We read Thales, Anaximander, and Heraclitus from the pre-Socratics, Plato's Republic (but only in order to refute it), and Aristotle's Metaphysics as a precursor to Hegel and Marx. We studied Descartes and the English empiricists, especially Locke, Berkley, and Hume, a demonstration in the futility of bourgeois idealism. (p. xi)

I can honestly say, with only slight embarrassment, that I did not read a single word from any of these authors until graduate school and, even now, I have yet to crack the spine on Anaximander. Clearly, Aronowitz sees his exposure to these writings as key to his own development, which only continued through his time at the New School, and in his participation in the Free University of New York and the Union Graduate School, where he earned his PhD. It is little wonder that Aronowitz sees curricular changes and a dumbing down of the university canon as a primary culprit in the destruction of "higher learning."

The Knowledge Factory: Then and Now

When Aronowitz (2000) coined the term *knowledge factory* to describe the repurposing and reshaping of U.S. universities within the neoliberal era and declared that there was already "little that would qualify as higher learning in the United States," the culture of the corporate model was already wreaking havoc on every aspect of the institution (p. xvii). Aronowitz explains that the knowledge factory "is a production site in which criticism of the status quo narrows with each passing year" and has reached such a level of reity that students and faculty alike "have had to take what they can and run" (p. 35).

Since these dire declarations, things have only gotten worse. The defunding of public universities; the resulting skyrocketing of tuition, housing, and fees; the constant creep of administrative bloat; the outsourcing and privatization of campus spaces; the vocationalization of an "accredited" curriculum; and the pathological assault on faculty tenure and shared governance have marched steadily forward. In every aspect, from the exploitation of contingent faculty to the privatization of campus housing to the pettiness of for-profit parking spots, higher education now pits the logic of the market against the public good at every possible level.

As Aronowitz has warned, real learning in universities continues to be eclipsed by the constant pressure to better prepare students for the job market. As students have been redefined as customers, the bulk of faculty have been reduced to an army of academic mercenaries whose primary way of maintaining their paychecks is by keeping those customers entertained and happy. Aronowitz provided a much-needed voice and brought attention to how the hegemonic assaults on higher education were not only being driven by the logic of capital, but also driven to establish ideological barriers against the possibility of a university dedicated to inspiring collective critical consciousness and mass resistance.

It is both amazing and depressing that the mountain of scholarship that has been produced since *The Knowledge Factory* has had so little impact on the actual policy and practices of higher education. And this lack of impact has not only been the case for the critiques offered from those on the left, like Aronowitz. As I mentioned previously, critiques of higher education have seemed to come from every possible ideological angle. It has practically become a cottage industry unto itself. All the clamoring and hyperbolic claims of "communist brainwashing" coming from the right have really done nothing more than pilfered more book profits from Donald Trump's base and provided us with more uber-dystopian book covers from the likes of Dinesh D'Souza. So too is the case for the liberal-centrists whose handwringing over rising student debt, outrage over systemic inequality, and demands for equal access have had virtually no impact on the realities of higher education. And, as I mentioned previously, there are some concerns that are universally criticized across the ideological spectrum.

For example, even though David Horowitz and those of his ilk often assert noble-sounding ideals—such as the defense of free speech, to justify their witch hunts—there is a kernel of reality at the core of their position, but not one that they care to acknowledge. Freedom of speech for students, academic freedom for professors, free choice of what to study for students, opportunity to engage in student activism, to name just a few, are undoubtedly being increasingly constrained. But, although these realities may well be the result of ideological homogeneity in some of the departments or colleges of the elite universities, it is a truly detached and idiotic case to make against the institutions of higher education that remain a teetering option for working-class students. Every instance in my 20-year career in which I have felt pressure to shape my course objectives or "align" my content has been at the demand of vocation, not ideology. At the so-called third-tier institutions, accreditation bodies are the true drivers of curricula, not the faculty nor the administration.

The faculty at these institutions have all but accepted their roles as mere delivery mechanisms of content that has been built to specification, and increasingly so, to maintain the accreditation of their programs. I can't speak to the impact of such efforts at the "first-tier" institutions, but my sense is that when a diploma has the name "Harvard" embossed on it, there is little added value offered by adding an accreditation seal of approval. There is little to no doubt that the Harvard graduate is going to get a job, or as Harvard graduates snootily prefer, "make a job." However, at a working-class institution, accreditation is seen as a vital addition—potential employers may not trust our judgment (or brand) for what makes a qualified accountant, but they can surely trust the Association to Advance Collegiate Schools of Business! For students (whom we claim benefit the most from such accreditation) this has had direct impacts on their access to the knowledge that both the critics on the left and right have argued is the gateway to the development of critical citizenship. But in spite of the chorus of critics, little to no change has occurred.

I have a theory as to why this has been and continues to be the case. It is undoubtedly rooted in the fundamental logic of the neoliberal era in which we currently find ourselves, where everything, including education, has been commodified and the consumer ethos coats every aspect of our existence (more on that later). But what has grown from that tainted soil is a vicious cycle that has proven impressively impenetrable to any critique or reform, regardless of how accurate the claims or how powerful the voice from which they are offered.

The baneful trinity of high cost and debt, corporate-minded leadership, and a disempowered faculty are the core spokes of the breaking wheel. The process moves something like this: (a) Defund or habitually low-fund higher education; (b) kill as many grant programs as you can and make loans the only real option or, as President Reagan described it, "place the burden of higher education back where it belongs"; (c) when the institutions begin to really struggle, it becomes "necessary" to hire presidents and administrations that are "business-savvy" or "entrepreneurially inclined"—rename them CEOs, so you don't tarnish their résumés; (d) in league with these new academic executives, conservatives in state legislatures are joined by neoliberal democrats in demanding that universities be held "accountable" and judged solely on the employment of their graduates—bourgeois magazines stoke the fire by offering annual rankings based on starting salaries of graduates; (e) in response to this pressure, universities begin to realign their programs to the demands of "future employers" and to prove their commitment to the cause, they spend millions of tuition dollars to buy window stickers that declare "Accredited by . . ."; (f) recognizing their new power, accreditation bodies begin to increase the specificity of their demands such that programs begin to have difficulty fitting all the required objectives, so the university introduces the new "career-oriented general education" program, in which majors can now dictate to students which literature class they choose as a freshman, electives dwindle and disappear, and the liberal arts fade into the background; (g) the majority of students, fearful of extra semesters and increased debt (and brainwashed in consumerism), welcome anything that will get them out in 4 years with a job, so they can pay back their loans—and who can blame them? As Rotfeld (2001) aptly describes,

> Once students are told to see themselves as customers for education degrees, they expect customer service with a smile. . . . Seeing graduation as a job certification, not a mark of education, students want the degree but not the education. They want to earn, not learn. (p. 416)

This is certainly not meant to shame the victim—and students and the democracy they hope to hold are undoubtedly the victims—but only to describe the student dispositions produced by the corporate university. Finally, (h) the faculty find themselves with little leverage as they have given up their power bit by bit and submitted to a new "shared governance" model, in which the height of their influence is merely "advisory." Adding to their impotence is the fact that they now find more than 75% of their brethren are unprotected (i.e., contingent faculty who have long since realized that the "customer surveys" that their students fill out at the end of each semester are the only thing standing between them and the breadline). Do they assign Anaximander to them? I think not. Giroux (2013) accurately describes the end result in the following:

> Welcome to the dystopian world of corporate education in which learning how to think, be informed by public values, and become engaged critical citizens are viewed as a failure rather than a mark of success. Instead of producing a generation of leaders worthy of the challenges, the dystopian mission of public and higher education is to produce robots, technocrats, and compliant workers. (para. 4)

The specifics may differ, but I have a strong hunch that if you're reading this as a faculty member—certainly at a state university—you can relate to much of what I just described. It's a vicious cycle and one that only seems possible to break from the ground upward by using the institution to encourage our students to *question* the institution and the power relations that they are currently built to maintain. If this even qualifies as a "solution," it is, perhaps, where I respectfully diverge from Aronowitz.

Acknowledging the Real Target

When asked to discuss the circumstances of U.S. education over the past 50 years, Noam Chomsky points to the neoliberal definition of, and agenda for, education, which was spelled out quite directly by the Trilateral Commission report, *The Crisis of Democracy* (Crozier et al., 1975). In making the case for "a greater degree of moderation in democracy," the commission expressed a special concern in regard to institutions of higher education, and the intellectuals housed within (p. 113). This was especially the case for what the commission labeled "values-oriented intellectuals" whom they deemed a threat to democracy: "the intellectuals and related groups who assert their disgust with the corruption, materialism, and inefficiency of democracy and with the subservience of democratic government to 'monopoly capitalism'" (p. 114). In theorizing both the cause and the cure for this "crisis," the authors describe a cyclical process of interaction in which:

1. Increased political participation leads to increased policy polarization within society.
2. Increased policy polarization leads to increasing distrust and a sense of decreasing political efficacy among individuals.
3. A sense of decreasing political efficacy leads to decreased political participation. (p. 84)

Depoliticization and apathy are, the commission argued, keys to restoring governmental authority and social order. Given the role that institutions of higher education played in the civil rights and antiwar movements of the 1960s—what the commission deemed the result of an "excess of democracy" on our campuses—little imagination is required to envision the changes the commission wanted to see in higher education.

However, these trepidations and prescriptions were clearly not concerned with, nor directed at, every class of institution or demographic equally. According to Chomsky (1981) the commission assessed that a clear threat to

> democracy is posed by the "previously passive or unorganized groups in the population," such as "blacks, Indians, Chicanos, white ethnic groups, students and women—all of whom became organized and mobilized in new

ways to achieve what they considered to be their appropriate share of the action and of the rewards." The threat derives from the principle, already noted, that "some measure of apathy and noninvolvement on the part of some individuals and groups" is a prerequisite for democracy. Anyone with the slightest understanding of American society can supply a hidden premise: the "Wall Street lawyers and bankers" (and their cohorts) do not intend to exercise "more self-restraint." We may conclude that the "greater degree of moderation in democracy" will have to be practiced by the "newly mobilized strata." (p. 115)

Critical thought, and even some level of radicalization, could be somewhat permitted as long as it emanated from the "right" place or from the "right" demographic. The children of the ruling class would continue to attend elite institutions of higher learning, where they may very well bump into the occasional "values-oriented" professor, who may actually inspire them to think critically. However, this was clearly not viewed as a safe allowance for the children of the working class. Crozier et al. (1975) and the commission make a recommendation that clearly defines the nature of higher learning to be prescribed to such students:

> What seems needed . . . is to relate educational planning to economic and political goals. Should a college education be provided generally because of its contribution to the overall cultural level of the populace and its possible relation to the constructive discharge of the responsibilities of citizenship? . . . If answered in the negative, then higher educational institutions should be induced to redesign their programs so as to be geared to the patterns of economic development and future job opportunities. (p. 132)

When combined with the previously shared sentiments of the commission, the intent is clear: Working-class institutions were to become 4-year vo-techs. Henry Giroux (2013) explains how the concerns of the Trilateral Commission have been carried forward:

> It is for these very reasons that higher education is increasingly under attack by the concentrated forces of neoliberalism. Self-confident critical citizens are viewed as abhorrent by conservatives who remember the campus turmoil of the sixties. Citizens who take their responsibility to democracy seriously now pose a dire threat to corporate power. Unsurprisingly, these same individuals daily face the suspicion of the new corporate university that appears willing to conceive of faculty only as entrepreneurs, students only as customers, and education only as a mode of training. (para. 3)

The Stanfords, the NYUs, and the Princetons of the world were never the target, nor were the students they traditionally serve. Children of the elite can be somewhat trusted with such criticality, but in the hands of the children of the working class, the risk is viewed as too great. The "inducement" the commission was looking for came in the form of skyrocketing costs due to a systematic defunding of public education, which is very much a class-specific concern. According to the U.S. Bureau of Labor Statistics, prices for college tuition and fees were 1414.61% higher in 2020 than they were in 1977. High cost and the threat of indebtedness, in combination with the triumph of neoliberalism, with its disdain for the very concept of a "public good," serve as the key ingredients that sustain the previously described vicious cycle.

The list of books that Aronowitz offers in the final chapter of *The Knowledge Factory* is amazing, but I'm not convinced that the transformation of our current "higher training" into the higher learning that we seek begins with an ideological shift in the canon. It simply fails to address the structural impediments that Aronowitz accurately describes in his work. Although the students of elite schools may very well be deprived of the reading list Aronowitz recommends, the working-class students who attend the regional, state schools (like the one I teach at) often find themselves unable to even choose a single elective course within their program of study, lest they be condemned to an extra semester or year of school and the resulting increase in debt. When they do manage to sneak in a course based on intellectual curiosity, there is a good chance they will be handed a syllabus that has been so derailed in the name of "career-oriented" education objectives that it will probably fall well short of the knowledge and inspiration for which they were hoping. Or, worse yet, if the course does inspire them and they discover a new passion, they are quickly faced with the reality of the contemporary working-class university—the degree programs of study are so narrowly prescribed that changing your major, even after the first semester, virtually assures an extra year of school and debt. I have had more than a few seniors sit in my office and admit that they realized they didn't want to become a teacher 2 years earlier, but it was too late to change. What a sad circumstance at a so-called liberal arts university. As I am sure he would agree, given Aronowitz's (2003) arguments in his excellent book, *How Class Works*, the neoliberal agenda for education cares little of what books are read in the lavishly ornate libraries of Columbia or NYU, but it has completely destroyed any potential for working-class students to experience a shadow of the "higher learning" that he promotes.

It is certainly not that I disagree with Aronowitz's valuation of a radical intelligentsia—the critical role of a vanguard class for social critique and transformation. As he makes clear in *Taking It Big: C. Wright Mills and the Making of Public Intellectuals*, autonomous intellectuals play a central role in identifying and alerting the public to the often hidden or obscured forces of power. For similar reasons, I have always held the work of the late Christopher Hitchens in high regard (something for which I have taken a bit of heat from my leftist friends). But Hitchens, like Mills, at his core stood for the right to think for one's self—to own the *wheels in the head*, in Max Stirner's (1907) terms—and the paramount responsibility of the public intellectual to speak to power and as publicly as possible. One of Hitchens's (2010) most famous quotes, speaking to university students, also made clear what I believe true higher learning should lead to:

> I want to live my life taking the risk all the time that I don't know anything like enough yet . . . that I haven't understood enough . . . that I can't know enough . . . that I am always hungrily operating on the margins of a potentially great harvest of future knowledge and wisdom. I wouldn't have it any other way. And I'd urge you to look at those who tell you, those people who tell you at your age, that you are dead until you believe as they do. What a terrible thing to be telling to children . . . and that you can only live by accepting an absolute authority. Don't think of that as a gift. Think of it as a poisoned chalice. Push it aside however tempting it is. Take the risk of thinking for yourself. Much more happiness, truth, beauty and wisdom will come to you that way. (1:40–2:35)

Like Mills and Hitchens, Aronowitz has been one of those public intellectuals who celebrates and preaches the great value of critical and independent thought—and its essential role in pursuit of collective human freedom and justice. I, like many others, am thankful for his work. But given where we currently find ourselves, I think challenging the deformed version of higher education being peddled to the 99% of us is where our work must begin.

From my experience, teaching working-class students at working-class institutions, the transformation absolutely must start with the issue of cost and student debt, followed by a reclaiming of a liberal arts–based general education, dedicated to the development of critical thought, logic, and reason, and allowing a high degree of student choice. A return to the days when students were required to be "nondeclared" until their junior year and majors were not allowed to dictate prerequisites in the general education program would be a move in the right direction. Virtually any changes at the level of the university will most certainly require a reclaimed role by faculty in regard to control over the curriculum and, at least, a disempowering of accreditation bodies to, at most, an advisory role—if not their complete deletion. Perhaps the millions saved in time and money in pursuit of accreditations could be used to assist in the first priority of bringing student costs down. Undoubtedly, Aronowitz is correct that there needs to be a transformation in what is happening in the classrooms as well. Who could argue, with a straight face, that academic rigor and the central goal of challenging students to think critically and dialectically hasn't been drained from our classrooms within the corporate knowledge factory? However, until we reclaim our "students" from their current state of hypnotized "customers," by removing the main motivator—fear of a life of indebtedness—and faculty reclaim some degree of autonomy and control over the curriculum, I am not sure even the greatest philosophical books in history will make a dent, at least not with the working-class students I am certain Aronowitz is very much concerned for.

References

Aronowitz, S. (2000). *The knowledge factory: Dismantling the corporate university and creating true higher learning.* Beacon Press.

Aronowitz, S. (2003). *How class works: Power and social movement.* Yale University Press.

Aronowitz, S. (2008). *What's it all for? Against schooling in the corporate university.* Paradigm.

Aronowitz, S. (2012). *Taking it big: C. Wright Mills and the making of political intellectuals.* Columbia University Press.

Busch, L. (2017). Knowledge for sale: The neoliberal takeover of higher education. MIT Press.

Chomsky, N. (1981). *Radical priorities.* Black Rose Books.

Crow M., & Dabars, W. (2015). *Designing the new American university.* Johns Hopkins University Press.

Crozier, M., Huntington, S., & Watanuki, J. (1975). *The crisis of democracy: On the governability of democracies.* New York University Press.

Ellis, J. (2020). *The breakdown of higher education: How it happened, the damage it does, and what can be done.* Encounter Books.

Fitzpatrick, K. (2019). *Generous thinking: A radical approach to saving the university.* Johns Hopkins University Press.

Giroux, H. (2013). Beyond dystopian education in a neoliberal society. *Fast Capitalism, 10*(1). https://www.uta.edu/huma/agger/fastcapitalism/10_1/giroux10_1.html

Giroux, H. (2014). *Neoliberalism's war on higher education.* Haymarket Books.

Hitchens, C. (2010, November 18). *Does a good god exist? A debate with William Dembski* [Video]. YouTube. https://www.youtube.com/watch?v=VYEV1B5R-2g

Horowitz, D. (2006). *The professors: The 1010 most dangerous academics in America.* Ragnery.

Horowitz, D. (2009). *Indoctrination U: The left's war against academic freedom.* Encounter Books.

Rotfeld, H. J. (2001). *Misplaced marketing.* Quorum Books.

Selingo, J. (2013). *College unbound: The future of higher education and what it means for students*. Houghton Mifflin.

Shapiro, B. (2010). *Brainwashed: How universities indoctrinate America's youth*. Thomas Nelson.

Stirner, M. (1907). *The ego and its own*. Benjamin R. Tucker Publishing.

Treadgold, W. (2018). *The university we need: Reforming American higher education*. Encounter Books.

Tuchman, G. (2009). *Wannabe U: Inside the corporate university*. University of Chicago Press.

10

NEWFIELD AS A *NEW FIELD*?

The Substance and Subjectivities of a Cross-Disciplinary Voice in the Public Domain

Cassie L. Barnhardt

Christopher Newfield has assumed the role of critic, philosopher, cynic, idealist, and advocate regarding how American universities enact their responsibility to educate, serve, and contribute to society. Conventionally, across the corpus of Newfield's work he presents a synthesis of the social institution of higher education where he tells a story of the organizational and administrative issues, controversies, structural disincentives, and barriers to affirming educational values such as quality, learning, access, and open inquiry. This chapter explores his contributions, but it does not simply characterize Newfield's arguments as the object of analysis. Rather, in evaluating Newfield's public work the scholar becomes the subject of the analysis. Tracing the patterns of Newfield's public scholarly footprint reveals some of the ugliness about inequalities that the academy produces, enacts, and resists. Further, in framing the scope and reach of this scholar's public discourse, I consider cleavages that present as opportunities for reimagining public engagement within and external to the university context.

The Scholar and the Public

Public intellectuals engage as experts, analysts, innovators, critics, cynics, provocateurs. Their efforts can inspire, infuriate, calm, inform, motivate, and demystify the topic or subject about which they communicate. The boundaries for defining what constitutes being a public intellectual are increasingly blurred as the modes, formats, and venues for sharing scholarly work products or discourse are more numerous. Similarly, the discursive spaces and networks that constitute the public are equally obscure and complex. Is it even possible to construct or define a uniform "public" audience when communicating in a socially fragmented world—one characterized by niche virtual communities and extreme algorithmic personalization?

Historically, universities' public intellectuals have capitalized on their referent or expert power positions (Manning, 2018). Public intellectuals amplify the activities born of the university by giving them life in contexts beyond a corporeal body. In the early 20th century, as the modern research and scientific apparatus took on an institutionalized form, the public heard from university presidents as well as intellectual leaders from the newly forming academic societies (Trattner, 1970). Simultaneously, newspapers reported on lectures and talks given by prominent scientists from U.S. campuses and those visiting from abroad. With the help of private foundations, the academic-public interface in the United States was further structured to assure that research would be translated to meet society's social and industrial needs for the purpose of governing (Barnhardt, 2017). With the creation of research entities such as the Social Science Research Council and the National Bureau of Economic Research, the formalization of public, scholarly influence was reflected in the policy agendas of multiple presidential administrations (Karl, 1985).

The matter of influence is central to any conception or discussion of a public intellectual. Essentially, the relative impact of a public intellectual can be gauged by the extent to which one's work and ideas becomes noticed by others. In attempting to assess whether one's work is noticed the questions become more numerous. How are audiences accessing the ideas—through what venues? Who (or which groups) engage with the ideas put forth by the intellectual? Is the substance of one's work shaping culture and public opinion? Or is the substance having a structural impact by virtue of its influence on policy, regulatory frameworks, or governance arrangements? With respect to both the cultural and structural influence of a public intellectual's contributions, why must we narrow our focus to the relative impact of one person? All intellectual ideas and discoveries have emerged from scientific and intellectual communities with distinctive ontologies, epistemologies, methods, and axiological frameworks—not to mention massive public and institutional investments and infrastructures dedicated to the production of intellectual work.

Newfield: A Case of the Public Intellectual

Christopher Newfield has become a marquis voice associated with an area of inquiry and analysis labeled "critical university studies" (CUS). Notably, this arena of intellectual thought has its own Wikipedia (2020) page, and a designated series category with an esteemed publisher (Johns Hopkins University Press). Practically speaking, the field of CUS is characterized as focusing on "critique of current trends and on providing analytical tools to rebuild colleges and universities internationally. The general aim is to allow universities to fulfill their higher social and intellectual ambitions" (Newfield, n.d.). Newfield does not claim to be the sole originator of CUS, but he certainly has become its steward.

Newfield has been writing on higher education topics since the mid-1990s. His major scholarly publications in this domain consist of three books: *The Great Mistake: How We Wrecked Public Universities and How We Can Fix Them* (Newfield, 2016), *Unmaking the Public University: The Forty Year Assault on the Middle Class* (Newfield, 2008), and *Ivy and Industry: Business and the Making of the American University 1880–1980* (Newfield, 2003). Each book offers a deep analysis of the structural and organizational issues that shape university activities, such as the delivery of the curriculum, the conduct of research, and the broader role that the university has as an institution in civic, cultural, economic, and political life. Across the corpus of CUS works, and particularly within Newfield's books, the analyses demonstrate the ways the logic of neoliberalism when applied to the public university have privileged managerialism, privatization, and reductionist quantification to the detriment of democratic values and shared decision-making, investing in civic and common goods, and adhering to complex and holistic conceptions of quality, learning, and human flourishing (through the provisions of education and research). Aside from Newfield's books, he has written for the popular press—the *HuffPost* (Newfield, n.d.), cofounded and curated a blog called *Remaking the University* (Meranze & Newfield, n.d.), and has authored several articles and chapters that span a range of publication types.

Newfield has stepped into the higher education discourse to make sense of and explain the very public critiques that were being asserted by political and ideological elites in the 1990s with coedited volumes on political correctness in 1995, and then on multiculturalism in 1996. In these works, the emphasis was on the humanities curriculum, a component of the academy that Newfield positions as essential for addressing cultural topics and tensions in American life, thereby being essential for democracy. His high regard for the humanities is a persistent theme in his writing on higher education; Newfield routinely expresses his faith in the humanities as crucial to preparing students for citizenship, but also for overcoming the problems of and within the university (unequal access, inclusion, participation, and declining creativity). The chapters Newfield and Strickland (1995) assembled in *After Political Correctness* display tangible examples of the ways neoconservative elites have pursued strategic actions in areas such as media, philanthropy, and public policy to reduce the public's esteem for humanistic and critical education. The essence of Newfield's efforts to bundle politics and curricula is consistent across his work. His scholarship documents how the legitimacy of the academy has been undermined in the public domain by conservative elites. The conservative ideological argument holds that humanities curricula have been disparaged on account of their embracing a deviation from traditional Western culture and representing the diversity and pluralism of contemporary culture. From the conservative viewpoint, these curricular dualities are viewed as irreconcilable and as evidence of changing/declining standards. Rather than expanding knowledge, Newfield argues that neoconservatives view variations from classic liberalism as niche politics of professors unchecked by academic management, threatening the quality of the academy. Further he asserts that attacking the multicultural elements of the humanities is part of a macro neoconservative and neoliberal strategy to divest from the welfare state. That is, efforts to undermine the legitimacy of the humanities make room for public money to flow toward workforce development, research for commercial application, or economic impact—all of which subsequently favor the interests of elite capital investors.

Newfield's trilogy of books take up different pieces of the ways in which the interests of neoconservative elites have coupled their ideology to support the proliferation of neoliberal management in higher education. He views the neoliberal administrative approach as working to inoculate campus governance, policy, and administrative practice from the influence of critical values, critique generally, and dissenting positions—or, stated more simply, the substance of what is typically voiced in faculty senates or shared governance bodies. *Ivy and Industry* offers an historical map of the rise of the modern-day university-sponsored research apparatus, one that has produced an administrative infrastructure devoted to advancing the interests of elite capital codified in policies and procedures related to patents, product development, royalties, technology transfer, and licensing. He frames universities' complex entanglements to raise concerns and offer hope. The concern is that the growth of public universities' administrative capacity to commercialize research has given private industry an outsized share of public universities' work products. The hope Newfield offers is that the robust and homegrown university administrative apparatuses associated with research have been able to somewhat insulate universities' independence from external influence, thereby sustaining scientific principles of truth, creativity, ethics, and quality.

In *Unmaking the University*, Newfield deals directly with public university funding in a way that he only inches up to in his prior works. In many respects this book is a tome on what emerged from the neoconservative cultural critiques he worked to document in the late 1990s. In *Unmaking* he situates neoliberal management of the university as deliberate "economic war," born of and amplified through the "culture wars." He argues that political elites' targeting of the university was deliberately designed to reduce the legitimacy of the institution, thereby justifying further public divestment from higher education and a redirection of public resources into private (elite) hands. He documents the constraints placed on public universities through policy, budget cuts, curricular reform, and donor preferences as part of a plan to situate power among the few, or the elite. Newfield highlights the political dimensions of the elites' economic war by reviving the democratic principles of public education as a mechanism of social uplift, empowerment, and opportunity for the masses instead of the few. With *Unmaking*, he gives greater specificity to what it means to dismantle the welfare state by explaining the changing university revenue processes in detail and with examples. Again, Newfield positions the intellectual tradition of the academy as sufficient armor to endure the elite attacks on the academy, thus reinforcing the need for humanism, deliberation, and a commitment to shared governance.

The Great Mistake continues to extend earlier themes of the consequences of neoliberal management that have resulted in shifting universities away from their democratic and civic purposes. Newfield offers a bit more practicality and pragmatism compared to his other works by using the example of the University of California system. His contribution comes in spelling out how political agendas, when enacted incrementally and under the cloak of organizational routines, amount to plausible deniability for elites. Instead of paying political consequences for cutting off public universities at their knees, reduced autonomy, financial decline, and public divestment are participatory and taken for granted by well-intentioned academic managers. He reveals a world where university leaders seem to have succumbed to the weight of the neoliberal agenda. In this book, he carefully draws on studies and reports to document the inaccuracies and myths associated with university operational costs and revenues. He actively works to debunk assumptions about the financial impact of research apparatus, academic labor, federal financial aid, and state budget austerity incentives, flipping the interpretation by looking at the evidence. Like his prior books, this book edges up to and then introduces the next phase of his thought process on public higher education. *The Great Mistake* dabbles in university rankings and reputation metrics as an instrument that has redirected universities from their uniqueness and creative capacities toward the neoliberal logics of standardization. Knowing that Newfield's current work is more expressly devoted to quantification schemes in higher education, or measuring the unmeasurable (learning), I anticipate that if he were to produce another book, quantification of educational phenomena from organizational performance to student learning and faculty quality would be the focus.

Across his writing, Newfield tends to be slim on articulating reforms, but he is big on advancing the argument that critical thinking, humanism, pluralism, and inclusion are essential for revitalizing democratic values and equal opportunity in education. Notably, Newfield's contributions, especially his books, have been the subject of many, many reviews by other scholars, and higher education scholars specifically. In my view, it would be somewhat narrow to simply address the content of his writing. To date, what is missing from prior analyses is situating Newfield and his work as a particular contributor and voice in public discussions of higher education.

Who Is Christopher Newfield?

The story of Newfield as a public intellectual within the discourse about higher education is important for a variety of reasons. For all intents and purposes, his formal academic preparation did not foretell he would emerge as a contributor to the specific subject matter of higher education. He is an English professor by training, and yet has ventured into the domain of higher education policy, practice, and impact. Essentially, Newfield's public take on higher education as a subject matter is uncommon for his field. English professors tend to focus on creative works or literature rather than social welfare provisions like education or science, public finance, or political battles in statehouses or within boardrooms. Also, Newfield seems to have been intentional about "going public" with his scholarship on higher education. To use a metaphor drawn from theatre, he has been successful in breaking the proverbial fourth wall of the proscenium, or has at least succeeded in lifting the curtain to give the audience a better look at the performance (of higher education). His intentionality in proactively creating or cultivating a public audience for his writing and scholarly analysis is something unique and not typical of people of his academic profile.

Modern academics, especially those at public institutions, are asked and expected to be translational, publicly engaged, community oriented, and entrepreneurial, ensuring that what they generate within the academy propagates into broader use and application. By in large, transfer and translation of academic work tends to be confined to discrete innovations, discoveries, or solutions, institutionalized in trademarks, patents, technology transfer, and entrepreneurial structures (Owen-Smith, 2011). It is rarely the case that conceptual "products" become components of the public's grasp—which is the reality of Newfield's case, and makes his public contribution distinctive.

The evidence and the argument, the meanings derived from them, and the critiques and analyses Newfield elaborates are regarded as his public contributions. Moreover, in examining Newfield's work I grapple with the subjectivity of who he is, and how these realities contextualize what he says, who listens to or absorbs it, and how all these elements contribute to a discourse about universities and higher education.

Academic Background

Christopher Newfield's academic background is firmly imprinted with the quintessential stamp of a liberal arts education. He earned his undergraduate degree at Reed College, a small, highly selective, private residential liberal arts college in Portland, Oregon. At Reed, academic engagement is baked into the culture and community with compulsory humanities courses, close engagement with faculty, and a decrial of traditional grading scales in favor of holistic assessments. By enrolling at Reed, the 'Reedies' have chosen to disavow the conventional sizzle of college athletics and fraternities, instead funneling their passions into consciousness raising, late night debates, language immersion, or global exploration. Soon after receiving his bachelor's degree Newfield leveraged his Reed talents and was admitted to an Ivy League graduate school, Cornell University, earning a master's and a doctorate there. He describes the focus of his graduate preparation as covering U.S. literature and intellectual history before 1865.[1]

Professionally, Newfield's academic degrees translated into full-time appointments as an English professor at large, selective universities—Rice University (2 years), Duke University (1 year), and the University of California Santa Barbara (UCSB) for the majority of his academic career (1989–2021). His academic trajectory fits the modern archetype of a faculty career. That is, following the conferral of a disciplinary doctorate (not a professional doctorate) he took a tenure-track assistant professor job where he earned tenure within 6 years, was promoted to associate professor, and was subsequently promoted to full professor within another 6 years. In fact, Newfield reached a pinnacle of the professoriate, achieving the title of "Distinguished Professor of Literature and American Studies" at UCSB. As of 2021, he holds the role of director of research at the Independent Social Research Foundation in the United Kingdom.

Newfield's personal academic story provides a bit of subtext to the substance of what he publicly professes about the changes and challenges that the higher education sector faces. When he entered the postsecondary sector in the mid-1970s as a student, a majority of faculty were employed full time by their universities, and most of them were part of the tenure stream (tenured or tenure-track) (Curtis, 2014). At places like Reed and Cornell, on account of their selectivity and traditions, these structural patterns were even more pronounced; students routinely were taught by career faculty who were employed full time at one university. The forum for learning that Newfield experienced was structured, and therefore resourced, in a manner that tightly coupled professors to students, so the learning could be deep, detailed, rich in feedback, and highly personalized, thereby extracting the maximum value and quality from the intensity of the investment by both parties (students and professors).

Throughout Newfield's professorial career his advancement was certainly predicated on the quality and merit of his scholarship and work products. Even so, his advancement cannot be understood without broader context. Universities' promotion structures have favored those with elite educational backgrounds (Burris, 2004; Clauset et al., 2015), and have been documented as being more conducive to the advancement of White males (Newfield externally presents as White and male) to the exclusion of other social identities, especially women (Leslie et al., 2015; Savigny, 2014) and people of color (American Association of University Professors [AAUP], 2018). Further, during the years Newfield was progressing along the tenure stream, the instructional workforce in higher education was realigning; he writes about these dynamics in his scholarship—although he does not necessarily personalize it. The share of full-time, tenure, and tenure-track faculty working in higher education declined by 15 percentage points (45% to 30%) between 1975 and 2015 (AAUP, 2018). As these part-time, contingent, and lower status instructional positions became more numerous, social stratification was further evident across academic ranks (Morrison et al., 2011). It has become increasingly evident that men comprise the lion's share of tenured and full professorships in the academy (U.S. Government Accountability Office [GAO], 2017). The divisions and stratification within academic labor currently stand in sharp contrast to the educational aspirations of inclusion, diversity, and equity.

His Work

Decidedly, Newfield approaches his scholarship of higher education with an integrative and analytical approach that is consistent with his training in the humanities, and specifically aligned with his disciplinary focus in English and its corresponding elements of literary analysis and criticism. Literary analysis and criticism as an academic specialization requires that scholars situate characters, narrative works, the writers themselves, or the writing process to particular histories, contexts, and cultures (Newfield & Strickland, 1995). In so doing, the scholar invites readers to reflect on the interplay between person or people, positions, and societal structures and norms. The task of bringing all these elements together is foundational to the ontological and epistemological foundations of the humanities—where truth is conceived of as whole and inaccessible when parsed or parceled. Further, the essence of literary analysis and critique is bringing forth insights about the virtues, morality, ethics, or worthiness of the conditions and characters.

Conventionally, literary scholars make characters, authors, novels, prose, or genres their point of entry to their humanistic analysis and inquiry. When literary scholars apply their form of inquiry and analysis to nonfiction, they end up binding the substance to its context, thereby situating social structures and institutions within the human experience. As such, Newfield's analyses and critiques of higher education, or about colleges and universities, are consistent with his academic training. He narrows in on structural and cultural dimensions of power in organizations as expressed in history, finance, ideology, decision-making/governance arrangements, and disciplinary traditions. However, along with these practical expressions of power he is deliberate in directing attention to philosophical and aspirational ideas about the role of education in a society and how it aligns with human capabilities and flourishing. He carefully maps the historical lineage of ideas and accompanying contextualized meanings that produce culturally normative meanings about the *proper* role of education in society, dominant norms that have fueled the substantive changes in the provision and delivery of U.S. higher education.

Compatible with the literary analysis form, Newfield writes to explain and connect, rather than to report and correct—a departure from a substantial share of the public reporting of empirical evidence on higher education. Because humanism obligates the writer to contemplate purpose, virtue, and morality, Newfield unforgivingly demands that readers stare at the democratic, civic, and public dimensions of higher education, invoking, albeit at times subtly, classical notions of liberty, the state, or the commons. Invoking a spanning philosophical discussion of ideals is rarely included in public/popular writing about reform in higher education. Moreover, Newfield approaches his work with the tenacity of an investigative journalist digging into the existing evidence, and he does so with the sophisticated and narrative prose of, well, an English professor. Essentially, he is an explainer and a storyteller who invites readers to *think* and *feel* something about higher education. Just as one is moved by a literary work of fiction, his writing style allows one to feel disgust, compassion, frustration, or familiarity and allows readers to see tangible connections between the tasks of teaching, learning, and discovery through the lens of ideals such as freedom, autonomy, human agency, solidarity, and/or self-actualization.

My remarks regarding how Newfield writes may come across as advocacy that his approach toward communicating about higher education should be scaled up and pursued by others. Although the merits of his approach are noteworthy and could be adopted by others, my intent is not to encourage the proliferation of his style, but rather to dissect his contribution as a means of contemplating what he distinctively adds to the higher education discourse. Personally, I view Newfield's work as insightful and well-crafted, but the substance of his assessment of higher education's problems and corresponding causes are not unfamiliar.

Preceding decades of rigorous empirical work produced by higher education scholars (many of whom are my personal intellectual heroes)—such as Walter Allen, Estela Bensimon, Eric Dey, Patricia Gumport, Sylvia Hurtado, Adrianna Kezar, Peter Maassen, Peter Magolda, Anna Neumann, Kris Renn, Gary Rhoades, Robert A. Rhoads, Daryl Smith, and William Tierney (and countless others that I certainly have overlooked)—have measured, documented, and carefully analyzed the material that Newfield synthesizes in his writings. The research generated by higher education scholars has been extensive and highly translatable. They have developed measures and interventions to assist campuses stakeholders, policymakers, governing boards, and frontline student services support administrators, all in an effort to be responsive to pressing educational needs and issues related to access, equity, inclusion, quality, affordability, capacity, governance, coordination, and mission. If the research coming out of education schools has been so useful and applicable to reforming and improving higher education, why have Newfield's contributions generated such broad interest?

Why Newfield?

There are multiple possible explanations that contribute to Newfield's emergence as public intellectual. To address these matters, I first consider why a Newfield-type of scholar landed on the subject of higher education, and then I consider why the field of higher education had space for a Newfield-type scholar to serve as a prominent messenger.

Newfield Needed Higher Education

The humanities are decidedly in decline, and increasingly so over the past several decades (Donoghue, 2008; Ikpe, 2015). In fact, a major feature of Newfield's writings has been documenting the structural and cultural changes within higher education that have produced this current state of affairs; the humanities have been experiencing declines in enrollments, limited job prospects for newly minted scholars, reduced funding, and a crisis of legitimacy as a consequence of the economic and vocational rhetoric in postsecondary policy and governance circles and the perennial culture wars. Newfield's early response to the cultural attacks on the humanities was to unabashedly "go public" with his work—even calling it that—thereby deliberately conjoining the humanities, aesthetic to issues and contentions of the day (Newfield & Strickland, 1995).

More specifically, prior to Newfield's single-authored trilogy of books on universities, he squarely inserted himself into the "political correctness" debates about the humanities and the college curriculum that characterized the 1980s and early 1990s postsecondary policy discourse coming out of the Reagan administration and championed by the National Endowment for the Humanities chairs at the time, William Bennett (who also served as Reagan's secretary of education) and Lynne Cheney. In those days, the conservative political narrative that gained media attention was that liberal humanities professors were ruining the college curriculum with overspecialization, a proximal term attributed to the growth of area and ethnic studies subfields and their corresponding analyses that addressed the intersecting dimensions of power, history, culture, language, identity, and struggle. Newfield and Ronald Strickland's (1995) edited volume emerged as a collection of essays written primarily by humanities faculty with the deliberate mission of "redesigning and expanding the social and cultural role of the academic humanities . . . to take active control of our relations to the rest of the world" (pp. 1–2), thereby "calling for the redevelopment of the humanities in the direction of public concern" (p. 3).

Since the 1995 book, Newfield's public contributions have been expanded. Along with his role in formalizing and codifying CUS, he has also generated work about nanotechnology and quantification studies or the "limits of the numerical," (UCHRI, n.d.) and he has ventured into film as an additional form of scholarly media. In recent years, his speaker biographies and the write-ups of his lectures indicate that his work addresses a far-reaching set of topics, including innovation theory, American political psychology, American intellectual and social history, multiculturalism, race relations, science studies, the future of solar energy, humanities-based approaches to economics, and the power of humanities-based investigation. One summary described him as a polymath (New, 2014), which seems fitting based on this list. It is also no wonder that 17 pages of his vita are devoted to documenting his public presentations and invited lectures at universities and to academic societies, along with pages devoted to documenting his radio program commentary about his work.

Data denoting the intellectual and popular footprint of a written work can be a bit imprecise. Even so, of the 1,990 total Google Scholar citations attributed to Newfield, 62% (1,242) are attributable to his trilogy of higher education books. As a point of reference, Slaughter and Leslie's (1997) *Academic Capitalism* book, which is also characterized as being part of the CUS genre (Williams, 2012) and has been in print longer, has 7,196 Google Scholar citations. For further reference, the more recent *Academic Capitalism and the New Economy* book by Slaughter and Rhoades (2004), a topically similar work to Newfield's, has 4,561 Google Scholar citations. Within the label "American Literature" Newfield is positioned within the top 10 most cited in Google Scholar, and under the label "Literary Theory" his citation count places him in the top 25. Overall, the top two U.S.-based scholars within the "American Literature" Google Scholar label have 72,800 (D. Quentin Miller) and 3,268 (Shirley Samuels) citations. Miller is seemingly an anomaly in American literature, for the top scholars tend to have thousands of citations, not tens of thousands. Comparatively, within the Google Scholar label of "Higher Education" the top U.S. scholars have 103,231 citations (Lee S. Shulman) and 68,034 (Ernest Pascarella).[2] These numbers make it evident that the citation of higher education scholarship is more robust compared to that of American literature. As a point of further reference, the top scholars in nanotechnology, the other area of inquiry that Newfield has written on, has scholars with 328,308 and 264,442 Google Scholar citations—and this topic has scores of pages of scholars with citation counts in the hundreds and tens of thousands. A last point with respect to citations counts, "critical university studies" is not currently a label with any citation counts attribution to any Google Scholar profile.

Beyond Google Scholar citations, another approach for examining how a community has responded to a scholarly work is to consider library holdings. Newfield's three books have received substantial attention from libraries worldwide. Using the WorldCat.org global database of library holdings, his higher education trilogy of books are held at 436 (*Ivy & Industry*), 598 (*Unmaking*), and 545 (*The Great Mistake*) libraries, primarily in the United States. This count pattern of academic library holdings is consistent with the number of libraries that have acquired Slaughter's books with Leslie (1997) and Rhoades (2004). By comparison then, the accessibility rate of Newfield's work, or an English professor's scholarship on higher education, is compatible to the accessibility rate of comparable books written by education professors.

All the metrics that I am using to make meaning of Newfield's work, something Newfield would likely not be fond of given his grant focused on the "Limits of the Numerical" (UCHRI, n.d., para. 4) in higher education, that questions whether quantification practices can ever serve as sufficient proxies for intangible qualities (like impact or learning) are intended to emphasize some of the very tangible conditions that English and literature scholars face. Their work tends to circulate on a smaller scale compared to other academic fields, which gives credence to the ambition of applying one's analytical capabilities to crossover areas in hopes of having a wider reach. If Newfield's aim is to "go public" with his brand of humanities, higher education is a wise topical choice. It is a social welfare provision, a human right by some definitions (see United Nations, 1976), and because it operates as a hub (Stevens et al., 2008), it connects many other societal sectors. Further, because professors are organizational insiders at their universities, intimately familiar with performing teaching, research, and service functions, readers tend to accept them as authoritative on the subject matter of higher education—whereas they might be perceived as less expert or ill-equipped to write on other public provisions like water, energy, municipal administration, health care, or even primary or secondary education. Moreover, higher education has inherent topical appeal for a broad audience. In the United States there 1.5 million faculty (NCES, 2020a) and 19 million enrolled students (NCES, 2020b, 2020c); 62% of the nation's population over the age of 25 has participated in postsecondary education at some level (U.S. Census Bureau, 2020). And if these numbers do not provide a sufficient rationale that there is a large audience interested in higher education, there are 44.7 million people in the United States who carry college student loan debt, amounting to $1.6 trillion (Friedman, 2020). This last number addressing student debt almost obligates anyone writing about U.S. higher education to pursue the subject critically, and to invoke questions about the morality of a culture and society that produces systemic indebtedness on such a massive scale.

U.S. Higher Education Needed Newfield

Turning to the field of higher education, it is important to closely examine the structure and scope of this field. In its 130-year history, the study of higher education has always been interdisciplinary (Goodchild, 2014; Jensen & Freeman, 2019). It is therefore multifaceted and pluralistic in its methods, theories, analytical frames, and philosophical influences and traditions. As a professional field (not a discipline), people who earn graduate degrees pursue a range of careers, from becoming tenure-track or clinical faculty or serving as campus administrators or senior managers to being policy analysts, employees of government agencies, researchers for various nonprofits or professional organizations, program officers or experts for educationally related foundations, or, increasingly now, designers or consultants for educational technology and management consulting firms. Rumbly et al. (2014) notes more than 450 higher education academic degrees are offered globally, of which the majority are attributable to programs in the United

States. Nearly all higher education academic programs are located within education schools of universities (Rumbly et al., 2014). The Association for the Study of Higher Education's (2020) directory includes 244 academic programs. Rumbly and colleagues further report that many of the current programs date back to the mid-1950s. Aside from the programs, there are 217 research centers globally devoted to the study of higher education, again with the majority located in the United States (Rumbly et al., 2014). More than one third of the 279 journals devoted to the field of higher education are also based in the United States (Rumbly et al., 2014). Jensen and Freeman (2019) report that the number of graduate degrees in higher education has increased dramatically in the past 35 years, with a 743% growth in master's degrees and 177% in doctoral degrees. Moreover, analysis of higher education is by no means a "scattershot enterprise" (Williams, 2012, para. 2); it is naïve or misinformed to deny its footprint within academe. Simply stated, the label might be novel, but its substance is not.

Conventionally, with its spanning scope, pliable boundaries, and compartmentalization of topics, higher education is best understood as a low-consensus field (Renn, 2020). The humanities are also a low-consensus domain where, like higher education, there is great heterogeneity in the application of methods, topics, and theory among scholars (Lee, 2004). (By contrast high-consensus fields are more uniform in their application of methods, theory, and the corresponding interpretations that flow from the work.) Renn (2020) carefully points out that a substantial downside of higher education being a low-consensus field is that "we lose a lot of our possibility to have an impact on policy and practice . . . when someone has a question they need answered—about institutional, state, federal policy, for example—they ask one question and get possibly dozens of answers" (p. 922). It seems then that the problem of "going public" with higher education is that the scholarship, data, analyses, and conclusions are multidimensional—so much so that to the outsider or nonexpert, explanations and solutions to enduring problems may seem confusing or specious. The challenge for higher education scholars then is one of translation, to find ways to weave the complexity of the variants across the range of research in an understandable and accessible way, without oversimplifying matters or coming across as either disaffected or zealous. Considering these realities, Newfield's emergence as a public voice seems almost inevitable; he has claimed space by passionately documenting a higher education story—a story that speaks to scores of disciplinary faculty and laypeople who have a desire to understand the problems of higher education: Why is it so expensive? Why can't everyone have an opportunity? Will it really help students succeed and live a fulfilling life? He does not get bogged down in the day-to-day implementation of interventions, policies, and pedagogy—he identifies the antagonists, sets the scene for a promising future, and invokes nostalgia as he presents examples, data, and anecdotes.

Beyond the study of higher education generally, it is essential to address the role that critical analysis of the university has (or has not) had in this field. Although I do not intend to reduce Newfield's scholarship or contributions and his application of a *critical* perspective, I am compelled to make sense of the interpretation that this analytical stance toward the university is innovative, or that CUS, an area for which Newfield is a founder, is a new area of inquiry (Williams, 2012). Such assertions feel flatly dismissive toward the work coming out of graduate education schools—particularly from the higher education programs and researchers. A practical explanation for overlooking the work of education schools may be that noneducation scholars have been encumbered by their disciplinary blinders. Or to be more cynical, those in the humanities and liberal arts may have been ensnared by a form of academic elitism that subordinates the work of education schools to the scholarship generated within the disciplines. Although critical scholars attribute the origins to legal analysis (Cabrera, 2018), the connections between the social institution of higher education and critical race theory were nearly requisite from the start. Affirmative action as a legal matter in the United States is intertwined with the subject of race, both as a practical matter of analyzing civil rights laws but also due to the social, historical, political, cultural, economic, and instrumental manifestations of race, racial categories, and racism that have been institutionally sanctioned or rebuked by schools, lawmakers, and courts. Moving from and through the legal dimension, scholars of higher education employ critical race theory (CRT) and other critical framings to study an array of subject matter applicable across individual, organizational, and institutional phenomena in the field (Patton, 2016). Citation patterns reveal that the topic of education generally, and higher education specifically, comprises a substantial share of the scholarly CRT discourse. Further, getting into "who did it first" turf disciplinary battles does not serve any productive purpose in the broader cause of advancing universities' responsibilities to educate, serve, and contribute to society.

As I previously elaborated the qualities of Newfield's work, I regard his humanistic literary analysis approach as distinctive, high quality, and substantively meaningful and rigorous. I also welcome his public position and scholarly contributions because they are complementary to and aligned with the constructivist approach taken by many scholars of higher education and student affairs—particularly higher education scholars who draw on not only CRT but poststructuralist, or queer theories, as well. Critical, CRT, poststructural, and/or queer paradigmatic orientations, as applied to higher education phenomena, have been both robust and profoundly important to understanding and trans/re/forming higher education—especially as it relates to making sense of the experiences and identities of students as well as instructional staff and faculty. These paradigms have been invaluable for observing, explaining, and predicting the ways in which colleges' and universities' policies and practices (and their corresponding personnel and students) have (re)produced oppression, repression, stratification, bias, bigotry, and all forms of identity-based social animus. Unfortunately however, scholars doing this critical work (many of whom hold marginalized identities themselves) are not necessarily easily embraced by the public—especially by audience members who find the changes and transformations articulated in the research as threatening to their power, privilege, position, or competence. Therefore, it is possible that the emergence of an archetypal English professor (Newfield) with an elite liberal arts pedigree, a quintessential progression through the academic ladder, and large measure of social privilege (derived from his race, sex, and gender) has contributed to the abundance of public attention his work has yielded. There is certainly a segment of the academy and the public who (either knowingly or unwittingly) use Newfield's professional and personal qualities as credibility markers, thus making them more receptive to his contributions. Even in the face of these functional consequences of prejudice that cannot be extracted from Newfield's work, I choose to be generally appreciative that his scholarly public orientation has drawn a larger audience to the topic of higher education. He has cultivated greater exposure to and acceptance of critical perspectives on the field. Further, my hope is that his public contributions to the discourse may operate as a bridge for newcomers (and perhaps old-comers as well) to engaging more reflexively and collectively with the broader corpus of critical work in higher education.

Together, for the Public

Newfield's rise as a public intellectual for his work on higher education in both its substance and form should not surprise anyone. The enduring and emerging challenges and problems in higher education are reflected in both its empiricism and sensibilities. In my assessment, Newfield has garnered public attention not for the novelty of his arguments but because he has been effective in synthesizing multiple strands of what constitutes the study of higher education into a narrative prose that possesses the familiarity and accessibility of a novel and the status of the academic old guard. Educational researchers often view their publics as educational practitioners, professionals, leaders, and lawmakers; this instrumental orientation (Lee, 2004) can, at times, be overly insider-focused and thus a bit blinded to other interested parties. When the provision of higher education is something of wide public interest, with troubles and successes that impact all of us, it is imperative that we assemble interdisciplinary viewpoints to muster all resources available in the pursuit of improvement and change. Higher education scholars should welcome the attention that Newfield or other humanities professors are focusing on the organizational structures, dynamics, and constraints that prevent universities from performing more effectively for their publics. Humanities scholars, and disciplinarians, should embrace and seek out the scholarly contributions of higher education researchers in education schools, and view them as collaborators in advancing the ideals of education for democracy, freedom, and self-actualization. Higher education for the public good requires an all-hands-on-deck approach where we move through ideation, discovery, and improvement together, with humility, passion, and clarity of purpose.

Notes

1. See https://www.isrf.org/2020/06/22/the-isrf-welcomes-its-incoming-director-of-research-christopher-newfield/.

2. Within "Higher Education" Henry Giroux of McMaster University in Canada has 120,837 citations. He holds the top position for both higher education and the label "Cultural Studies" in Google Scholar. Christopher Newfield has also adopted the label "Cultural Studies," but his citation count of 1,990 places him within the top 100 under that label.

References

American Association of University Professors. (2018). The annual report on the economic status of the profession, 2017–18. *Academe, 104*(2), 4–30. https://www.aaup.org/sites/default/files/ARES_2017-18.pdf

Association for the Study of Higher Education. (2020). *Higher education program directory*. https://www.ashe.ws//Files/Higher%20Ed%20Program%20Directory/Higher%20Ed%20Directory%2011-19-2020.xlsx

Barnhardt, C. L. (2017). Private philanthropic foundations' social agendas and the field of higher education. In M. B. Paulsen (Ed.), *Higher education: Handbook of theory and research* (pp. 181–257). Springer. http://doi.org/10.1007/978-3-319-48983-4_5

Burris, V. (2004). The academic caste system: Prestige hierarchies in PhD exchange networks. *American Sociological Review, 69*, 239–264. https://doi.org/10.1177/000312240406900205

Cabrera, N. L. (2018). Where is racial theory in critical race theory? A constructive criticism of the Crits. *The Review of Higher Education, 42*(1), 209–233. https://doi.org/10.1353/rhe.2018.038

Clauset, A., Arbsman, S., & Larremore, D. B. (2015). Systematic inequality and hierarchy in faculty hiring networks. *Science Advances*, *1*(1), 1–6. https://doi.org/10.1126/sciadv.1400005

Curtis, J. W. (2014). *The employment status of instructional staff members in higher education, fall 2011*. Association of University Professors. https://www.aaup.org/sites/default/files/files/AAUP-InstrStaff2011-April2014.pdf

Donoghue, F. (2008). *The last professors: The corporate university and the fate of the humanities*. Fordham University Press.

Friedman, Z. (2020, February 3). Student loan debt statistics in 2020: A record $1.6 trillion. *Forbes*. https://www.forbes.com/sites/zackfriedman/2020/02/03/student-loan-debt-statistics/?sh=1baf878c281f

Goodchild, L. F. (2014). Higher education as a field of study: Its history, degree programs, associations, and national guidelines. In S. Freeman, L. S. Hagedorn, L. F. Goodchild, & D. A. Wright (Eds.), *In quest of doctoral degree guidelines—Commemorating 120 years of excellence* (pp. 13–50). Stylus.

Ikpe, I. B. (2015). The decline of the humanities and the decline of society. *Theoria: A Journal of Social and Political Theory*, *62*(142), 50–66. https://philpapers.org/rec/IKPTDO

Jensen, D., & Freeman, S., Jr. (2019). Stepping to center stage: The rise of higher education as a field of study. *The Journal of Educational Foundations*, *32*(1), 24–48. https://eric.ed.gov/?id=EJ1240068

Karl, B. D. (1985). Philanthropy and the social sciences. *Proceedings of the American Philosophical Society*, *129*(1), 14–19. https://www.jstor.org/stable/986976

Lee, J. J. (2004). Comparing institutional relationships with academic departments: A study of five academic fields. *Research in Higher Education*, *45*(6), 603–624. https://doi.org/10.1023/B:RIHE.0000040265.86668.1a

Leslie, S. J., Cimpian, A., Meyer, M., & Freeland, E. (2015). Expectations of brilliance underlie gender distributions across academic disciplines. *Science*, *347*(6219), 262–265. https://doi.org/10.1126/science.1261375

Manning, K. (2018). *Organizational theory in higher education* (2nd ed.). Routledge.

Meranze, M., & Newfield, C. (n.d.). *Remaking the university*. https://utotherescue.blogspot.com/

Morrison, E., Rudd, E., & Nerad, M. (2011). Onto, up, off the academic faculty ladder: The gendered effects of family on career transitions for a cohort of social science Ph.D.s. *Review of Higher Education*, *34*(4), 525–553. https://doi.org/10.1353/rhe.2011.0017

National Center for Education Statistics. (2020a). *Characteristics of postsecondary faculty*. U.S. Department of Education, Institute of Education Sciences, Integrated Postsecondary Education Data System (IPEDS). https://nces.ed.gov/programs/coe/indicator_csc.asp

National Center for Education Statistics. (2020b). *Postbaccalaureate enrollment*. U.S. Department of Education, Institute of Education Sciences, Integrated Postsecondary Education Data System (IPEDS). https://nces.ed.gov/programs/coe/indicator_chb.asp

National Center for Education Statistics. (2020c). *Undergraduate enrollment.* U.S. Department of Education, Institute of Education Sciences, Integrated Postsecondary Education Data System (IPEDS). https://nces.ed.gov/programs/coe/indicator/cha

New, J. (2014, April 25). Christopher Newfield penetrates "humanities crisis." *Iowa Now.* https://now.uiowa.edu/2014/04/christopher-newfield-penetrates-humanities-crisis

Newfield, C. (n.d.a.). Contributor. *HuffPost.* https://www.huffpost.com/author/christopher-newfield

Newfield, C. (n.d.b.). *Critical university studies.* University of California, Santa Barbara. https://ihum.innovate.ucsb.edu/critical-studies

Newfield, C. (2003). *Ivy and industry: Business and the making of the American university, 1880–1980.* Duke University Press.

Newfield, C. (2008). *Unmaking the public university: The forty year assault on the middle class.* Harvard University Press.

Newfield, C. (2016). *The great mistake: How we wrecked public universities and how we can fix them.* Johns Hopkins University Press.

Newfield, C., & Strickland, R. (1995). *After political correctness: The humanities and society in the 1990s.* Westview Press.

Owen-Smith, J. (2011). The institutionalization of expertise in university licensing. *Theory and Society, 40,* 63–93. https://doi.org/10.1007/s11186-010-9136-y

Patton, L. D. (2016). Disrupting postsecondary prose: Toward a critical race theory of higher education. *Urban Education, 51*(3), 315–342. https://doi.org/10.1177/0042085915602542

Renn, K. (2020). Reimagining the study of higher education. *The Review of Higher Education, 43*(4), 917–934. https://doi.org/10.1353/rhe.2020.0025

Rumbly, L. E., Altbach, P. G., Stanfield, D. A., Shimmi, Y., de Gayardon, A., & Chan, R. Y. (Eds.). (2014). *Higher education: A worldwide inventory of research centers, academic programs, and journals and publications* (3rd ed.). Boston College Center for International Higher Education.

Savigny, H. (2014). Women, know your limits: Cultural sexism in academia. *Gender and Education, 26*(7), 794–809. https://doi.org/10.1080/09540253.2104.970977

Slaughter, S., & Leslie, L. (1997). *Academic capitalism: Politics, policies, and the entrepreneurial university.* Johns Hopkins University Press.

Slaughter, S., & Rhoades, G. (2004). *Academic capitalism and the new economy: Markets, state, and higher education.* Johns Hopkins University Press.

Stevens, M. L., Armstrong, E. A., & Arum, R. (2008). *Sieve, incubator, temple, hub: Empirical and theoretical advances in the sociology of higher education.* Annual Review of Sociology, 34, 127–151. https://nces.ed.gov/programs/coe/indicator_cha.asp https://doi.org/10.1146/annurev.soc.34.040507.134737

Trattner, W. I. (1970). *Crusade for the children: A history of the National Child Labor Committee and child labor reform in America.* Quadrangle Books.

United Nations. (1976). *International covenant on economic, social and cultural Rights*. Office of the High Commissioner on Human Rights. https://www.ohchr.org/en/professionalinterest/pages/cescr.aspx

UCHRI. (n.d.). *Awards. The limits of the numerical: metrics and the humanities in higher education*. https://uchri.org/awards/the-limits-of-the-numerical-metrics-and-the-humanities-in-higher-education/

U.S. Census Bureau. (2020, March 3). *Educational attainment in the United States: 2019*. https://www.census.gov/content/census/en/data/tables/2019/demo/educational-attainment/cps-detailed-tables.html

U.S. Government Accountability Office. (2017, October). *Contingent workforce: Size, characteristics, and work experiences of adjunct and other non-tenure-track faculty (GAO-18-49)*. https://www.gao.gov/products/GAO-18-49

Wikipedia. (2020, October 20). *Critical university studies*. https://en.wikipedia.org/wiki/Critical_university_studies

Williams, J. J. (2012, February 19). An emerging field deconstructs academe. *The Chronicle of Higher Education*. https://www.chronicle.com/article/deconstructing-academe/

II

CONSUMER DEMAND AND THE STATUS-SEEKING SOCIETY

David F. Labaree on the American Higher Education System

Timothy Glander

Among the many distinctive aspects of David F. Labaree's historical analysis is the clarity with which he expresses his argument that market forces and consumer behavior are responsible for the character of our colleges and universities. Throughout his writings he carefully defines the parameters of his theoretical perspective. He explains to the reader what is, and what is not, constitutive of this theoretical perspective, where this perspective begins and ends, what it includes, and what areas and matters it does not treat. This judicious approach is a hallmark of each of his five books on the history of American schooling, including *How to Succeed in School Without Really Learning: The Credentials Race in American Education* (1997), *The Trouble With Ed Schools* (2004), and *Someone Has To Fail: The Zero-Sum Game of Public Schooling* (2010). It is especially evident in his most recent book, *A Perfect Mess: The Unlikely Ascendancy of American Higher Education* (2017). Here he makes clear that his aim is to understand the evolution of colleges and universities as economic and social institutions independent of any educational purposes they may purport to advance or serve. He writes:

> My focus in this book is on schooling rather than education. I'm not arguing that learning doesn't matter or that education doesn't take place in schools. I'm only arguing that you can understand the development of school systems in liberal democracies without recourse to ideas such as education or learning. These things may be happening in schools, but they are not necessary for understanding how the system of schooling has come to take the form that it has. (Labaree, 2017, p. 100)

In the end, what matters most is the demands that consumers place on colleges and universities as they seek to use these institutions to attain or maintain social status. "My point is that consumers of schooling have been less interested in learning than in gaining or holding social position. And in the history of schooling in the United States, the consumer is king" (Labaree, 2017, p. 100).

Labaree remains consistent with this approach throughout his book and refrains from addressing the difficult issues relating to educational aims or the meaning of liberal education. He also chooses not to extensively address the larger contextual circumstances at work during the so-called American century—the 20th century—the period in which colleges and universities flowered in American life and eventually rose to international ascendancy. "I choose not to focus on these powerful contextual factors," he writes. "Instead, I examine the structural elements within the system of American higher education itself that allowed this system to capitalize on the opportunities granted it by wealth, power, linguistic dominance, geographic isolation, and government investments" (Labaree, 2017, p. 4). Again, it is not that these larger 20th-century historical and contextual factors are insignificant or do not matter; it is rather that his argument does not require an analysis of these factors, so he generally leaves them out of the discussion.

Labaree provides a kind of large-scale systems analysis of the structure of American higher education. He operates with broad strokes, synthesizing other scholarship in unique ways, yet always returning to the theme that student consumer demand is the linchpin and central determinant. Although he examines individual schools as case studies, his goal is to flesh out the dynamics and patterns that have formed the interlocking and significantly stratified system of higher educational institutions in the United States. The higher education system we have inherited is not the result of any plan. "It just happened," he writes. Nevertheless, this higher education system "has a well-defined structure and a clear set of rules that guides the actions of the individuals and institutions within it." The system is more akin to "a solar system guided by the laws of physics" than a political or social system guided by constitutional principles and human design. The history of the higher education system in the United States "is not a deliberate construction but an evolutionary process" (Labaree, 2017, p. 2).

Labaree's argument is insightful, consistent, and persuasive. He offers a novel and compelling way to think about the colleges and universities we have inherited and continue to occupy. Surveying the landscape in the United States today, one cannot help but find ample evidence in support of Labaree's thesis. One cannot fail to recognize how thoroughly higher education has become a commodity. Everywhere one looks one finds colleges and universities surrendering to the values of our consumer culture, operating as businesses, infantilizing students and treating them as consumers, joining the emphasis on advertising and brand identification, and touting return on investment and other narrow instrumentalist and financial measures.

The great American educational philosopher John Dewey was among those early 20th-century thinkers who expressed serious alarm at the increasing commodification of higher education. "That which prevents the schools from doing their educational work freely is precisely the pressure—for the most part indirect, to be sure—of domination by the money-motif of our economic regime," Dewey wrote in 1930. Because of this wholesale submission of schools to dominant pecuniary and business values,

> the distinguishing trait of the American student body in our higher schools is a kind of intellectual immaturity. This immaturity is mainly due to their enforced mental seclusion; there is, in their schooling, little free and disinterested concern with the underlying social problems of our civilization. (Dewey, 1930/1999, p. 62)

Much later contemporary essayist Mark Edmundson (2013) brought this concern up to date:

> Midway through the last decade of the twentieth century, American higher education changed. Colleges and universities entered a new phase in which they stopped being intellectually driven and culturally oriented and began to model themselves on businesses. They sought profit; they sought prestige: the more the better. To be sure, there had always been a commercial side to American higher education. But in the mid-nineties, universities began dropping pretenses and putting profit ahead of intellectual and (dare one say it?) spiritual values. (p. vii)

For Labaree, however, none of this is really new. This consumerist orientation has been the defining feature of U.S. higher education from the start. His work assists us in understanding that what we see around us today is simply the manifestation of dynamics at work at the founding of America's colleges and universities, and which continued as these institutions proliferated during the 19th century, and which by the second half of the 20th century made this system, in his view, the envy of the world.

Although Dewey, Edmundson, and countless others have recognized and lamented the increased commodification of higher education, Labaree chooses to look on the bright side. His is a fundamentally celebratory view of the American system of higher education, even though a latent critical perspective seems to inform much of his analysis. As Labaree (2017) writes in the introductory chapter,

I could easily write this book as a critique, focusing attention on the system's failings, but instead I choose to write it as an appreciation, examining the distinctive institutional dynamics that enable it to be all things to all people. In its organizational complexity, multiple functionality, and breadth of support, the system inspires awe. (p. 24)

The American system of higher education is "a perfect mess," or what he referred to in one interview as a "hustler's paradise" (Jaschik, 2017, para. 15). It is contradictory, wasteful, and on some profound levels terribly unjust, but it seems to function adequately by conforming to the rules and values of the marketplace. Therefore, the worst thing we can do, according to Labaree (2017), is to try to reform it—to try to mess with this perfect mess. "We need to leave it alone," he concludes, "in order to enjoy its benefits" (p. 196).

So the strengths of Labaree's interpretation can be found in the explicit way he delineates his approach: He attends to schooling rather than education. He focuses on the system-wide structural dynamics and developmental patterns of higher educational institutions rather than on the 20th-century context in which they evolved. And he chooses to praise rather than critique the system as we now find it.

In the next section, I will try to identify a few key observations that emerge from his analysis. This has no pretense of being a summation of his complex and nuanced argument, which I encourage readers to encounter on their own. Again, I find his analysis to be an important contribution to our understanding, even if his focus has evident and acknowledged limitations. Finally, in the concluding section I will pose some questions that arise as a result of these limitations and ask the reader to consider ways in which we might build upon them: How might we think about the current state of liberal education—which is to say, "liberating education"—in light of the history of schooling he has presented? How might a contextual analysis of World War II and the Cold War enrich our understanding of these culturally important educational institutions? How might a critical perspective illuminate other ways of considering (and, perhaps, shaping) the system of higher education we have inherited?

Observations and Analysis

Labaree's analysis hinges on several key dualisms, or "tensions" as he often refers to them (e.g., schooling as a private good versus schooling as a public good, use value versus exchange value, liberal learning versus professional training, public schooling versus private schooling, etc.). It is the interplay between these polarities that manifests the contradictory aspects of American higher education and serves as the basis for the messy character of the system he observes. Again, he has no desire to try to resolve or synthesize the competing forces at work but rather to describe how they come to function, somewhat (and strangely) harmoniously despite these conflicts and essential tensions. Broadly speaking, a "functionalist" label would not be misapplied to him, though, again, his is a complex and nuanced view.[1] In many ways, his perspective is that of a sociologist who, having surveyed the present state of higher education, regards it in a mostly deterministic fashion and finds it mostly agreeable, and then uses historical study of these perennial tensions to describe why this is so.

The most fundamental dynamic at work, according to Labaree (2017), is "a basic tension that lies at the heart of liberal democracy." It is the enduring ideological dichotomy between equality and liberty. "This is the tension between democratic politics, with its willingness to constrain liberty in order to maximize social equality, and liberal markets, with their willingness to tolerate inequality in order to maximize liberty" (pp. 4–5). For American higher education this essential conflict is displayed in the dialectic between *access* to college (for the many) and the *advantage* it provides (to the few). On the one hand, there is the ongoing movement for access to colleges and universities, which serves as a powerful motivator for those in the lower and middling strata of society. On the other hand, the conflict becomes the catalyst for those in the upper strata of society as they seek to maintain their position of advantage in the social order. Those seeking access see higher education as a means of social mobility, a means of achieving equality through educational opportunity and a chance of reaching a social status long denied. Those seeking the advantage higher education provides see it as a means of protecting their elite status, an assertion of their liberty in the marketplace, and (perhaps) a rationalization for their superior place at the top of the social heap.

The higher education system in America modulates these competing forces by maintaining *many* institutions with very open and inclusive access, thereby promoting a spirit of equal educational opportunity, and *very few* institutions with high selectivity and exclusivity that give distinct advantages to the already privileged. "What allows us to accommodate both our democratic and our liberal tendencies in higher education is stratification," he writes. "We can make universities both accessible and elite by creating a pyramid of institutions in which access is inclusive at the bottom and exclusive at the top" (Labaree, 2017, p. 5). It is this highly stratified character of the system that provides its dynamics for change and maintenance. The system does offer something to everyone, but it does so unequally. It gives the economic elite an avenue to maintain their privileged status, while giving the rest of society a conveyor belt (mostly illusory) for social mobility.

Labaree maps out a four-tiered pyramidal system of higher education. At the top of the pyramid is the research university, and at the bottom the community college. Public and private bachelor's degree-granting colleges and universities occupy the second tier and those colleges primarily focused on the training of teachers (historically linked to the normal school) occupy the third tier. There is considerable overlap among these tiered institutions, but they serve distinct roles in balancing the push and pull between access and advantage. Although consumer demand is pervasive throughout the system, it is most in evidence among those at the middle and bottom of the social order. The bottom-up demand for access spurred the historical development of colleges and universities in the three bottom tiers of the four-tiered system. Yet it is the ideal of the research university, in part emanating from the German university model (though modified to meet the needs of the American market), that sets the tone and defines the aspirations for the system. Driven by the demands of the market, American higher education created a hierarchy of institutions with four distinct tiers. "These tiers are distinguished from each other by degree of social access (greatest at the bottom) and degree of social advantage (greatest at the top)," Labaree writes. "But one thing the three top tiers have in common is convergence around a single organizational ideal, the research university" (Labaree, 2017, p. 13).

Labaree describes a society pervasively (if not perversely) motivated to seek social status. Status-seeking is our dominant cultural motif and, presumably, our essential psychological dynamic. Status-seeking is rampant not only among individual educational consumers, but also among the colleges and universities themselves as well as the faculty who are employed in them. Labaree (2017) writes "Consumers' interest in higher education is social mobility" (p. 88). And institutionally "everyone wants to be Harvard" (p. 13). But these remain little more than pipe dreams for most individuals and institutions. "Most universities end up as pale imitations of the real thing," he writes (p. 13). And although the

> system offers students the possibility of upward mobility through higher education . . . the probability for students to attain a substantial rise in social position is low. A substantial number will wash out of the system with no degree and major debt. Others will attain a degree at a lower tier and move into a lower tier white-collar job; some will gain a degree that ushers them into a middle-tier position; and a few will grab the brass ring. (p. 170)

The pattern of status-seeking is reflected as well in the professional careers of faculty and is mirrored in the inevitable disappointments. "It's much the same with faculty," Labaree concludes, as only a few academic aspirants will grab the brass ring of establishing tenured careers at prestigious research universities (p. 170). Most others will have to settle for careers at lower tiered schools, join the ranks of extremely exploited adjunct faculty, or be washed out of academia altogether.

With each historical development one sees these tensions and subsequent patterns at work in creating and sustaining a highly stratified system. The elite colonial colleges of the 17th and 18th centuries (e.g., Harvard, Yale, Penn) begat the spread of hundreds of less prestigious, private, sectarian colleges throughout small towns in the early part of the 19th century (e.g., Middlebury College, among countless others), as well as the creation of what would become public flagship universities (University of Michigan, etc.) and then finally the more pragmatically oriented land-grant institutions (Michigan State, etc.). These upstart institutions sought prestige in various ways. The lowly normal schools that proliferated in the mid-19th century to train teachers for the burgeoning common school movement sought full college status, eventually becoming the regional state universities we see throughout the land. The 19th-century private colleges, nearly all tied to one religious tradition or another, sought to spread denominational faith. But perhaps even more importantly, according to Labaree, their establishment was a way to raise the visibility and status of the small towns in which they were housed. The creation of a small liberal arts college, modeled on the prestigious liberal arts colleges of the past, put a small town "on the map" both literally and figuratively.[2]

For the most part, these small private colleges lacked not only academic eminence but academic credibility, and as tuition-dependent institutions they were forced to learn how to attract students, especially in the period before higher education was recognized as the primary means of social mobility in American society. Yet they learned this lesson well. Like all colleges and universities in the system, they became entrepreneurial, flexible, and sensitive to the demands of students who were increasingly seen as consumers. These institutional attributes would be highly rewarded as colleges moved into the consumerist-oriented 20th century. Colleges tended to mold their educational vision and practice according to the prevailing markers of social status. And they learned to adapt to the consumerist desires of undergraduates (the financial cash cow for even the prestigious research institutions) in all areas of academic and social life. Labaree (2017) writes:

> Schools in the system learned how to attract tuition-paying students, give them the college experience they wanted, get them to identify closely with the institution, and then milk them for donations when they graduate. Football, fraternities, logo-bearing T-shirts, and fund-raising operations all paid off handsomely. Colleges and universities learned how to adapt quickly to trends in the competitive environment. (p. 157)

Labaree describes a ragtag system of higher education that grew from the bottom up, beholden to no single authoritarian state entity or religious denomination. This autonomy wasn't without its benefits, but it also meant that colleges and universities did not have stable sources of revenue to rely upon. As primarily tuition-dependent institutions, they had to cater to student consumer demands. Colleges and universities were compelled to throw their lot in with the marketplace. As a result, Labaree argues, invoking another perennial dualism, American higher education has been historically driven to achieve "private goods" (i.e., social mobility and status maintenance) rather than to achieve "public goods," in which some larger social or public goal is pursued. Again, for Labaree this orientation toward "private goods" is systemic; it has dominated American higher educational institutions from the start. State universities have always had to submerge the rhetoric of their loftier social and cultural goals to the private goals of their student consumers. And even the strongly held denominational beliefs among various religious traditions had to bend to the private student demands for social status climbing. The primacy of "private goods" over "public goods" cuts across both public and private institutions. For Labaree, the aims of American higher education have always been essentially private in nature.

The exception to this rule, for Labaree, occurred during the middle of the 20th century when the United States entered World War II and began the 45-year Cold War. The Second World War and ensuing Cold War placed demands on colleges and universities as never before, and these institutions took the temporary turn of operating toward achieving "public goods." World War II pulled the United States out of the economic depression of the 1930s even as it initially negatively impacted college and university enrollments. But the war established the pattern for significant government funding in the physical and social sciences at research universities across the country, which continued throughout the Cold War years. As massive military contracts flowed to research universities during this period, returning veterans flocked to colleges and universities with the tuition benefits awarded under the G.I. Bill. According to Labaree, this period represents the first and only time in history the American system of higher education was seen as primarily serving the public good. Enrollments soared throughout the four-tiered system, while government funding to research universities, largely for military-related research, continued to grow.

This period is regarded by many as the "golden age" of American higher education. Flush with external funding and well-funded students, American higher education was on the move and growing in status and prestige. But for Labaree this period must be understood as an historical aberration. All of this has now come to an end as the government largess has shriveled, and students take on more individual financial responsibility for their schooling. "Now we are back to the place we have always been," Labaree (2017) writes, "where the university's primary role is to provide individual consumers a chance to gain social access and social advantage" (p. 142). Barring another national crisis on the scale of World War II and the Cold War that will again define higher education as a public good, the success of American higher education will depend on its ability to satisfy the demands of consumers. Labaree claims we need to accept this as a structural law of nature. The primary purpose of higher education in our liberal democracy is to advance private ends.

Limitations and Questions

And who can deny it? Our colleges and universities are increasingly indistinguishable from other institutions that offer a commodity or service, always oriented toward growth and aiming to satisfy the needs of student consumers in the most efficient, cost-effective, and economically profitable way. Like other levels of schooling in American society, our colleges and universities have ceased envisioning themselves as distinct and special kinds of learning communities and instead take on the character of the generic shopping mall or bank.[3] In a culture so thoroughly saturated with consumerist values (a culture in which social status is so thoroughly tied to these consumerist values), it is certainly not surprising to find colleges and universities operating according to the machinery and purpose of the marketplace. Labaree describes a situation that is commonplace and readily apparent, and he provides a useful historical lens for explaining how the institution of schooling was shaped by tensions inherent in a highly stratified liberal democracy and capitalist economy. Clearly, we can see at work many of the dynamics he colorfully describes. We owe him a debt for this; and although his analysis has obvious limitations, it nevertheless provides a basis from which to build.

First, it is important to keep in mind that Labaree's focus is on schooling rather than on education. The whole point of his study is to understand our colleges and universities as social and economic institutions. He does not explore the philosophies of education and social ideologies that were at work in the founding of American higher educational institutions. For the most part, he abjures engaging in normative analysis. He doesn't seriously treat educational aims and purposes, and his analysis is limited by reducing educational aims to the two large conceptual categories of "public goods" and "private goods." The social (and epistemological, aesthetic, ethical, etc.) ideas of the communities of people who founded, and taught in, our colleges and universities are not explored in his work. Even the implications of the deeply held religious convictions that pervaded so many of these early institutions do not factor extensively into his considerations.

His interest is in schooling at the higher levels and not in the higher educational ideals that originally animated our colleges and universities. To state it most baldly, he uses historical inquiry in the service of a sociology of schooling and not a philosophy of education.

This is, of course, an entirely justifiable and appropriate focus, and it yields important insights. But, then, we are still left with many key questions: How are we to attend to, and account for, the serious social, cultural and intellectual aims that historically inspired the commitment to colleges and universities? And how might we regard the liberal education ideal in light of Labaree's thesis?

One can certainly agree with Labaree that the institutional apparatus of schooling is shaped by the demands consumers place on it as they seek to achieve or maintain social status. And we may also concede that any educational ideas and philosophies initially orienting these schools were no match for the strength and pressure of mounting student consumer demands. But one still needs to contend with the way in which education was originally conceived in these institutions we call colleges and universities, and to ask in what ways these educational institutions were corrupted by conforming to the necessities of the marketplace. What was lost as our educational institutions morphed into business institutions? What was lost as our colleges and universities internalized the values of the marketplace? Beyond the social and economic implications, what are, and have been, the particular "educational" consequences of this transformation?

Let us be clear: The people who created the colleges and universities we inherited did so with particular and specific educational aims and values in mind. Even the most cursory historical examination will bear this out. Frederick Rudolph (1962) recognized this in his classic study and noted that in their early years, American colleges and universities "would be governed less by accident than by certain purpose, less by impulse than by design" (p. 3). They also articulated definite social and cultural goals, advancing what historian Charles Dorn (2019) has recently identified as a near universal desire to contribute to the common good.

Although it may be tempting to treat these aims and values as quaint (or even to regard them as largely oppressive, as some contemporary perspectives do), they still must be reckoned with as they gave our nascent institutions their meaning and reasons for being. These educational and social purposes were varied and diverse in the American context, and Labaree is correct to note that the collection of higher educational institutions we received from our ancestors was not the consequence of any system-wide plan. Nevertheless, these unique educational and social purposes guided individual colleges and universities in making important decisions regarding the academic program: curriculum, resource allocation, standards of scholarship, admissions, and other policies. The colleges and universities we inherited were animated by distinct principles, and they were successful insofar as the community of people who populated them (faculty, students, and staff) were committed to these principles and were willing and able to make sacrifices in support of these principles. A more comprehensive historical view would reveal the tenuous balance sometimes achieved as these principles tempered consumer desires.[4]

In describing a system compelled by consumer demand and social status-seeking, Labaree also assists us in understanding some of the mechanisms at work in the ongoing assault on the value and meaning of liberal education. Although not making this point explicitly, Labaree's analysis demonstrates just how one-dimensional and narrow our cultural markers of social status and success have become. As this flattening of what constitutes social status and success continues, it is not surprising to see a parallel flattening of the purposes of education. We are in the midst of what philosopher Martha Nussbaum (2012) has aptly called a "silent crisis." At all levels of schooling, the purpose of education has been reduced to preparing workers, and education has been increasingly constricted to those technical skills assumed to be economically profitable in the short term. Vocational education, in its most narrow meaning, is insurgent everywhere one seems to look today, as the notion of social progress is reduced to the single measure of gross national product.

Educational policy follows suit by valuing only the kind of learning regarded to be quantifiable and measurable, as reflected in so many accountability schemes. Increasingly devalued, marginalized, and lost are all those largely intrinsic ways of learning and knowing that we associate with liberal education, which is to say "liberating education," an education whose primary purpose is to make us free. Moreover, liberal education, especially as it is manifested in the arts and humanities, has historically been conceived as necessary for the creation and maintenance of a democratic and just social order. These ways of knowing humanize us; these ways of knowing make us more fully human by encouraging the capacity for empathy through widening and expanding our apprehension of the human experience.

In our competitive, status-hungry culture, however, narcissism becomes the dominant character type. For Nussbaum (2012), a central purpose of liberal education should be to mitigate this narcissism. Instead, we find that schools in our culture tend to actually encourage the development of a narcissistic personality.[5] Although clearly not his intention, Labaree's thesis goes part of the way explaining why this is so. A society trapped in a race for narrow and private aggrandizement will have little regard for (or even tolerance of) a purpose of education that calls this orientation of social status climbing into question. In a superficial, image-based culture success and achievement are more about appearance than substance. Schools become credentialing factories (a perceptive and recurring theme in Labaree's work) and not communities where authentic and intrinsic learning is cultivated and honored.

Labaree's position on the impact of World War II and the Cold War might also be fruitfully expanded. Labaree is astute to note that they represented social crises to which American colleges and universities were forced to respond. Yet as a structural, rather than a contextual, analysis, his investigation never goes further than observing that these institutions temporarily shifted from meeting private goods to public goods. What is essentially and normatively "good" about these "goods" is not investigated. Yes, colleges and universities demonstrated remarkable flexibility in adapting to the needs of the nation at war. The money flowed and these institutions grew in size, influence, and prestige. American colleges and universities learned to "love the bomb," as Labaree puts it. But he leaves unexplored what a strange love this would turn out to be. He simply does not explore how the problems of a nation at war (more or less, permanently and totally) would socially construct knowledge at these institutions of higher learning. He chooses not to explore how turning the attention of our physical and social scientists to military problems would shape the institutions in which they worked. Nor does he explore how the culture of war would impact the essential cultural function of higher education.

Yet this historical context matters for any kind of adequate understanding of the development of our higher educational institutions. The Second World War was the watershed moment in the development of these institutions—as it was for American society more generally—demarcating what could have been from what came to be. Shortly before the end of the war, neohumanist scholar Norman Foerster (1944) understood what hung in the balance:

> When our young men—and young women—return from the wars, many of them will return to the university. What kind of university will it be then? Will it be a university they remember, unchanged by the most violent storm in human history? Will it be the meaningless prolongation of the wartime university, a university focusing its forces upon the destruction of human beings? (p. 26)

It was during this war that university-based researchers gave birth to not only the atom bomb and other instruments of physical destruction but also spawned the development of technologies and ideologies of social control and surveillance. The war legitimized and made urgent many war-related problems, and it created social networks among like-minded university researchers and sources of power and influence. At the end of the war, those researchers returned full time to their universities, bringing war-related problems (and attendant war values) and their new social networks with them. The ensuing extended period of Cold War enshrined these war-related problems and values, while reviving fears of a dormant Red Scare. Loyalty oaths and blacklisting became common practices on college and university campuses throughout this period, shaping these institutions in ways about which we remain only vaguely aware. The Cold War thus established a specific climate of status and prestige by underwriting some perspectives while pushing others to the periphery, or excising them altogether.

In the end, one is compelled to pose a variety of questions: How did the massive, and frequently covert, funding of national security–related research impact the character and purposes of American colleges and universities? What educational purposes and values were promoted or marginalized by the influences of this dominant war culture? How did this funding shape disciplinary knowledge? How did it shape the culture of higher learning? In what ways did this war-related funding influence the orientation of academic programs and curricula, the hiring of faculty and administrators, the setting of academic policies, the expression of academic freedom, the dominant pedagogy, the prevailing ideology, and so on? What is the normative "good" about the militarization of our colleges and universities that occurred during this extended period of war? Labaree's analysis unintentionally compels these and other questions related to the historical context in which colleges and universities developed during the American Century. Pursuing them would add depth and comprehension to our ways of seeing them in both the past and present.

Finally, a word must be said about Labaree's overall deterministic theoretical orientation and the generally positive view he comes to hold about the present state of our American higher education system. Labaree certainly recounts and catalogs many of the shortcomings and injustices of this system. Yet there is something oddly Panglossian about Labaree's view, as if our present situation represents "the best of all possible worlds" where colleges and universities are concerned. At least this appears to be the political implications Labaree encourages his readers to draw from his analysis. Echoing a theme from his earlier work, *Someone Has to Fail*, Labaree discourages attempts to reform the system of schooling, a system that he characterizes as manifesting an incurable *syndrome*. These system dynamics exist outside of human control, and attempts at engineering them are destined to fail and will likely make matters worse. Instead, he invites the reader to find beauty and awe in the remarkable flexibility and adaptability of the system and how, among other things, it balances the competing social demands between access and advantage.

To be sure, there are dimensions and degrees of beauty and wonder to be found in the system of colleges and universities he examines. The unplanned system of colleges and universities has proven to be highly adaptable, and the march toward greater access to higher education can only be regarded as a positive, an expression of progress in our profoundly unequal society. Yet there should be no mistaking the fact that colleges and universities are institutions of cultural reproduction, which mirror some of the most mindless and destructive aspects of the larger society. Labaree's analysis begs the question about the meaning of this educational access. His sociological analysis throws light on the question of the dynamics of who is seeking access, and under what market conditions they are seeking it. He does not, however, pose or investigate the questions of what this access is *to* and what this access is ultimately *for*. Again, posing critical foundational questions about the purpose of education, and treating those questions with the gravity they require, would greatly extend his insights.[6]

Given the near total commercialization of our culture, it is no easy task to imagine how our colleges and universities might be animated by alternative educational and social purposes. But an historical analysis that downplays or denies the reality of these alternatives in the past can only serve to abet this impoverished imagination. Alternatives abounded in the thinking and practice of those who came before us. One key function of historical scholarship is to retrieve from obscurity these lost alternatives.

Similarly, it is difficult not to be persuaded by Labaree's argument that our system of higher education has been determined, inevitably, by the structural force of ubiquitous consumer demand and status-seeking behavior. Many of our contemporaries do seem to be driven by such superficial, narrow, and self-centered impulses, and the historical record is replete with evidence of such shallow and mechanical behavior. But that same history also demonstrates much contrary evidence, undercutting the claim that all is determined by a regulatory law of nature. And looking around us we can clearly see that not all our contemporaries are so thoughtlessly driven to grab the same brass ring. A disposition critical of the present system of American higher education would enable us to use historical inquiry to reclaim alternative expressions of the meaning of higher learning from the past, even as it would enrich our imaginations about alternatives to the pervasive narcissism we see around us today. Critical perspectives on the present may empower us to recover hidden possibilities from the past.

Notes

1. The functionalist perspective on schooling is well defined by Feinberg and Soltis. They note that functionalism derives its primary theoretical orientation from the biological sciences and examines social institutions in light of the functions various institutions serve to the survival of the social organism. Adopting a quasiscientific outlook, which attempts to explain the present in causal, and largely deterministic, ways, "functionalists tend to look at social institutions and practices in terms of their contribution to the adaptation and adjustment of the total system" (Feinberg & Soltis, 2009, p. 14).

2. Labaree (2017) writes: "With a college, a town could claim that it deserved to gain lucrative recognition as a stop on the railroad line, the county seat, or even the state capital. These consequences would elevate the value of land in the town, which would work to the benefit of major landholders. In this sense, the nineteenth-century college, like much of American history, was in part the product of a land development scheme" (pp. 25–26). Little has changed with this part of the "hustler's paradise" as real estate developers continue to circle like sharks around colleges and universities, while representatives of construction firms and other potential vendors finagle their way onto college boards of trustees. Not surprisingly their firms are frequently rewarded with new building construction contracts and other lucrative opportunities. This practice, if not legally corrupt, certainly corrupts the educational mission of the institution by diverting funds away from its core academic mission. "Mission creep," indeed!

3. Such schools, philosopher Kenneth Strike (2010) points out, "tend to privatize the goals they serve, present a curriculum that lacks coherence, and cope with cultural diversity by affirming tolerance and equality while standing for nothing else of educational substance. They seek to equip students to pursue self-chosen lives by providing knowledge and skills that are economically valuable, but they convey little about how to lead a good life and little about what is just or worthwhile. The people they serve are viewed as members of the species *homo economicus*. Many schools have a tacit ethic: Get an education to get a job to get money to get stuff. They teach 'possessive individualism.' Such schools are more like banks or shopping malls than communities" (p. 10).

4. It is not possible to overstate the centrality of the notion of *community* to the historical development of colleges and universities. Sometimes referenced as the "community of scholars," or the "learning community," the notions of college, collegium, university, *studium generale*, and scholastic guild are all historically rooted in the principle of a self-governing community, anchored around the pursuit of shared intellectual interests and fundamentally bound together by mutual trust and respect. As Paul Goodman (1962) noted more than 50 years ago, the colleges and universities we have inherited are in fact the result of unique adaptations of a singular institutional model, "a literal historical succession from a tiny number of medieval teaching-learning companies, guilds of either the students or the teachers, 'the spontaneous product of that instinct of association which swept over the towns of Europe in the course of the eleventh and twelfth centuries'" (p. 174). Spanning roughly

1,000 years, the notion of a self-generating, self-regulating, and self-renewing community of scholars served as a founding and guiding principle of our colleges and universities.

5. Some of the most insightful thinking on the social and psychological dynamics of narcissism, and the importance of higher education in holding this narcissism in check, was done by Erich Fromm in the mid-20th century. Fromm (1964/2010) understood that democracy and science required the diminution of narcissism, and he also noted that all the great religious traditions of the past held the elimination of narcissism as a central tenet and goal: "The essential teachings of all the great humanist religions can be summarized in one sentence: It is the goal of man [sic] to overcome one's narcissism" (p. 85).

6. A good starting point for this would be Alfred North Whitehead's (1929/1967) brilliant essay "Universities and Their Function." Here Whitehead argues in defense of the upstart business school at Harvard University and makes the case for including the study of business as a legitimate and important area of study at the university. Yet he warns against operating the university as a business corporation: "The management of a university faculty has no analogy to that of a business organization . . . the heart of the matter lies beyond all regulation" (p. 99). Simply and beautifully put "the justification for a university is that it preserves the connection between knowledge and the zest of life, by uniting the young and old in the imaginative consideration of learning. The university imparts information, but it imparts it imaginatively. At least this is the function which it should perform for society. A university which fails in this respect has no reason for existence" (p. 93).

References

Dewey, J. (1999). *Individualism old and new*. Prometheus Books. (Original work published 1930)
Dorn, C. (2019). *For the common good: A new history of higher education in America*. Cornell University Press.
Edmundson, M. (2013). *Why teach? In defense of a real education*. Bloomsbury.
Feinberg, W., & Soltis, J. (2009). *School and society* (5th ed.). Teachers College Press.
Foerster, N. (1944). A university prepared for victory. In N. Foerster (Ed.), *The humanities after the war* (pp. 26–31). Books for Libraries Press.
Fromm, E. (2010). *The heart of man: Its genius for good and evil*. American Mental Health Foundation Books. (Original work published 1964)
Goodman, P. (1962). *Compulsory mis-education and the community of scholars*. Vintage Books/Random House.
Jaschik, S. (2017, May 3). Author discusses new book about how American higher education has always been a "perfect mess." *Inside Higher Ed*. https://www.insidehighered.com/news/2017/05/03/author-discusses-new-book-about-how-american-higher-education-has-always-been
Labaree, D. F. (1997). *How to succeed in school without really learning: The credentials race in American education*. Yale University Press.

Labaree, D. F. (2004). *The trouble with ed schools*. Yale University Press.
Labaree, D. F. (2010). *Someone has to fail: The zero-sum game of public schooling*. Harvard University Press.
Labaree, D. F. (2017). *A perfect mess: The unlikely ascendancy of American higher education*. University of Chicago Press.
Nussbaum, M. C. (2012). *Not for profit: Why democracy needs the humanities*. Princeton University Press.
Rudolph, F. (1962). *The American college and university: A history*. Vintage Books/Random House.
Strike, K. A. (2010), *Small schools and strong communities: A third way of school reform*. Teachers College Press.
Whitehead, A. N. (1967). *The aims of education and other essays*. The Free Press. (Original work published 1929)

PART THREE

ON EDUCATION AND SOCIAL CHANGE

12

#REALCOLLEGE

The Work and Activism of Sara Goldrick-Rab

Carrie Freie

In the film *Hungry to Learn* Sarah Goldrick-Rab appears wearing a "#RealCollege" t-shirt. On the back of the shirt is written "it's not ALL about Harvard," referring to the work of the #RealCollege movement in breaking down stereotypes of the privileged college student in order to reveal the reality of what college is like for a growing number of students from poor, working-class, and middle-class backgrounds. Today's college students are, increasingly, not the stereotype of a carefree college student but instead struggling to make it through school while juggling financial and familial responsibilities. Goldrick-Rab's work has not only uncovered this important reality but works to draw attention to it in order to create change.

Research: Investigating Real Experiences of College Students

This chapter examines the work of Sara Goldrick-Rab and her characteristic approach as a scholar-activist. Her work assesses and often challenges taken-for-granted ideas both inside and outside of the academy. Specifically, this chapter focuses on her research and how it impacts her activism and work with higher education policy, particularly the ways her work addresses ideas and assumptions that underlie higher education policy decisions regarding accessibility and affordability of college, redefining opportunity, and rethinking the role of higher education within American society.

Goldrick-Rab's work joins research examining the unique experiences of poor and working-class college attendees (Bozick, 2007; Stich, 2012; Stuber, 2011). Scholars have examined aspects of access (Bailey & Dynarski, 2011; Christie & Munro, 2003; Lehman, 2016) and how students fare academically (Arum & Roska, 2011, Stinebrickner & Stinebrickner, 2003). Each is studying higher education at a time when the push for democratization of higher education has resulted in greater access in terms of students from more diverse racial, ethnic, and socioeconomic backgrounds attending colleges and universities (Ellwood & Kane, 2000). Yet despite the implied promise of access, which exists alongside narratives of "college for all" and increased acknowledgment of the necessity of a college degree, significant concerns continue about completion, debt, and the inequality of experiences within the system of higher education (Bozick, 2007; Christie & Munro, 2003; Pascarella et al., 2004; Stich & Freie, 2016). With the backdrop of increasing college tuition, stagnation of financial aid, and more students from poor and working-class backgrounds attending college, Goldrick-Rab's body of work contributes to our understanding of the experiences of college students' lived realities and hidden struggles. Goldrick-Rab's work forces us to address the changing demographic of today's college student as tuition, fees, and room and board costs continue to rise and financial aid fails to keep pace, or results in overwhelming debt, at a time when a college degree is more essential than ever. This work also pushes us to understand the struggles and experiences of this group as individuals as well as being representative of college students more generally (Goldrick-Rab, 2006, 2016a; Goldrick-Rab et al., 2015). In this way her work not only gives us an in-depth structural analysis of the current college climate but asks us to consider ways the system could change in order to ameliorate the dire situation many students face both during and after college.

Scholarship: Uncovering Real Struggles of College Students

While at the University of Wisconsin–Madison Goldrick-Rab worked on the Wisconsin Scholar's Longitudinal Study, which followed 6,000 college students and studied the roles of financial hardship and financial aid in their college experiences. The findings of this study are presented in *Paying the Price: College Costs, Financial Aid and the Betrayal of the American Dream*, in which Goldrick-Rab (2016a) describes an obsolete financial aid system that leaves many students struggling to get through college or worse, wracked with debt and no degree to show for it. The book received positive reviews (Abad, 2018; Reed, 2018), led to Goldrick-Rab being awarded the 2018 Grawemeyer Award in Education (Grawemeyer Awards, n.d.), and was groundbreaking for drawing attention to the depth of hardship that was hidden from view on college campuses. Using the students' own voices, *Paying the Price* details the difficulties students from poor and working-class backgrounds endure as they navigate higher education and pursue a degree. Goldrick-Rab (2016a) shares the stories of college students who are skipping meals, working multiple jobs, and experiencing poverty as they try to complete their studies. She points out how the financial aid system falls short of acknowledging the reality of all students—for example, the student who works in order to contribute to their family's income, a phenomenon the financial aid system has never considered in its determination of "need," which she argues is based on obsolete assumptions and formulas.

Paying the Price is significant for its findings, the ways it draws attention to the unrecognized suffering of college students who struggle financially, and its proposals for change. One of the most striking findings from this study was the number of college students experiencing food and/or housing insecurity—students who were skipping meals or falling asleep in class because they weren't able to find a good place to sleep the night before.

Whereas the hardship caused by student debt had received media attention, this issue had not (Comedy Central, 2016). Among Goldrick-Rab's significant findings are details of the ways the Federal Student Aid system falls short, including requirements of the Free Application for Federal Student Aid (FAFSA) form itself (e.g., asking for a parent's financial information regardless of the parent's intended support or immigration status) and built-in assumptions, such as the idea that money moves from parents to children. Goldrick-Rab interviewed students who work to provide money to support their parents and families and needed to continue to do so even while in college, yet formulas used to calculate financial aid assume the opposite is true, that parents are able to contribute to their student's education and do not rely on their income. The book also illuminates the real struggles of students who work at low-wage jobs that are often inflexible and incompatible with attending classes and studying (Goldrick-Rab, 2016a).

Goldrick-Rab outlines the ways in which financial aid and how it is awarded has failed to keep up with the modern reality of who attends college and how they do it, as well as the ways disinvestment in state-funded higher education has exacerbated the situation and resulted in steep increases in tuition, room, board, and other fees and expenses (Goldrick-Rab, 2016a; Goldrick-Rab & Miller-Adams, 2018). In order to address this, she proposes a number of policy changes including expansion of the National School Lunch Program, which now serves kindergarten through 12th grade (K–12) students in the United States. She also backs changes to the Supplemental Nutrition Assistance Program (SNAP), which currently has a work requirement of 20 hours per week in order to qualify. She argues this rule should be changed for college students. In addition, she proposes that colleges and universities address housing insecurity with their housing policies, including setting aside emergency housing for students in need. Other recommendations include more transparent and fair information on tuition, pricing, and financial aid packages, as well as clear explanations for students and families about how different types of aid work (Goldrick-Rab, 2016a).

Finally, Goldrick-Rab concludes that a college education should be free or partially free. Her proposals for this include making community college free, making the first 2 years of college free, and making the "first degree free," using a model that would award an associate's degree as part of the process of earning a bachelor's degree (Goldrick-Rab, 2016a, 2016b). To pay for this, one part of her proposal includes rethinking the Federal Financial Aid system to favor public colleges and universities and increasing public investment in higher education (Goldrick-Rab, 2016a). She argues that this is a common-sense approach similar to providing high school education as a public good. In a TEDxPhiladelphia talk Goldrick-Rab (2019, 17:57) said,

> We've done this before . . . we decided to make high school free, and it wasn't easy, and it didn't happen overnight, but we did it and it changed our entire country. It is increasingly hard to imagine where we would be if we had not done that. (17:57–18:24)

She further proposes that a move toward free college will not only benefit poor students but middle-class students who increasingly struggle with college affordability, working while attending school, and student loan debt. While free college may be important to encourage low-income students to attend at all, for middle-class students who are more likely to pursue higher education, free college can interrupt downward mobility and increase overall social equity. In response to reports from The Education Trust and the Institute for Higher Education Policy, Goldrick-Rab and Miller-Adams (2018) write,

> The lack of college affordability for middle-class students helps explain downward mobility for the middle class, the looming student-loan debt problem, and a growing crisis of food and housing insecurity on college campuses. A college degree can be a ticket to a more secure future, but only if students can complete degrees free from crushing debt. (para. 8)

When Goldrick-Rab first began to write about the idea of free college, it was a somewhat marginal idea. However today, while still debated, it has become mainstream as some political leaders have taken up the mantle of free college tuition in various forms (Arnett, 2018; Hartig, 2020). Programs such as Tennessee's Promise Scholarship and New York's Excelsior Scholarship have attempted to reach the goal of a tuition-free degree

(Goldrick-Rab & Miller-Adams, 2018; Quinlan, 2017). Though Goldrick-Rab generally promotes the idea of free college, particularly the idea of a "first degree free," she offered harsh criticism of the Excelsior Scholarship for its many requirements, including a postgraduation residency requirement that stipulates graduates work in the state for the same amount of time they claimed the scholarship or risk their scholarship turning to a loan (Quinlan, 2017). More generally, her critiques of free college programs center around the ways most of these programs operate on a "last dollar" basis, in which need-based grant aid is applied first before any "free college" scholarship money. This, she and Miller-Adams (2018) claim, leaves many students with still unmet needs, such as living expenses, and does nothing to stop the seemingly continual tuition increases.

Regarding these debates Goldrick-Rab (2016b) says,

> The whole concept of higher education is under debate in America today—public versus private versus for-profit, preprofessional versus liberal arts, in-person versus online. One thing, however, should be clear to all: when large numbers of people can't afford college at all, the system is broken. (para. 3)

She argues for focusing on community colleges and the state systems of higher education as sites for change. This is in line with the comparison she makes between the K–12 public education system and higher education. If higher education mimicked the current K–12 system, would it be one in which the majority of students attend public institutions, leaving a privileged minority at private institutions? The ways this might change the landscape of higher education is largely left unaddressed in her work. In addition, important questions arise about how this might exacerbate or ameliorate the current inequalities and stratification within higher education. One significant difference between the K–12 versus higher education models of funding is that the higher education model, as Goldrick-Rab (2016b) envisions it, relies primarily on federal funding as opposed to state and local funding. While inequities in the K–12 system are exacerbated by the reliance on local funding, relying on federal funding itself does not ensure equity. Goldrick-Rab's (2016a) example of the high levels of need found at University of Wisconsin–Milwaukee, compared to Madison, attest to the different levels of need found in the student body at separate locations, even within one state system. She found the students at Milwaukee not only had greater need but that the school received less funding for programs such as work study.

Nevertheless, she stridently maintains that funding a first degree is not only an investment society can make in an individual student's life and the lives of their children but one that our society cannot afford not to make, as the necessity of a college degree has increased over the years

(Comedy Central, 2016). Particularly in her public speaking, Goldrick-Rab frames a college degree as a necessity in today's economy, but one whose cost can cause poverty for students (Goldrick-Rab, 2016b, 2019). In much of her public speaking she focuses on the economic importance of a college degree and on job readiness. For example, she says in her 2019 Tedx talk in Philadelphia that "the data are really clear. 80% of the good jobs in this country require at least some education after high school . . . even mechanics now need at least some education after high school. . . . That education comes in the nation's community colleges" (3:48–4:26). Critics argue against narrowly focusing on job skills; "the real curriculum of preparation for work should not be on job skills" (Worthen, 2012, p. 191). The argument Worthen mounts against Goldrick-Rab's focus is not one against vocational education, but instead argues that education offers much more than job skills and this greater purpose of higher education needs to be valued and talked about as a contribution to our larger society and collective good (Goldrick-Rab, 2012; Worthen, 2012). This is part of the challenge of a public intellectual and scholar-activist—balancing the ways to communicate complicated research-based proposals to a broad audience.

Goldrick-Rab's findings from *Paying the Price* led her, often with collaborators, to focus on both educational policy as well as federal, state, local, and university policies and practices that play a role in the struggles of the students she studies. In work with Peter Kinsley, they examined the impacts of requirements attached to the Pell Grant, such as number of credits and maintenance of a minimum grade point average (GPA). They found that recipients of the grant were often strategically making decisions about courses, credit loads, and even majors based on maintaining their qualifications for receiving the grant. Kinsley and Goldrick-Rab (2016) learned that Pell recipients in their survey cared deeply about their education and had ambitious goals. They also learned that the recipients carefully considered the number of credits they took because of the GPA requirements of the grant. "The Pell recipients we studied appear to be utilizing information about their grades to decide how many credits to attempt in the next term—the worse they are doing, the fewer credits they take" (p. 106). Although this seems like a logical step, it can have unintended consequences. Kinsley and Goldrick-Rab (2016) point out that taking fewer credits will increase time to completion of their degree, increase their debt, and even reduce their chance of degree completion. Looking at the ways in which policy design impacts the real lives of students, their decisions, and achievements provides a more comprehensive picture of the impact of these policies.

Another example of Goldrick-Rab's examination of the impact of policy on students' lives and college outcomes is on the issue of food insecurity experienced by college students (Broton & Goldrick-Rab, 2018). Her work with Freudenberg and Poppendieck (Freudenberg et al., 2019) declares that "college students are a new population at risk for food insecurity" (p. 1652). They studied SNAP, asking questions about why the food assistance program often fails college students. They argue that though we see more low-income college students who are struggling with food insecurity, SNAP policies fall short of providing for them. The authors then critique the current system of aid, noting that the success of enrolling more students in college without solid support to keep these students in school (or even to keep them from going hungry) is work left half done. "In sum, a problem created by a significant policy success—expanded enrollment of low-income students in college—was followed by the failure of federal policy to address two other trends: rising college costs and reduced financial assistance" (p. 1654). The authors then offer policy recommendations in some detail—including both SNAP-specific changes (such as eliminating the college student exemption, which would allow college students to qualify for the program) and other changes such as expanding school lunch and breakfast programs, currently used in public schools, into higher education.

Activism: #RealCollege and Drawing Attention to the Experiences of College Students

Goldrick-Rab's focus on creating change goes further than her academic research and publications. Although she eschews being referred to as an advocate, preferring the term *scholar-activist*, much of her focus recently has been working in the vein of a public intellectual, sharing the work of the Hope Center for College, Community, and Justice. She clarifies,

> Scholarly activism is not advocacy. Let me say that again, since in my experience people have trouble hearing this. I am a scholar-activist, but not an advocate. The difference is critical. An advocate begins with a core and guiding goal—not a theory—and pushes for changes to achieve that goal. In contrast, a scholar-activist begins with a set of testable assumptions, subjects these to rigorous research, and once in the possession of research findings seeks to translate those findings into action. (Supiano, 2016, p. 7)

Goldrick-Rab defines herself as an applied sociologist who comes by her activism though her research, and her research has led her to conclude that the system of funding of higher education, and many of our assumptions about the system, need to change (Gandbhir, 2020). Building off of the concept that students cannot apply themselves when their basic needs are unmet (Maslow, 1970), she has taken up the mantle of the #RealCollege movement.

As part of the Hope Center for College, Community, and Justice (2020), #RealCollege is a movement whose goals include encouraging institutions of higher education to focus on the basic needs of college students (food, housing, transportation, childcare, and mental health). In its first iteration, the Harvesting Opportunities for Postsecondary Education (HOPE) Lab originated at the University of Wisconsin–Madison. With new funding the project reemerged as the Hope Center at Temple University, where Goldrick-Rab moved after leaving the University of Wisconsin–Madison. Goldrick-Rab describes it as the "first laboratory for translational research aimed at improving equitable outcomes in postsecondary education, and finding innovative ways to make college more affordable" (Santovec, 2017, p. 6).

Goldrick-Rab's work at the Hope Center reinforced her reputation as a public intellectual and scholar-activist who is frequently in the public eye with activities such as giving TED talks, promoting #RealCollege, contributing to the documentary *Hungry to Learn*, and maintaining an active online presence (Goldrick-Rab, n.d., 2019, 2020). Having a public presence also comes with criticism, and sometimes attacks, particularly online. While at the University of Wisconsin–Madison she publicly spoke out against then governor Scott Walker's cuts to the public system of higher education and efforts to weaken the tenure system. Her criticism happened alongside protests to Walker's budget cuts to education, including deep cuts to both the university system and public education more broadly (Diverse Staff, 2015; Jaschik, 2015; Punzel, 2015). Her vocal presence on Twitter and a series of tweets made around this time gained public attention and resulted in online debates and to her being harassed (Jaschik, 2015). Perhaps most significant, she was not backed by the university, where some administration officials as well as the executive committee of the university's faculty senate issued statements critical of her speech (Wilson, 2015). Although Goldrick-Rab issued an apology for one controversial tweet, other tweets addressed to a prospective student—questioning the ability of the university to maintain high-quality education as a result of Walker's proposed changes—were the focus of the university's reprimand (Diverse Staff, 2015). Shortly after this Goldrick-Rab, who at that time had earned the rank of full professor, left for Temple University, where she is professor of sociology and medicine.

At Temple University Goldrick-Rab has expanded her public profile as she continues to work with the Hope Center. She remains active on Twitter and other social media platforms and has increased her public speaking to include audiences outside of academic or higher education circles and appearances in popular media (Gandbhir, 2020; Goldrick-Rab, 2019). By doing this she has drawn public attention to the plight of college students living in poverty, struggling with food and housing insecurity, and been able to present her case for free college education. Using the #RealCollege hashtag is one example of how the Hope Center communicates its larger messages and goals to a wider audience, working to bridge the spaces between academic research and policy action.

Conclusion

Goldrick-Rab's work and activism is most successful when it challenges us to think in new ways about how higher education policy shapes opportunities for college students. Her perspective of looking at not only the quantifiable impacts of higher education policy but at the ways policy impacts the everyday lives and potentials of college students gives Goldrick-Rab's work authority and accessibility. Her work appeals to both academic and popular audiences. Through her scholarly contributions such as her book *Paying the Price: College Costs, Financial Aid, and the Betrayal of the American Dream*, as well as her outreach work, including founding of the Hope Center for College, Community and Justice, she has challenged both academics and policymakers to reassess their thinking about who college students are, the purpose and role of college within society, the function of the state in providing a safety net, and the societal benefits of greater educational opportunity.

References

Abad, A. (2018). *Paying the price: College costs, financial aid, and the betrayal of the American dream* by Sara Goldrick-Rab [Review]. *The Review of Higher Education, 42*(1), E7–E10. https://doi.org/10.1353/rhe.2018.0041

Arnett, A. (2018, January 8). *3 years ago, President Obama first proposed making community college tuition free: Here's where we stand.* Education Dive. https://www.educationdive.com/news/free-community-college-its-not-just-democrats-making-the-push/512845/

Arum, R., & Roska, J. (2011). *Academically adrift: Limited learning on college campuses.* University of Chicago Press.

Bailey, M. J., & Dynarski, S. M. (2011). Gains and gaps: Changing inequality in U.S. college entry and completion. In G. Duncan & R. J. Murnane (Eds.), *Whither opportunity? Rising inequality and the uncertain life chances of low-income children* (pp. 117–132). Russell Sage Foundation Press.

Bozick, R. (2007). Making it through the first year of college: The role of students' economic resources, employment, and living arrangements. *Sociology of Education, 80*(3), 261–284. https://doi.org/10.1177/003804070708000304

Broton, K., & Goldrick-Rab, S. (2018). Going without: An exploration of food and housing insecurity among undergraduates. *Educational Researcher, 47*(2), 121–133. https://doi.org/10.3102/0013189X17741303

Christie, H., & Munro, M. (2003). The logic of loans: Students' perceptions of the costs and benefits of the student loan. *British Journal of Sociology of Education, 24*(5), 621–636. https://doi.org/10.1080/0142569032000127170

Comedy Central. (2016, September 27). Exclusive—Sara Goldrick-Rab extended interview [Video]. *The Daily Show With Trevor Noah.* http://www.cc.com/video-clips/uurxys/the-daily-show-with-trevor-noah-exclusive---sara-goldrick-rab-extended-interview

Diverse Staff. (2015, July 13). Gov. Scott Walker uses education as platform for presidency. *Diverse Issues in Higher Education.* https://diversepodium.com/article/76293/

Ellwood, D., & Kane, T. J. (2000). Who is getting a college education? Family background and the growing gaps in enrollment. In S. Danzinger & J. Waldfogel (Eds.), *Securing the future* (pp. 283–324). Russell Sage Foundation Press.

Freudenberg, N., Goldrick-Rab, S., & Poppendieck, J. (2019). College students and SNAP: The new face of food insecurity in the United States. *American Journal of Public Health, 109*(12), 1652–1658. https://doi.org/10.2105/AJPH.2019.305332

Gandbhir, G. (Director). (2020). *Hungry to learn* [Film]. Good Docs.

Goldrick-Rab, S. (2006). Following their every move: An investigation of social-class differences in college pathways. *Sociology of Education, 79*(1), 61–79. https://doi.org/10.1177/003804070607900104

Goldrick-Rab, S. (2012). Comments on Mike Rose's essay "Rethinking remedial education and the academic-vocational divide." *Mind, Culture, and Activity, 19*, 26–28. https://doi.org/10.1080/10749039.2011.632054

Goldrick-Rab, S. (2016a). *Paying the price: College costs, financial aid, and the betrayal of the American dream.* University of Chicago Press.

Goldrick-Rab, S. (2016b). The economy needs more workers with associate degrees. *Education Next, 16*(1). https://www.educationnext.org/economy-needs-more-workers-with-associate-degrees-forum-community-college/

Goldrick-Rab, S. (2019, May). *College is creating poverty* [Video]. TED Conferences. https://www.ted.com/talks/sara_goldrick_rab_college_is_creating_poverty

Goldrick-Rab, S. (2020). *Sara Goldrick-Rab.* http://saragoldrickrab.com

Goldrick-Rab, S. [@saragoldrickrab]. (n.d.). *Tweets* [Twitter profile]. https://twitter.com/saragoldrickrab?ref_src=twsrc%5Egoogle%7Ctwcamp%5Eserp%7Ctwgr%5Eauthor

Goldrick-Rab, S., Kelchen, R., Harris, D., & Benson, J. (2015). *Reducing income inequality in educational attainment: Experimental evidence on the impact of financial aid on college completion* (IRP working paper 1393-12). Institute for Research on Poverty.

Goldrick-Rab, S., & Miller-Adams, M. (2018). Don't dismiss the value of free-college programs: They do help low-income students. *The Chronicle of Higher*

Education. https://www.chronicle.com/article/dont-dismiss-the-value-of-free-college-programs-they-do-help-low-income-students/

Grawemeyer Awards. (n.d.). *Home page.* http://grawemeyer.org/

Hartig, H. (2020, February 21). *Democrats overwhelmingly favor free college tuition, while Republicans are divided by age, education.* Pew Research Center. https://www.pewresearch.org/fact-tank/2020/02/21/democrats-overwhelmingly-favor-free-college-tuition-while-republicans-are-divided-by-age-education/

Hope Center for College, Community, and Justice. (2020). *Home page.* hope4college.com

Jaschik, S. (2015, July 17). Who crossed the line? *Inside Higher Ed.* https://www.insidehighered.com/news/2015/07/17/debate-escalates-over-twitter-remarks-sara-goldrick-rab-professor-wisconsin-madison

Kinsley, P., & Goldrick-Rab, S. (2016). Making the grade: The academic side of college life among financial aid recipients. In A. E. Stich & C. Freie (Eds.), *The working classes and higher education: Inequality of access, opportunity and outcome* (pp. 87–109). Routledge.

Lehman, W. (2016). Influences on working-class students' decision to go to university. In A. E. Stich & C. Freie (Eds.), *The working classes and higher education: Inequality of access, opportunity and outcome* (pp. 13–29). Routledge.

Maslow, A. H. (1970). *Motivation and personality* (2nd ed.). Harper and Row.

Pascarella, E. T., Pierson, C. T., Wolniak, G. C., & Terenizini, P. T. (2004). First-generation college students: Additional evidence on college experiences and outcomes. *Journal of Higher Education, 75*(3), 249–284. https://doi.org/10.1080/00221546.2004.11772256

Punzel, D. (2015, February 15). Protesters express no love for Scott Walker's budget cuts at UW rally. *Wisconsin State Journal.* https://madison.com/wsj/news/local/education/university/protesters-express-no-love-for-scott-walkers-budget-cuts-at-uw-rally/article_2f8e0ea2-d832-59e1-ac1b-fe93c548cc18.html

Quinlan, C. (2017, April 10). *There are a lot of strings attached to New York's tuition-free plan.* Think Progress. https://archive.thinkprogress.org/https-thinkprogress-org-there-are-a-lot-of-strings-attached-to-new-yorks-tuition-free-plan-e01db-2fabe8f/

Reed, M. (2016, September 13). Paying the price: A review. *Inside Higher Ed.* https://www.insidehighered.com/blogs/confessions-community-college-dean/paying-price-review

Santovec, M. (2017, April). An activist for students: A profile of Dr. Sara Goldrick-Rab. *Women in Higher Education, 26*(4), 6–12. https://doi.org/10.1002/whe.20423

Stich, A. E. (2012). *Access to inequality: Reconsidering class, knowledge and capital in higher education.* Lexington Books.

Stich, A. E., & Freie, C. (2016). *The working classes and higher education: Inequality of access, opportunity and outcome.* Routledge.

Stinebrickner, R., & Stinebrickner, T. R. (2003). Working during school and academic performance. *Journal of Labor Economics, 21*(2), 473–491. http://dx.doi.org/10.1086/345564

Stuber, J. (2011). *Inside the college gates: How class and culture matter in higher education.* Lexington Books.
Supiano, B. (2016). The many battles of Sara Goldrick-Rab. *The Chronicle of Higher Education.* https://www.chronicle.com/article/the-many-battles-of-sara-goldrick-rab/
Wilson, K. (2015, July 17). In defense of Sara Goldrick-Rab. *Academe Blog.* https://academeblog.org/2015/07/17/in-defense-of-sara-goldrick-rab/
Worthen, H. H. (2012). A different curriculum of preparation for work: Commentary on Mike Rose, Sara Goldrick-Rab, Kris Gutiérrez and Norton Grubb. *Mind, Culture, and Activity, 19*(2), 190–195. https://doi.org/10.1080/10749039.2012.678541

13

LORI PATTON DAVIS

Mapping the Landscape of African American Postsecondary Education

Sabrina N. Ross

This chapter reviews the scholarly work of Lori Patton Davis and articulates the means through which it exemplifies the intellectual activist strategy of contesting existing relations of power within the context of U.S. higher education. A review of Patton's scholarly work is provided. Specific attention in this review is given to ways that Patton's individual and collaborative inquiry projects offer a critical mapping of the African American postsecondary educational landscape by challenging deficit-oriented perspectives and constructing new knowledge about African Americans, their postsecondary educational experiences, and the higher education policies and initiatives that support social justice goals for African Americans and other socially marginalized groups.

Introduction

Educational inquiry on topics related to African American education is often informed by deficit-oriented perspectives that frame African Americans, their experiences, and their cultural ways of knowing as problems (Dumas, 2016; Joseph et al., 2017). Through a singular focus on rectifying problems, deficit-oriented educational research on African Americans and other racially marginalized groups lends support to racist ideologies, offering seeming justifications for disparate educational outcomes (Solorzano & Yosso, 2002). Not only does deficit-based research fail to honor the complexity of African American lived educational experiences, but it also limits possibilities for social justice by shifting focus away from structural causes of educational inequity and the educational policies and practices that could address them.

Increasingly, critical race scholars have responded to problematic representations of African Americans in educational research through engagement in critical race counter-storytelling (Solorzano & Yosso, 2002) that intentionally counters deficit-based perspectives of African Americans and their formal and informal educational experiences. Such critical race inquiry represents a form of intellectual activism. Patricia Hill Collins (2013) discusses two strategies critical scholars often employ for intellectual activism and explains the ways that power is wielded in both. The first strategy, speaking truth to power, represents scholarship that "harnesses the power of ideas toward the specific goal of confronting existing power relations" (Collins, 2013, p. xii). The second strategy, speaking truth to the people, seeks to empower marginalized groups through interpersonal interactions and through scholarship whose main audience is the public (Collins, 2013). While, the boundary-crossing work of Lori Patton Davis (identified as Patton in her scholarly work) exemplifies both strategies of intellectual activism, emphasis in this chapter will be placed on Patton's use of the strategy of contesting existing relations of power manifested within the context of U.S. higher education. Specific focus in this chapter is placed on ways that Patton's scholarship challenges deficit-oriented knowledge and constructs new knowledge about African Americans and their postsecondary education experiences.

Challenging Taken-for-Granted Understandings and Constructing New Knowledge Through Intersectional Analysis

Although Patton is well-known for her scholarship on campus culture centers and for her scholarship related to student development theory and practice (Ciccone, 2020), Patton's major contribution to higher education research is, arguably, the dissemination of methodologically rigorous intersectional analysis. Most often, this analysis is devoted to examining the multiple and interlocking experiences of oppression of Black women and other socially marginalized groups that are derived through the inhabitation of multiple stigmatized markers of identity (Crenshaw, 1991). The work of Patton and colleagues that engages intersectional analysis to challenge taken-for-granted understandings and to develop new knowledge is discussed in the following sections.

Intersectional Analyses of the Experiences of Black Women in Higher Education

Notable among scholarly works by Patton and colleagues is the use of intersectional analysis to highlight the complexity of the lived experienced of Black women across postsecondary education settings. Patton and Croom's (2017) edited work, *Critical Perspectives on Black Women and College Success*, exemplifies this dedication to understanding the complexity. Comprised of diverse chapters that purposefully resist essentializing stereotypes of Black womanhood, the text is a continuation of Patton's ongoing efforts to chart the contours and complexities of African American experiences on college and university campuses. In the introduction, Patton and Croom (2017) articulate the corrective role they envision their text playing in the debunking of stereotypical and disempowering information about Black undergraduate women. They write,

> Today, there are many fantasies about Black women in higher education that must be critically interrogated and examined to illuminate the complexities of our experiences across the higher education landscape. This project is one effort devoted to the interruption of epistemic violence enacted to silence, marginalize, and dehumanize Black women, particularly at the undergraduate level. Scholars and practitioners know little about the experiences of Black undergraduate women, and what is presumed to be known has in large part been constructed outside Black women's communities, devoid of a critical lens, and treated as insignificant. (p. 1)

The notion of scholarship as a corrective to deficit-oriented and essentialized knowledge about Black women's educational experiences is also prevalent in the scholarship by Patton, discussed next. Focus in this scholarship is on Black women's mentoring experiences, Black women's tenure and promotion experiences, and media coverage of missing Black college women.

Challenging Knowledge About Mentoring Practices

Patton (2009) examines Black women's mentoring experiences within predominantly White institutions and their perceptions of the significance and availability of Black women mentors to support their graduate schooling experiences. A number of findings emerge from this study that challenge taken-for-granted knowledge about mentoring practices. First, participants emphasized a distinction between mentors and advisers. Participants viewed mentors as individuals they could openly share educational and life struggles with. When such mentors were not available within their own academic departments, some participants actively sought external mentors while continuing to receive advising assistance from their formally assigned mentors (Patton, 2009). Additionally, participants experienced trust issues with mentors who did not share cultural congruence with them (i.e., did not share the participants' racial and gender identities). A number of the participants in Patton's study expressed fear that formally assigned mentors who lacked cultural congruity would be unable or unwilling to understand and relate to their postsecondary education experiences. Participants who did have culturally congruent mentors compared the mentoring relationships to familial connections and sometimes viewed their mentors through the lens of fictive mothers.

Through her research on Black women's mentoring experiences, Patton challenges ideas about the presumed neutrality of university mentoring practices. Mentoring for the participants in Patton's study was context-specific. The participants required advisement to help them understand and navigate their racialized and gendered university experiences, but were reluctant to seek such assistance if their formal advisers lacked cultural congruence. Some participants sought "other mentors" to fill their mentorship void while others went without the additional mentoring help they required. The participants' needs and mentor-seeking behaviors were likely unnoticed by their formally assigned mentors, suggesting that securing appropriate mentoring relationships is an additional, and often invisible, hurdle for Black women graduate students.

Challenging Knowledge About Promotion and Tenure Practices
In a conceptual piece exploring inequities in the promotion process for Black women seeking promotion to the rank of full professor, Croom and Patton (2012) trouble notions of equity and fairness in promotion and tenure decisions. Compiling statistics and research on the tenure and promotion experiences of Black women faculty, they highlight the existence of racial and gender hegemony within collegiate spaces and explain how this hegemony maintains the status quo of disproportionately low numbers of Black women faculty who obtain the status of full professorship. Importantly, Croom and Patton argue for a reframing of understandings of the tenure and promotion process, not as neutral and merit-based, but as politically charged with intersecting issues of power that disadvantage tenure-track Black women faculty. Inquiry by Croom and Patton (2012) offers a corrective to research that either implicitly or explicitly links the dearth of Black female full professors to problems inherent in Black women. The authors argue that the disproportionately low numbers of Black female professors across higher education

settings be viewed as glaring evidence of systemic racism and gender discrimination. In this way, Croom and Patton's intersectional analysis of the lack of Black women full professors contests notions about the objectivity and neutrality of tenure and promotion decisions.

Challenging the Presumed Neutrality of Media Coverage of Missing College Women

Patton and Ward (2016) utilize critical race feminist methodology—an approach to inquiry that identifies challenges experienced by "racially minoritized bodies" (p. 332) and intentionally centers those groups in intersectional analysis—to explore differences in police responses and media coverage associated with Black and White college women who are missing. The authors identified greater media coverage and less public scrutiny over the lives of non-Black missing college women. Their work highlights ways that intersecting identity markers of race, class, and gender shape overall messaging, media coverage, and public responses to missing Black women in ways that support the devaluing of Black women's lives both within and beyond college campuses.

Intersectional Analysis of LGBTQi and Gender-Nonconforming African American Students at Historically Black Colleges and Universities

Despite their valuable contributions to the education of African American students and to the general system of U.S. postsecondary education, historically Black colleges and universities (HBCUs) are frequently depicted "from a deficit perspective, without balanced or nuanced consideration of their assets" (Williams et al., 2018, p. 558). In this light, intersectional analysis of African American students enrolled at HBCUs by Patton and colleagues contributes to a complex discourse surrounding these institutions. Negative social depictions of HBCUs notwithstanding, illumination of the complexities of LGBTQi student experiences within HBCUs, whether or not those experiences cast HBCUs in a negative light, serve social justice goals by affirming the full humanity of these students. Through individually authored and collaborative projects, Patton has made important contributions to discourses surrounding gender and sexuality within historically Black campuses by highlighting the salience of multiple and complex identity formations for students attending HBCUs. A review of work by Patton and colleagues that corrects erroneous notions and shares new knowledge about the perceptions and lived experiences of LGBTQi students at HBCUs follows.

Challenging Preconceived Notions and Creating New Knowledge About LGBTQi Students and Gender-Nonconforming Students at HBCUs
Patton and Simmons (2008) explored the experiences and perceptions of five first-year Black female students who self-identified as lesbian and also attended an HBCU. The authors examined intersectional experiences of race, gender, and sexuality and the resulting "triple consciousness" (Patton & Simmons, 2008, p. 204), or acknowledgement of experiences of intersecting oppressions due to their racial, gender, and sexual orientation that participants' perceived through their learning and interactions within HBCU spaces. Patton and Simmons also explored their sense of belonging within the HBCU context. Participants felt accepted on campus based on their identity markers of Blackness, but perceived themselves as outsiders based on their sexual identities. Findings from the study resist romanticized depictions of HBCU campuses by calling attention to the ambivalence lesbian students perceive about their sense of belonging on the HBCU campus.

In another work on gender and sexuality, Patton (2011) examined the experiences, perceptions, and sexual disclosure decisions made by six African American males enrolled in an HBCU who self-identified as either gay or bisexual. Findings challenged taken-for-granted assumptions about gay and bisexual men within HBCU contexts. For example, race emerged as a significant identity marker for all of the participants. Based on this racial significance, the participants perceived the HBCU that they attended as an overall supportive environment, though they experienced challenges in publicly expressing their sexuality on campus. Findings from this study challenge the presumed universality and applicability of traditional understandings of the coming out process for Black LGBTQi students. Additionally, this study contests the heteronormativity of HBCU environments, calling for increased information provided to HBCU academic communities related to the needs of LGBTQi students.

In a conceptual piece that explores ways that power operates through implicit messaging in university policy, Patton (2014) used critical discourse analysis to examine ways in which the Morehouse College Appropriate Attire Policy, though ostensibly apolitical, encouraged prescriptive understandings of masculinity and respectability that served to marginalize Black men attending the HBCU who did not conform to cisgender expectations. In highlighting ways that policies presumed to be neutral actually serve oppressive goals for Black male HBCU students who are gender-nonconforming, Patton's work again troubles romanticized views of HBCUs as safe havens for all students. By calling attention to ways that intersecting issues of gender physiology and gender identity complicate understandings of the impact of campus policies such as the Appropriate Attire Policy, her work also creates new knowledge about the importance of attending to the complexity of identities at HBCUs.

Patton et al. (2020) again tackle issues of gender and sexuality experienced within HBCU campuses by exploring the experiences of LGBTQi students in negotiating campus spaces that supported their racial identities but posed challenges to their expression of sexual identities. Participants of the study were all undergraduates enrolled in one of three HBCUs and identified as either lesbian, bisexual, or gay. Similar to findings from Patton (2011), emergent themes from the Patton et al. (2020) study brought into stark relief ways that HBCUs operate as sites of both support and oppression for LGBTQi students. Students in the study simultaneously experienced racial affirmation and marginalization based on their sexual identities within their respective HBCUs. Recognizing the embeddedness of heterosexism and homophobia in central aspects of HBCU culture, Patton et al. use their scholarly work to advocate for social justice, recommending LGBTQi support services for students at HBCUs and training for all faculty and students to improve the HBCU campus climate.

Comprehensive Literature Reviews of Intersectionality Studies in Higher Education

Patton's use of intersectionality research extends beyond empirical and conceptual studies. Publishing with colleagues, she has also made intellectual activist contributions through two comprehensive literature reviews of intersectionality research that are discussed next.

Challenging the Presumed Social Justice Aims and Political Impact of Intersectionality Research

To examine the extent to which higher education researchers engaging in intersectionality research were doing so in support of social justice goals, Harris and Patton (2019) conducted a content analysis of 97 peer-reviewed higher education publications that utilized the term *intersectionality*. Some of the research analyzed merely utilized intersectionality as a buzzword, failing to engage in thoughtful analysis that honored the complexity of marginalized identities or that recognized the interlocking systems of oppression impacting marginalized lives (Harris & Patton, 2019). Harris and Patton found that less than half of the articles reviewed used citation practices that recognized the women of color who coined the term *intersectionality* or who popularized its usage in academia. A major consequence of the "erroneous definitions and applications of intersectionality" (Harris & Patton, 2019, p. 365) employed in the reviewed articles is an erasure of the historical and social context within which women of color developed and modeled the concept of intersectionality. Findings by Harris and Patton call attention to and challenge uncritical uses of intersectionality research in postsecondary education.

In a meta-analysis that examined 30 years (i.e., 1986–2016) of empirical, peer-reviewed intersectionality research, Haynes et al. (2020) sought to examine ways that intersectionality as a methodology has been used to understand the experiences of Black women in postsecondary education contexts. Of the research published about Black women in postsecondary contexts, less than 4% (23 out of 680 articles) utilized intersectionality as a research methodology (Haynes et al., 2020). The authors identified the dearth of intersectionality research as perpetuating the invisibility of Black women and their college and university experiences. Additionally, the authors found that when adopted, the intersectional methodologies that framed the articles were insufficiently utilized to develop interventions supportive of Black women's liberation within colleges and universities. Thus findings from the Haynes et al.'s (2020) meta-analysis call attention to the lack of intersectional research about Black women published in refereed outlets and the underusage of intersectionality as an emancipatory tool for enhancing the well-being and material conditions of Black women in higher education. In this way, work by Haynes et al. highlights the pervasive disconnect between academic uses of intersectionality and intersectionality's emancipatory aims.

Challenging Taken-for-Granted Understandings and Constructing New Knowledge About Social Justice Initiatives and Practices Within U.S. Higher Education Institutions

In addition to her intersectionality research, Patton is also committed to inquiry and public work that supports social justice by shifting culture and improving campus climates (Ciccone, 2020). Remaining sections of this review discuss work by Patton and colleagues that addresses the possibilities and challenges of transforming postsecondary education spaces for social justice.

Challenging Knowledge About Predominantly White Postsecondary Education Settings

In a piece intended to critique the status quo in higher education, Patton (2016b) calls attention to ways in which racism and White supremacy pervade all aspects of postsecondary education, influencing curriculum, policy, and student access. Decrying the "ordinary, predictable, and taken for granted ways in which the academy has functioned for centuries as a bastion of racism and White supremacy" (Patton, 2016a, p. 315), Patton offers three propositions that link contemporary educational inequities to (a) a history rooted in racism; (b) a system that is enabled by imperialist and capitalist processes that facilitate the oppression of marginalized groups; and (c) knowledge production that generates racism/White supremacy. After offering support for these propositions through examples related to higher education inquiry, curriculum, policy, and programming, Patton offers critical race theory as a significant tool for social justice advocates who are committed to transforming college and university spaces. In naming ways that White supremacy continues to stall work for access and equity in education, Patton introduces an uncomfortable but necessary discussion within the context of U.S. postsecondary education.

Challenging Knowledge About Social Justice Initiatives and White Allyship

Higher education institutions increasingly respond to changing enrollment demographics and to diversity-related student protests by implementing formalized initiatives related to diversity, inclusion, equity, and justice (DIEJ). Patton et al. (2019) explore the substance of these programmatic and policy-related initiatives through a review of postsecondary DIEJ initiatives published in peer-reviewed educational research journals over a 50-year span (i.e., 1968 to 2018). Of the 45 articles included in the analysis, Patton et al. found that most policies and initiatives lacked any critical engagement with issues of power and oppression. Additionally, the programmatic and curricular revisions described in the articles relied on additive rather than systemic approaches to implementation, making institutional transformation unlikely.

Patton et al. (2019) intimate a connection between the lack of published DIEJ research they found and a generalized notion among university administrators that meaningful implementation of DIEJ initiatives is unnecessary. The authors surmise that in the absence of a preponderance of published DIEJ research, "institutional leaders may be simply operating in ways that make the implementation of DIEJ initiatives nothing more than performance of political correctness, rather than a deeply conscious effort to shift the campus climate and address injustices on campus" (Patton et al., 2019, p. 189). Patton et al. challenge the status quo within colleges and universities in the United States through research that refuses to take higher education policies and practices at face value. Instead, the authors' scholarship encourages careful review of ways in which DIEJ policies and practices are actually connected to social justice goals.

Through data collected from semistructured interviews, Patton and Bondi (2015) analyze the understandings of allyship and the specific work for social justice engaged by 12 White males employed within university settings. All of the participants were identified by their colleagues as social justice allies. The ally work that most participants engaged was individualized (e.g., teaching courses infused with diversity content, mentoring and advising, focusing on issues of social justice in their research, etc.) and did not disrupt systemic power structures (Patton & Bondi, 2015). Though participants did not alter systems of oppression within U.S. higher education settings through their ally work, they did receive individual benefits from their allyship. Due to their identities as White males, the participants received accolades and respect for engaging social justice work, even though their efforts required little risk-taking (Patton & Bondi, 2015). Emphasizing the privileges and lack of overall impact apparent in the ally work of the participants, Patton and Bondi (2015) write, "The participants viewed themselves as working toward social justice in the situations they chose, but such efforts become negligible if they do not disrupt structural inequities" (p. 505). Research by Patton and Bondi (2015) is important because it raises essential questions surrounding the power dynamics associated with allyship and also challenges the notion that allies can further social justice goals in education through individualized actions and good intentions.

Creating New Knowledge About Institutional Transformation

In a conceptual piece articulating the limitations of dominant models of institutional change, Patton and Haynes (2018) question prevalent institutional change models that fail to address the intersectional realities of individuals situated within U.S. postsecondary education settings. The authors also critique institutional leadership strategies that focus on single axis identity politics to achieve social justice goals within collegiate spaces. Patton and Haynes argue that, given their intersectional experiences, Black women are often optimal role models for institutional transformation, yet are typically ignored in this respect due to social stereotypes that reduce Black women's work to the labor they provide within campus settings. Patton and Haynes' work draws connections between Black women's individual experiences within institutions and the overall health of institutions by illuminating ways that the undervaluing of Black women's experiences within university spaces diminishes broader efforts toward institutional transformation.

The Significance of Lori Patton Davis's Scholarship: Concluding Thoughts

Lori Patton Davis is a prolific scholar whose inquiry her earned her the Outstanding Contribution to Literature and/or Research award (2020) from the National Association of Student Personnel Administrators and the Contribution to Knowledge award (2020) from the American College Personnel Association. Despite these and other national scholarly recognitions, of foremost importance to Patton Davis is her role as a publicly engaged scholar whose research impact is felt beyond the formal boundaries of U.S. colleges and universities (Ciccone, 2020). As a critical race feminist whose work contests interlocking structures of oppression, scholarly critiques of Patton's work are, perhaps surprisingly, few. Points of criticism are largely directed at Patton's earlier scholarship and include a perceived over-reliance on personal experiences instead of empirical research to support knowledge claims about campus culture centers (Shek, 2011) and inadequate attention to issues of social class and dis/ability in Patton's early scholarship on college student development (Abes, 2011).

Much more common have been internal critiques and resistance to Patton's public work. One example is the considerable resistance Patton received from stakeholders of Indiana University-Purdue University at Indianapolis (IUPUI) when she and colleagues began organizing workshops and other educational activities as part of the White Racial Literacy Project designed to help White people engage one another to address racial issues on college and university campuses (Jenkins, 2020). Reflecting on the project, Patton characterized her experiences of resistance from IUPUI stakeholders as "exhausting." She elaborates on the pushback she received in relation to the White Racial Literacy Project at IUPUI by stating:

> You know the resistance is out there but the ways that you see it . . . you know . . . they're really interesting. And it's hard to implement a project like that at a predominantly White institution where the structures in and of themselves, you know, don't allow for . . . you know, such a project . . . I think the leadership was really supportive, but the reality of it is . . . you know, how do you try to do work around undoing White supremacy in a structure that supports White supremacy, right? So you anticipate all of these things that are going to happen. (Patton, quoted in Jenkins, 2020)

Patton's experiences of resistance at IUPUI highlight the emotional labor that often accompanies social justice–oriented scholarly work.

Much of Patton's research centers the higher education experiences of Black women. As discussed in this chapter, however, her scholarship also broaches topics such as college and university policy, processes of college student identity formation, higher education leadership, and diversity initiatives developed within postsecondary education institutions. As a result, one broader critique offered of Patton's work might be the seeming lack of connection among her wide-ranging research pursuits. However, Patton's inquiry is largely unified through a methodology of critical race counterstorytelling and a focus on issues of knowledge construction and power and their impact on the lived experiences of socially marginalized groups. Understood from this perspective, each area of her inquiry makes important contributions to educational research. Patton's scholarship related to Black women in postsecondary education centers Black women's intersectionality and complicates understanding of Black women's lived realities within these educational spaces. Patton's intersectional analyses of LGBTQi and gender non-conforming student experiences at HBCUs expands the limited research on these groups and on experiences of homophobia and heterosexism within HBCU campuses. Patton's broader intersectionality research calls attention to the emancipatory potential of intersectionality research, the infrequency of employment of intersectionality research in higher education to enhance Black women's lives, and the political consequences that can arise from uncritical uses of intersectionality as a framework for inquiry. Taken as a whole, Patton's scholarly work is a reminder of the need to move beyond superficial acceptance of social justice–aligned labels and instead interrogate the relevance, impact, and the beneficiaries of the research, policies, and practices implemented within postsecondary education spaces. Her work illuminates how issues of power pervade all aspects of postsecondary education and also opens spaces for broader discourse about social justice within colleges and universities in the United States.

References

Abes, E. S. (2011). Book review of *Student development in college. Theory, research, and practice* (2nd ed.), by N. J. Evans, D. S. Forney, F. M. Guido, L. D. Patton, & K. A. Renn. *NACADA Journal, 52*(1), 131–133.

Ciccone, J. K. (2020). *Lori Patton Davis' influence in higher education earns her new honors.* The Ohio State University College of Education and Human Ecology. https://ehe.osu.edu/news/listing/lori-patton-davis-joins-ohio-state-leadership-role/

Collins, P. H. (2013). *On intellectual activism.* Temple University Press.

Crenshaw, K. W. (1991). Mapping the margins: Intersectionality, identity politics and violence against women of color. *Stanford Law Review, 43*(6), 1241–1299. http://blogs.law.columbia.edu/critique1313/files/2020/02/1229039.pdf

Croom, N. N., & Patton, L. D. (2011). The miner's canary: A critical race perspective on the representation of black women full professors. *Negro Educational Review, 62/63*(1–4), 13–39.

Dumas, M. J. (2016). Against the dark: Antiblackness in education policy and discourse. *Theory Into Practice, 55*, 11–19. https://doi.org/10.1080/00405841.2016.1116852

Harris, J. C., & Patton, L. D. (2019). Un/Doing intersectionality through higher education research. *Journal of Higher Education, 90*(3), 347–372. https://doi.org/10.1080/00221546.2018.1536936

Haynes, C., Joseph, N. M., Patton, L. D., Stewart, S., & Allen, E. L. (2020). Toward an understanding of intersectionality methodology: A 30-year literature synthesis of Black women's experiences in higher education. *Review of Educational Research, 90*(6), 751–787. https://doi.org/10.3102/003465320946822

Jenkins, T. (Host). (2020, September 2). *Dear White people: Reimagining Whiteness in the struggle for racial equality*. In The Faculty Lounge. https://anchor.fm/toby-jenkins/episodes/Dear-White-People-Reimagining-Whiteness-in-the-Struggle-for-Racial-Equality-ej1f7b

Joseph, N. M., Hailu, M., & Boston, D. (2017). Black women's and girls' persistence in the P–20 mathematics pipeline: Two decades of children, youth, and adult education research. *Review of Research in Education, 41*(1), 203–227. https://doi.org/10.3102/0091732X16689045

Patton, L. D. (2009). My sister's keeper: A qualitative examination of mentoring experiences among African American women in graduate and professional schools. *The Journal of Higher Education, 80*(5), 510–537. https://doi.org/10.1353/jhe.0.0062

Patton, L. D. (2011). Perspectives on identity, disclosure, and the campus environment among African American gay and bisexual men at one historically Black college. *Journal of College Student Development, 52*(1), 77–100. https://doi.org/10.1353/csd.2011.0001

Patton, L. D. (2014). Preserving respectability or blatant disrespect?: A critical discourse analysis of the Morehouse College appropriate attire policy and implications for conducting intersectional research. *International Journal of Qualitative Studies in Education, 27*(6), 724–746. https://doi.org.10.1080/09518398.2014.901576

Patton, L. D. (2016a). Missing Black undergraduate women and the politics of disposability: A critical race feminist perspective. *The Journal of Negro Education, 85*(3), 330–349.

Patton, L. D. (2016b). Disrupting postsecondary prose: Toward a critical race theory of higher education. *Urban Education, 51*(3), 315–342. https://doi-org.libez.lib.georgiasouthern.edu/10.1177/0042085915602542

Patton, L. D., Blockett, R. A., & McGowan, B. L. (2020). Complexities and contradictions: Black lesbian, gay, bisexual, and queer students' lived realities across three urban HBCU contexts. *Urban Education*, 1–28. https://doi.org/10.1177/0042085920959128

Patton, L. D., & Bondi, S. (2015). Nice White men or social justice allies?: Using critical race theory to examine how White male faculty and administrators engage in ally work. *Race, Ethnicity, and Education, 18*(4), 488–514. https://doi.org/10.1080/13613324.1000289

Patton, L. D., & Croom, N. N. (2017). *Critical perspectives on Black women and college success.* Routledge.

Patton, L. D., & Haynes, C. (2018). Hidden in plain sight: The Black women's blueprint for institutional transformation in higher education. *Teachers College Record, 120*(14), 1–18.

Patton, L. D., Sanchez, B., Mac, J., & Stewart, D. L. (2019). An inconvenient truth about "progress": An analysis of the promises and perils of research on campus diversity initiatives. *The Review of Higher Education, 42,* 173–198. https://doi.org/10.1080/13613324.1000289

Patton, L. D., & Simmons, S. L. (2008). Exploring complexities of multiple identities of lesbians in a Black college environment. *Negro Educational Review, 59*(3–4), 197–215.

Shek, Y. L. (2011). Review: *Culture centers in higher education: Perspectives on identity, theory, and practice* edited by Lori D. Patton. *InterActions: UCLA Journal of Education and Information Studies, 7*(2), 1–4. https://doi.org/10.5070/d472000704

Solorzano, D., & Yosso, T. (2002). Critical race methodology: Counter-storytelling as an analytical framework for education research. *Qualitative Inquiry, 8*(23), 22–44. https://doi.org/10.1177/107780040200800103

Williams, K. L., Burt, B. A., Clay, K. L., & Bridges, B. K. (2018). Stories untold: Counter-narratives to anti-Blackness and deficit-oriented discourse concerning HBCUs. *American Educational Research Journal, 56*(2), 556–599. https://doi.org/ 10.3102/0002831218802776

14

EQUITY AND ADVOCACY

The Scholarship of Marybeth Gasman

Pietro A. Sasso, Cheron H. Davis, and Adriel A. Hilton

The scholarly examination of diverse institutional types such as minority serving institutions (MSIs) or historically Black colleges or universities (HBCUs) has largely been overlooked, especially those that serve students of color. But from James Anderson's seminal work on the history of Blacks in the South to the scholarship of Marybeth Gasman, the role of the HBCU and MSI has been solidified across American higher education. While disclosing their own positionality, the authors will review, interrogate, and offer a critique of this important area of scholarship. The chapter will conclude with reflective perspectives and recommendations that are particularly valuable for those who are interested in, and care about, the present and future of MSIs and HBCUs.

The authors of this chapter begin by disclosing their own positionality to better offer transparency regarding their assumptions and affiliations with MSIs and HBCUs. All three authors come from working-class backgrounds. The first author (Pietro A. Sasso) identifies as a cisgender, Latino male with a bicultural orientation. He has experience in constructing collaborative partnerships for graduate education between HBCUs and predominantly White institutions (PWIs), as well as professional experience working at an MSI. The second author (Cheron H. Davis) identifies as a cisgender Black female. Deeply connected to her African American familial roots, she now teaches at an HBCU after attending a PWI for college. The third author (Adriel A. Hilton) identifies as a cisgender Black male and attended HBCUs, where he earned all of his degrees, except for an additional graduate degree from a PWI.

Each author considers the constructs of ethnicity and culture through intersecting identities of race, gender, and social class. They acknowledge their privilege and power as well as the responsibility that comes with those identities to deconstruct internalized hegemonies and reconstruct new ways of being that promote social justice and liberation. They are committed to scholarship examining HBCUs and MSIs to creating equitable educational experiences for Black, Indigenous, and people of color (BIPOC) across PWI and HBCU settings. These positionalities allow the authors to provide a distinctive and nuanced perspective about the scholarly impact of Marybeth Gasman as a public intellectual. The last two authors are products of her mentorship and one is a product of her leadership development program. In this chapter, the authors will provide an overview of MSIs and HBCUs and highlight the scholarship and advocacy of Marybeth Gasman.

The role of HBCUs as incubators for Black intellectuals existed in isolation and liminality for much of the 19th century and was ignored by mainstream scholars. Research on HBCUs and other MSIs was not well explored and received little attention from higher education scholars beyond investigating the undergraduate student experience and student identity. However, Gasman's scholarship centers the pivotal place of the HBCU across the scope of American postsecondary education. Her research includes exploring the history of HBCUs, their philanthropic activities, inquiry into the student experience, and her perspectives on other MSI institutional types.

HBCUs were created to offer equity and advocacy for Black Americans who were largely excluded from American higher education (Allen, 1992; Fleming, 1984; Gurin & Epps, 1975; Nettles, 1988). Although racial integration began in the 1960s and some private colleges offered limited admissions, minority enrollment at public state-supported institutions were not common until the early 1970s, with the implementation of federal financial aid, especially the Pell Grant program (Pulliam & Sasso, 2016). Over time, the role of financial aid challenged the role of the HBCU as many Black students shifted their enrollment to public state-supported colleges and universities. HBCU enrollment dropped during the latter decades of the 20th century and into the early 21st century.

In the contemporary context, it is assumed that this enrollment change occurred because of increased access (Bensimon & Malcom, 2012). However, the idea of increased access is a facade because most colleges may not be set up for the holistic success of students of color (Fries-Britt & Turner, 2002; Museus & Jayakumar, 2012; Turner, 1994). Many of the educational three "P's" of policy, protocol, and procedure (such as affirmative action, bridge programs, and other educational opportunity programs) have been rolled back or now have unsustainable support (Sasso & Maldonado, 2015; Sasso et al., 2019). These approaches build capacity for enrollment for students of color and other marginalized communities and create pipelines to present a welcoming campus, particularly for Black students (Pulliam & Sasso, 2016).

HBCUs exist as a federal designation under the umbrella classification of the MSI program of the Department of Education in the Office of Postsecondary Education (OPE) under Title III of the Higher Education Act (HEA) of 1965. It is also a category under the Carnegie Classification System, which serves as the standard American institutional typology and nomenclature. These also include Hispanic serving institutions (HSI), tribal colleges and universities (TCU), Asian American and Pacific Islander serving institutions (AAPISIs), Alaska Native-serving institutions, Native Hawaiian–serving institutions, and Native–American-serving nontribal institutions, as well as predominantly Black colleges. To be classified as an MSI, an institution must enroll "significant percentages of undergraduate minority students" under part F of the HEA, "Investment in historically Black colleges and universities and other minority-serving institutions."

The Higher Education Act of 1965 originally defined an HBCU as

> any historically black college or university that was established prior to 1964, whose principal mission was, and is, the education of Black Americans, and that is accredited by a nationally recognized accrediting agency or association determined by the Secretary [of Education] to be a reliable authority as to the quality of training offered or is, according to such an agency or association, making reasonable progress toward accreditation. (Section 322[a])

There are currently just over 100 federally recognized HBCUs, including 2-year colleges. They comprise 3% of all American postsecondary institutions, enroll 16% of Black college students, and are credited with approximately one quarter of Black college graduates (Arroyo & Gasman, 2018).

HBCUs began with the founding of the Institute for Colored Youth (now Cheyney University) as a farm outside of Philadelphia in 1837. Lincoln University (Pennsylvania) was founded as the Ashmun Institute in 1854, and present-day Wilberforce University (Ohio) was founded as the first private HBCU in 1856 as a coeducational institution for those who escaped slavery through the Underground Railroad. The HBCU purpose has evolved from the early debate between W.E.B. Du Bois and Booker T. Washington on liberal versus vocational education to the "Atlanta Compromise," which advocated for the politics of respectability and accommodationism leading to a greater emphasis on industrial, applied, and professional education for Black undergraduates. Now they serve a contemporary role of advocacy and racial and economic uplift as a form of social mobility. The historical legacy in facilitating college access for Black college students is undeniable, as Allen (1992) suggests:

> In short, African-American students' relative lack of access to and success in U.S. higher education is not shrouded in mystery. It is the result of the same historical, political, economic, social, cultural, and psychological patterns that have perpetuated Black subjugation and oppression since Blacks arrived on these shores in 1619. (pp. 41–42)

On campuses that are now termed PWIs, Black students have been largely treated as "guests in the house" or as "academic immigrants" (Arroyo & Gasman, 2018). They have often lacked a sense of belonging and have not been granted full participation (Fries-Britt & Griffin, 2007; Seider & Hillman, 2011). Decades of qualitative research, consisting of focus groups and individual interviews, have suggested "an insufficient sense of belonging at the institution [that] stifles engagement and diminishes one's inclination to persist toward baccalaureate degree attainment" (Harper, 2009, p. 700). Even high-achieving and academically talented Black college students have continually self-reported having to justify their earned place within their academic institution, such as having to resist negative stereotypes and being expected to serve as spokespersons for their race (Fries-Britt & Griffin, 2007). Overall, at a PWI, Black students experience racism and feel ostracized (Fries-Britt & Turner, 2002; Novick et al., 2011).

The cultural cost of attending a PWI is often referred to as the *Black tax* (Prince, 2017). The constant experience of paying the Black tax often leads to battle fatigue; students must navigate microaggressions, systemic racism, and even instances of overt racism. In a response to negotiate this sense of racial battle fatigue, Allen (1992) notes, "Black students [at PWIs] often find it necessary to create their own social and cultural networks in order to remedy their exclusion from the wider, White-oriented university community" (p. 29). This is ironically similar to the systems of oppression and marginalization that facilitated the creation of HBCUs.

Black students often exist as second-class citizens at PWIs (Thompson et al., 2010). There are separate, inequitable outcomes among Black students and other marginalized populations (Latinx, Native American) at PWIs (Fries-Britt & Turner, 2002). There is a lack of equitable outcomes in climates of safety, relationships, teaching, and learning for these marginalized populations (Benismon & Malcom, 2012; Museus & Jayakumar, 2012). Allen (1992) conducted a seminal comparative study of 2,500 Black college students at PWIs and HBCUs that revealed little has changed in the decades since that research. However, at an HBCU there are differential outcomes for Black students as compared to a PWI. A main goal of the HBCU is to provide a sense of belonging, cultural transmission, and social mobility (Palmer & Gasman, 2008; Palmer et al., 2011).

Overview of MSIs and HBCUs

As the Jim Crow era continued to stymie the progress and evolution of Black southerners, they soon realized education was their most viable path to empowerment, opportunity, and achievable success. This awareness resulted in more than 90 institutions of higher learning being established between 1861 to 1900 to educate Black Americans. The Morrill Act of 1890 also facilitated this didactic endeavor as it required states, particularly former Confederate states, to provide land grants for Black educational institutions. Today, the U.S. Department of Education recognizes HBCUs, and with the Higher Education Act of 1965 and sequential reauthorizations, and reclassified them along with other MSIs, based on their Title IV identification, historical origin, and percentage of minority enrollment. The College Cost Reduction and Access Act of 2007, signed into law by President George W. Bush, further recognized MSIs to include Asian American and Pacific Islander colleges, Native American–serving, nontribal institutions, Hispanic-serving institutions, tribal colleges and universities, predominantly Black institutions, and those serving a majority student population of Alaskan/Hawaiian natives. This is important in that these educational institutions received much needed funding for teacher education, engineering and other academic curricula, tutoring, lab equipment, and STEM programming, as well as providing a large percentage of underrepresented and/or low-income students with federal financial aid or Pell Grants (National Association of Student Financial Aid Administrators [NASFAA], n.d.).

Without HBCUs and MSIs, many BIPOC would not be able to attain social mobility. This is fundamentally due to a cultural context that exists within MSIs that allows BIPOC access to academic and cocurricular experiences that often pose barriers or reduced capacities at a PWI. According to a report of the Center for Minority Serving Institutions (Gasman, 2013), these institutions provide diverse faculty and staff, which is particularly comforting to first-generation college students. They offer same-race role models and mentoring. MSIs provide environments that significantly enhance student learning by providing programs of study that challenge them, while also recognizing and addressing potential precollege academic underpreparation as a result of systemic educational inequities.

MSIs and HBCUs often introduce BIPOC students to civil activism and political mobilization as well as open students to a network that serves them professionally and personally through clubs, fraternities, sororities, community service, and other extracurricular activities. These institutions are dedicated to preparing the BIPOC student to be successful in the workforce, with many continuing on to earn graduate and professional degrees. Particularly, HBCUs are a cultural transmitter and repository of African American achievement, which is needed in the 21st century to advance and protect the diversity of the United States (Brown, 2001; Brown-Scott, 1994; Fleming, 1976; Hale, 2006; Morris et al., 1995; Williams & Ashley, 2004).

This role of the MSI, and specifically the HBCU, was often ignored due to racism and assumptions about their significance or relevance as PWIs opened access during the 1960s and into the early 1970s. Critics propounded a postracial critique of these institutions to suggest that the HBCU was no longer necessary because America had expanded college access through its loosely coupled system of higher education. However, this assumption has been challenged, thanks, in part, to the public discourse and scholarly publications of Marybeth Gasman.

The Scholarship of Marybeth Gasman

In a 2014 TedX talk, Gasman recounted her childhood experiences as a White woman from a working-class background who was raised in a racist home and a patriarchal community that told her the best she could aspire to be was a secretary. Gasman grew up on a farm in northern Michigan, the daughter of two working-poor parents and one of nine children. She often wore the hand-me-down clothes of others, and she depended on charitable donations about which others made fun of her lack of current fashions. Her father was a racist who blamed the economic hardships and marginalities of their family on "Black people." Her family did not necessarily understand that they were "poor" because they were White—an "impossibility" from their privileged perspective. Her family home was lost to fire when she was in eighth grade, and she sought solace in books. In high school, the messaging she received was that she should pursue careers that were more acceptable and traditional to women. Her high school counselor suggested that she should become a secretary because she could type rapidly.

Gasman's academic career began at St. Norbert College, where she found her way largely on her own accord. There were many barriers to her undergraduate education because she was a first-generation female from a low-income background. She attended Indiana University in Bloomington for her master's and doctoral programs, where she studied under the historian James Anderson.

Anderson is the author of *The Education of Blacks in the South, 1860–1935* (University of North Carolina Press, 1998), a seminal text that explores the history of southern Black education from Reconstruction to the Great Depression. The book focuses on both K–12 and higher education. It highlights the tensions with regard to the influences of Northern philanthropic groups on HBCUs and the Atlanta Compromise, where it specifically considers the significance of the Tuskegee Institute. This seminal work, coupled with existing gaps in the literature, influenced Gasman to produce more than 250 scholarly publications, including book chapters and journal articles as well as 25 texts. (A summary is included in the next paragraphs but is not included in the references list.)

These texts cover Blacks in STEM (Gasman & Nguyen, 2019), Black/African American studies, foundations of higher education, other different MSIs, HBCUs, and HBCUs' philanthropy in education. The philanthropy texts (Gasman & Bowman, 2011, 2013; Gasman & Sedgwick, 2005; Gasman, Anders & Anderson-Thompkins, 2003; Ginsberg & Gasman, 2007; Walton & Gasman, 2008) served as the initial foundation for much of her early scholarship. Gasman has also been prolific in terms of journal articles and book chapters. Her journal articles have been widely cited in the field of higher education, with more than 7,000 citations by other researchers (see Google Scholar), and they have been selected in many of the top-tier journals in the disciplines of education, teaching, and higher education.

Her earlier scholarship focuses on the history of HBCUs, especially Fisk University in Nashville. Fisk is one of the earliest HBCUs, founded immediately following the American Civil War. It was distinctive because of its commitment to the liberal arts compared to others that emphasized vocational or professional education.

Gasman's scholarship transitioned to HBCU and MSI philanthropy. Her scholarship has evolved to further describe other pieces of the HBCU culture and experience. These include exploring challenges in HBCU leadership or HBCU governance. Gasman has elucidated the HBCU student experience with regard to persistence factors and student success. She has also explored curriculum related to teacher preparation and STEM, including Black graduate education, medical education (Gasman et al., 2017), and Black law schools (Hilton et al., 2012, 2015).

Other areas of her research involve critical scholarship and interrogating issues of race. As a trained historian, some of her scholarship includes historical methods and social foundations of education (Gasman et al., 2015). Gasman has published with some of the foremost current scholars in higher education, including Shaun Harper, Laura Perna, Terrell Strayhorn, and John Thelin. Her scholarship includes more than 50 book chapters focused on National Pan-Hellenic Council (NPHC) fraternities and sororities, critical race theory, the HBCU experience, history of higher education, MSI issues, and many contributions to other texts in forewords and epilogues. What is most noteworthy is that a majority of her scholarship over the last 8 years has been coauthored with her own doctoral and other graduate students whom she has individually mentored. She can be credited with guiding approximately 10 current faculty members.

Therefore, her scholarly impact extends beyond the traditional boundaries of citations and numbers of publications by many other researchers. Her research impact is particularly evident in her disciplining and proliferating the study of the HBCU and MSI. This work established research on the HBCU as an area of scholarship within American higher education.

As a public intellectual, Gasman has translated her research for accessible use in public discourse, thus elevating public consciousness about HBCUs, particularly for important private foundations and other governmental decision-makers. She serves on a number of HBCU governing boards and those of other significant leadership associations. Gasman has authored over 450 opinion articles for the nation's newspapers and magazines in print and digital formats. Such output frequently led to her ranking as one of the 10 most influential education scholars in the nation by *Education Week*. (This is an annual ranking of the most prolific and impactful "thought leaders" who affect public discourse, policy, and practice.) The proliferation and range of her scholarship facilitates Gasman's participation in the public arena, reflecting her comfort with larger audiences, a hallmark of a public intellectual. That role is elucidated in the next section.

Scholarly Impact

A network analysis by Manuel Canché from the Rutgers Center for Minority Serving Institutions (2018) that measured the centrality of the scholarship on MSIs during 1955–2018 (1,333 total publications, 2,985 authors, and 5,074 collaborations in total) suggests that Gasman has had a significant impact as progenitor of that area of research. Her work has also contributed to her commitment to the preparation of faculty and educational leaders at HBCUs and MSIs through her research center initiatives. Gasman endeavors to empower her students, particularly those from minoritized populations, in such ways they realize they are capable of being change agents. Gasman has acknowledged in various public media interviews that she still teaches about systems of Whiteness as forms of oppression but does not privilege or center it in her scholarship. Gasman's purview extends beyond her publications and public discourse toward her efforts at founding and staffing a fully funded research center that further contributes to the study of MSIs and HBCUs.

Previously, Gasman founded the Center for Minority-Serving Institutions (CMSI) at the University of Pennsylvania. However, the center moved to Rutgers University when she became the Samuel Dewitt Proctor Endowed Chair in Education as a distinguished professor. At Rutgers, she is also the executive director of the Samuel Dewitt Proctor Institute for Leadership, Equity & Justice, which is a component of CMSI. These centers host faculty fellows, early career mentor programs, and leadership development initiatives for those who aspire to study and serve in administrative leadership positions at MSIs or HBCUs.

A number of programs, such as ELEVATE, which is a faculty development initiative, provide early-career MSI faculty with a unique professional development experience that supports, equips, and trains them to enrich learning, enhance visibility, and optimize resources. The ELEVATE alumni represent a diverse range of disciplines, and many have gone on to publish, present at conferences, or earn tenure and promotion at their respective institutions.

Another signature program of the CMSI is the Frederick Douglass Global Fellowship program. Intended to increase study abroad at MSIs, these scholarship funds cover 100% of the program fees and travel costs for 10 students from MSIs as they take part in a summer study-abroad program designed to enhance their leadership and intercultural skills. CMSI awards the study-abroad scholarship annually based on a combination of financial need, academic achievement, and nomination by the college president. The outreach from Gasman's CMSI reaches both early career professionals and minority students who are matriculating in bachelor's degree programs.

The MSI Aspiring Leaders and Presidential Leaders programs, supported by $825,000 from ECMC Foundation, the Kresge Foundation, Apple, Hewlett Packard (HP), Pinterest, Samsung, Intel, and the Penn Executive Doctorate in Higher Education Management program, bring together prominent MSI leaders to engage with midcareer aspiring leaders from education, nonprofit, and business sectors in an effort to prepare the next generation of MSI presidents. A brief glance at the list of presidential leaders highlights the likes of Michael Sorrell, the 34th president of Paul Quinn College; Elmira Mangum, the first female president in Florida A&M University's 130-year history; and Roslyn Clark Artis, the first female president in Benedict College's 148-year history.

These kinds of programs have impacted one of the authors of this chapter. Cheron H. Davis matriculated through the ELEVATE program. She further describes the impact of Gasman's scholarship through a brief first-person narrative.

Perspectives From Cheron H. Davis

Gasman recently posted pictures on her personal social media page of a cottage in which she and her daughter stayed on a road trip through rural Pennsylvania. I responded that it was reminiscent of the bed and breakfast where I stayed in Philadelphia during ELEVATE in 2015. I reminded her that the encounter with her, and everyone at CMSI, had such a profound impact on me. It had not only changed my life, but indeed the trajectory of my entire career.

Gasman's work as a scholar and a philanthropist, having not only written about but also having visited countless HBCUs, speaks to the commitment and embodiment of social justice that she carries with her in her daily life. She has taught me many lessons as a woman. One of these lessons includes using my voice to challenge patriarchy in the academy. Another is that it is important to face adversity with boldness.

When asking her to recount her career trajectory, she tells the story of conceptualizing the center. Her center originally was founded at the University of Pennsylvania as the Center for Minority Serving Institutions, which has since transitioned to Rutgers University. At Rutgers, it is a component of the Samuel DeWitt Proctor Institute for Leadership, Equity, & Justice. Gasman suggested that she wanted to begin a center that sponsors programming and disseminates research about MSIs. She initially hoped this would build a network of scholars and advance the research about MSIs. Several of her trusted mentors told her that because she was a woman, there would be significant barriers. Gasman has dispelled these barriers as a prolific scholar and public intellectual.

In fact, she would tell each of us that the capstone of her scholarship cannot be summed up in the minimal biography she offers up when requested. Gasman's work has been both intriguing and questionable to me, as a Black female scholar. I spent many hours as a rookie graduate student in awe of the star scholars in the field, catching glimpses of them at conferences, hoping for a handshake, wishing to get a business card, and only dreaming of meeting them in person.

A 2015 email from Adriel Hilton regarding a professional development opportunity for early career faculty at CMSI provided the perfect opportunity for me to ask Gasman the one question that had intrigued me since discovering she was White—"Why the hell do you care so much about Black students?" As I sat in a West Philly restaurant having dinner with Gasman, her teenage daughter, and a myriad of the most brilliant multicultural early career faculty of color from various MSIs across the country, she shared with me the parallels in our quest to find answers to questions; pointedly, the question she finally asked her father before he died was "Why did you hate Black people so much?"

A staunch proponent of MSIs, specifically HBCUs, Gasman is also a White woman who has never attended an MSI or HBCU. When asked in a 2019 Higher Ed Jobs Careers interview, "What keeps you engaged working in higher education in your areas of expertise?" she answered,

> I care about opportunity, justice, and equity. I grew up intensely poor without opportunity and only because of my uneducated mother and mentors (mainly people of color) did I move out of that poverty. Over the course of my life (even today), people have not believed in my potential. I want to ensure that others don't have that experience. HBCUs give opportunity to so many and that matters to me. (Hibel, 2019, para. 12)

Besides her strong belief in the importance of these schools, Gasman emphasizes the shifting demographics in higher education as another significant factor in justifying the pressing need for MSIs. The importance of teaching in inclusive ways is magnified as the landscape of diversity within classrooms continues to evolve and transform. In looking at student equity through the lens of critical race theory (CRT), Gasman stresses that an introspective look must be taken into account about what can be done to improve learning among all students. One bold illustration defines CRT as representing racial analysis, intervention, and critique of traditional civil rights theory on the one hand, and critical legal studies on the other (Crenshaw et al., 1995). If CRT is a surety within American life and institutions, then extraordinary measures must be taken to ensure that college teachers are prepared to meet the collective needs of an ever-changing, diverse student body.

Furthermore, the racial, class, and cultural parallels often found within MSIs can lead to a more equitable educational experience. Simply put, the backgrounds of minority students, as a result of slavery and multigenerational oppression, differ from their White counterparts and their education also needs to differ. This is what so clearly distinguishes the mantras and the missions of MSIs from that of PWIs. BIPOCs are more likely to feel embraced, empowered, and heard in these educational settings. Gasman gives an example of such student empowerment in that same 2019 interview:

> I've been on the campuses of 103 of the 105 HBCUs, and I think the feeling has to do with a combination of being surrounded by African-American history in such a pronounced and unapologetic way and seeing so many African-American students craving learning in one place. One of

the best examples I've seen is while visiting Xavier University of Louisiana. Xavier boasts generations of African Americans who are now doctors and large numbers of students who want to be doctors. When we talked to students at Xavier for our forthcoming book "Making Black Scientists" (Harvard University Press with Thai-Huy Nguyen), students told us that the faculty and staff at Xavier believe in them more than they even believe in themselves and that being surrounded by successful black alumni who are doctors is inspirational, even when filled with self-doubt. (Hibel, 2019, para. 9)

Thus, as our global society becomes more diverse, the need for MSIs and HBCUs will increase. As some of these schools continue to suffer setbacks like many other smaller 2- and 4-year colleges, Gasman's scholarship will serve as a lifeline within this particular educational sphere. Without allies from different races and backgrounds willing to help the cause, the uphill climb for HBCUs and MSIs will continue to be difficult.

What I realized during that conversation with Gasman at the ELEVATE dinner in 2015, and since, is that her commitment to her work around HBCU and MSI students is as much her professional role as it is a personal obligation she made to herself long ago at her dying father's bedside. She realized that, in those moments, there are humanistic opportunities for redemption, and that there is a space in the world for people to be tragically flawed, and yet still make a tremendous contribution to the greater good. I believe that our parallel missions to find answers converge on that very road—the road where human hearts meet the goal of changing the educational and career outcomes for marginalized students. Both Gasman and I found answers to our questions on that road. And I am inclined to believe that our travels are far from over. As a scholar and public intellectual, Gasman's travels will continue as she has persisted to provide answers in setting directionality for American higher education.

Future Directions and Thoughts

More than 10 years ago, Gasman was given some unsolicited career advice—namely, to drop her research on HBCUs because "research of this nature would be ghettoized" (Nealy, 2010, para. 1). At that time, Gasman was an associate professor at the University of Pennsylvania, hitting the lecture trail as the author of a new book, as well as having approximately hundreds of articles and book chapters on the subject in her academic and public intellectual corpus. She had even received an invitation from *The New York Times* to guest blog about HBCUs. Needless to say, staying true to herself, Gasman ignored that counseling and today is consistently ranked among the most influential scholars in America. However, her vast impact has also been wrought with critiques and detractors.

Gasman's career ascension has not come without its fair share of challenges and criticism. A simple Google search reveals these commentaries and criticisms. We, as authors, do not wish to gloss over what some would consider a mishap in Gasman's career. She has a prolific scholarly record; however, she cannot always control for her own positionality. Some fellow scholars and former students are quick to criticize her research and scholarly advocacy of MSIs and HBCUs. Nevertheless, none of this can invalidate her research and scholarly impact.

Furthermore, the authors do not seek to paint Gasman as a "White savior." Rather, she has always been very transparent about her positionality. And then there is the obvious—she is indeed a White woman who did not attend an HBCU but for which she is deemed an expert on its history and philanthropy. However, Gasman has taught at an MSI (Georgia State), served on several dissertation committees at HBCUs, was a commencement speaker at Jackson State (an HBCU), and gave guest lectures in numerous HBCU courses.

There is much gratitude for Gasman's scholarship, advocacy, and passion for HBCUs and MSIs, particularly as they incur difficult times. An article in *The New York Times,* "H.B.C.U.s' Sink-or-Swim Moment," discusses how these institutions are on the "brink of financial ruin" (Smith-Barrow, 2019). The article lists rising college costs, the student loan crisis, decreasing endowments, a 42% decline in federal funding, and plunging enrollment. It concludes that "a large majority of HBCUs are facing existential threats and will need to be transformed, reinvigorated to ensure their futures are as vibrant as their pasts" (Smith-Barrow, 2019, para. 5).

The year 2020 brought with it a global pandemic that some contend "has permanently changed higher education" (Rosowsky, 2020, para. 1). The *Forbes* article "Where Does Higher Education Go Next?" suggests that the pandemic has cost higher education hundreds of millions of dollars in 2020 alone (Rosowsky, 2020). Those with medical schools or large research infrastructures are reporting collective losses in the billions.

If the pandemic has had this kind of astronomical effect on large PWIs, one can only imagine the strain it has added to many of the nation's HBCUs and MSIs already dealing with financial difficulties. If ever HBCUs have had the need for an activist with the knowledge and influence of Marybeth Gasman, it is now. Her work helps to crystallize "views and positions on the definition of a degree, time and path to degree completion, admissions criteria, industry engagement, experiential education, and more" (Rosowsky,

2020, para. 8), particularly in terms of HBCUs and MSIs. According to the previously described *New York Times* article:

> Any school ultimately has three funding streams. Of those three, public sources (grants, and federal, state and local appropriations) for HBCUs have been slashed, private investment is low, and HBCUs' ability to raise tuition and fees—without either violating their core mission or suppressing the number of students who will even apply—is limited. (Smith-Barrow, 2019, para. 6)

Gasman helped emphasize the relevance of MSIs and HBCUs and their contribution to American higher education, yet their future still needs additional support.

Conclusion

The authors of this chapter attempted to foreground both MSI and HBCU institutions in this chapter by highlighting the scholarly impact and advocacy of Marybeth Gasman. Her influence is seen in both her research and leadership in developing emerging scholars programs. This chapter has not been singularly about her, but about how her scholarship has solidified the contributions and relevance of these venerable institutions. Moreover, if significant, rapid change in higher education is indeed in the future, then HBCUs and MSIs will not just need Marybeth Gasman but also the concerted efforts of those she has influenced. They will need to remain diligent in pressing legislators and news outlets on behalf of HBCUs and MSIs. The latter will require experienced voices in the rooms of administrators and board members who will be well-versed in conversation on a new age of education. Those voices should not just be from outside the MSI and HBCU campuses, but from within as well.

References

Allen, W. R. (1992). The color of success. African-American college student outcomes at predominantly White and historically Black public colleges and universities. *Harvard Educational Review, 62*(1), 26–44.

Arroyo, A. T., & Gasman, M. (2018). Toward an afrocentric expansion of the dynamic student development metatheodel for Black American students. In M. Frederick, P. A. Sasso, & J. Maldonado (Eds.), *The dynamic student development meta-theory: A new model for student success*. Peter Lang.

Bensimon, E. M., & Malcom, L. E. (Eds.). (2012). *Confronting equity issues on campus: Implementing the equity scorecard in theory and practice*. Stylus.

Brown, C. M., II. (2001). Collegiate desegregation and the public Black college: A new policy mandate. *The Journal of Higher Education, 72*(1), 46–62. https://doi.org.10.2307/2649133

Brown-Scott, W. (1994). Race consciousness in higher education: Does sound educational policy support the continued existence of historically Black colleges? *Emory Law Journal, 43*(1), 13–14.

Canché, M. (2018). *MSIs coauthor network, 2- and 4-year sector effects*. Rutgers Center for Minority Serving Institutions.

Crenshaw, K., Gotanda, N., Peller, G., & Thomas, K. (Eds.). (1995). *Critical race theory*. The New Press.

Fleming, J. (1976). *The lengthening shadow of slavery: A historical justification for affirmative action for Blacks in higher education*. Howard University Press.

Fleming, J. (1984). *Blacks in college*. Jossey-Bass.

Fries-Britt, S., & Griffin, K. (2007). The Black box: How high-achieving Blacks resist stereotypes about Black Americans. *Journal of College Student Development, 48*(5), 509–524. https://doi.org.10.1353/csd.2007-0048

Fries-Britt, S., & Turner, B. (2002). Uneven stories: Successful Black collegians at a Black and a White campus. *Review of Higher Education, 25*(3), 315–330. https://doi.org.10.1353/rhe2002/0012

Gasman, M. (2013). *The changing face of historically Black colleges and universities* [Report]. The Center for Minority Serving Institutions. https://cmsi.gse.rutgers.edu/sites/default/files/Changing_Face_HBCUs.pdf

Gasman, M., Nguyen, T-H., & Conrad, C. (2015). Lives intertwined: A primer on the history and emergence of minority serving institutions. *Journal of Diversity in Higher Education, 8*(2), 120–138. https://doi.org/10.1037/a0038386

Gasman, M. & Sedgwick, K. (Eds.). (2005). *Uplifting people: African American philanthropy and education*. Peter Lang.

Gasman, M., Smith, T., Regla, A., & Nguyen, T-H. (2017). Historically Black colleges and universities and the production of doctors. *AIMS Public Health, 4*(6), 579–589. https://doi.org/10.3934/publichealth.2017.6.579

Ginsberg, M. S. & Gasman, M. (2007). Collaborations for gender equity in the context of policy and system-wide change: An interview with the editors. In Ginsberg, A. E. & Gasman, M. (Eds.), *Gender and educational philanthropy*. Palgrave Macmillan.

Gurin, P., & Epps, E. G. (1975). *Black consciousness, identity and achievement: A study of students in historically Black colleges*. Wiley.

Hale, F. W., Jr. (2006). *How Black colleges empower Black students: Lessons for higher education*. Stylus.

Harper, S. R. (2009). Niggers no more: A critical race counternarrative on Black male student achievement at predominantly White colleges and universities. *International Journal of Qualitative Studies in Education, 22*(6), 697–712. https://doi.org/110.1080/0951839080333889

Hibel, A. (2019). *Why historically Black colleges and universities matter*. Higher Ed Jobs. https://www.higheredjobs.com/HigherEdCareers/interviews.cfm?ID=1858

Hilton, A., Gasman, M. & Wood, J. L. (2015). The impact of the one Florida initiative on Florida's public law schools: A critical race theory analysis. *Journal of Educational Foundations, 27*(3/4), 103–116.

Hilton, A., Gasman, M. & Wood, J. L, & Williams, M. (2012). The relevance of Black law schools. *Southern University Law Review, 40,* 145–156.

Higher Education Act of 1965, 20 U.S. Code § 1067q

Morris, A., Allen, W. R., Maurrasse, D., & Gilbert, D. (1995). White supremacy and higher education: The Alabama higher education desegregation case. *National Black Law Journal, 14*(1), 59–91.

Museus, S. D., & Jayakumar, U. M. (2012). *Creating campus cultures: Fostering success among racially diverse student populations.* Routledge.

National Association of Student Financial Aid Administrators. (n.d.). *Overview of the College Cost Reduction And Access Act (CCRAA).* https://www.nasfaa.org/news-item/2379/Overview_of_the_College_Cost_Reduction_And_Access_Act_CCRAA

Nealy, M. J. (2010). *Who is Marybeth Gasman?* https://www.diverseeducation.com/article/13940/

Nettles, M. (Ed.). (1988). *Toward Black undergraduate student equality in American higher education.* Greenwood.

Novick, S., Seider, S., & Huguley, J. (2011). Engaging college students from diverse backgrounds in community service learning. *Journal of College & Character, 12*(1), 1–8. https://doi.org/10.2202/1940.1639.1767

Palmer, R. T., Davis, R., & Maramba, D. C. (2011). The impact of family support for African American males at an historically Black university: Affirming the revision of Tinto's theory. *Journal of College Student Development, 52,* 577–597. https://doi.org.10.1353/csd.2008.0002

Palmer, R. T., & Gasman, M. (2008). It takes a village to raise a child: The role of social capital in promoting academic success for African-American men at a Black college. *Journal of College Student Development, 49*(1), 52–70. https://digitalcommons.odu.edu/ape/vol2/iss2/7

Prince, J. T. (2017). "Can I touch your hair?" Exploring double binds and the Black tax in law school. *Penn Law: Legal Scholarship Repository, 20*(1), 29–49.

Pulliam, N., & Sasso, P. A. (2016). Building institutional capacity for college access and success: Implications for enrollment management. *Journal of Higher Education Politics & Economics, 2*(1), 1–37.

Rosowsky, D. (2020.) Where does higher education go next? *Forbes.* https://www.forbes.com/sites/davidrosowsky/2020/09/05/where-does-higher-education-go-next/?sh=674a89549b74

Sasso, P. A., & Maldonado, J. (2015). The effectiveness of U.S. summer bridge programs in supporting minority student college admissions. In V. Stead (Ed.), *International perspectives on higher education admission policy* (pp. 222–233). Peter Lang.

Sasso, P. A., Nasser, M., & Price-Williams, S. (2019). Improving bridge programs on American college and university campuses. In P. Blessinger, J. Hoffman, & M. Makhanya (Eds.), *Strategies for facilitating inclusive campuses in higher education: International perspectives on equity and inclusion* (pp. 197–207). Emerald Publishing.

Seider, S. C., & Hillman, A. (2011). Challenging privileged college students' othering language in community service learning. *Journal of College & Character*, *12*(3), 1–7. https://doi.org/10.2202/1940.1639.1810

Smith-Barrow, D. (2019). H.B.C.U.s' sink-or-swim moment. *The New York Times*. https://www.nytimes.com/2019/10/21/opinion/hbcu-college.html

Thompson, K. V., Lightfoot, N. L., Castillo, L. G., & Hurst, M. L. (2010). Influence of family perceptions of acting white on acculturative stress in African American college students. *International Journal for the Advancement of Counseling*, *32*(2), 144–152. https://doi.org/10.2202/1940.1639.1810

Turner, C. (1994). Guests in someone else's house: Students of color. *Review of Higher Education*, *17*, 355–370.

U.S. Department of Education. (n.d.). *White House Initiative on historically Black colleges and universities*. https://sites.ed.gov/whhbcu/one-hundred-and-five-historically-black-colleges-and-universities/

Walton, A. & Gasman, M. (2008). *Philanthropy, volunteerism, and foundraising in higher education*. Pearson.

Williams, J., & Ashley, D. (2004). *I'll find a way or make one: A tribute to historically Black colleges and universities*. HarperCollins.

15

AFFIRMATIVE ACTION IN HIGHER EDUCATION

The Perspectives of Randall Kennedy

William L. Nuckols and Dennis E. Gregory

Affirmative action in the United States and American higher education has been a shifting subject since its inception. Created by legislation and shaped by jurisprudence, affirmative action has tried to address the racial inequality that has scarred American history. This chapter will discuss affirmative action as a policy and then discuss how this policy is viewed by public intellectual Randall Kennedy. Before doing so, however, we provide a brief overview of the history of affirmative action so that readers can understand its development and how it stands today. We hope this will allow them to understand the impact of affirmative action and to better comprehend why Kennedy views it as he does. Readers can then decide whether they agree with how this policy is interpreted by this important figure in American legal thought.

A History of Affirmative Action in Higher Education

The term *affirmative action* first appeared in 1961 when President John F. Kennedy created the Committee on Equal Employment Opportunity (Carlton, 2020). It came into common use in 1966 when President Lyndon Johnson, in an executive order, wrote that federal contractors must "take affirmative action to ensure that applicants are employed, and that employees are treated during employment, without regard to their race, color, religion, sex, or national origin" (Exec. Order No. 11246, 1965). Subsequently, President Nixon and other presidents sought to create affirmative action as it applied to federal employees and contractors. Affirmative action came into the higher education lexicon in the late 1960s as part of efforts by selective universities to provide more diversity in their student bodies (Carlton, 2020). A listing of major decisions related to affirmative action, in both the workplace and higher education, may be found at History of Affirmative Action (AAAED, n.d.).

The first legal challenge related to affirmative action came in 1971 in *DeFunis v. Odegaard* (1974). Here, DeFunis applied to the University of Washington Law School but was denied admission. He claimed that he was denied based upon his race and asked for injunctive relief from the Washington state court, claiming that the decision was in violation of the Equal Protection Clause of the 14th Amendment to the United States Constitution. Relief was granted by the court and DeFunis began his legal study. On appeal, the Supreme Court of Washington reversed the lower court. By this time, DeFunis was in his 2nd year of law school. DeFunis sought to appeal his case to the U.S. Supreme Court, which granted *certiorari* in November of 1973. The case was not heard by the Court until November of 1974 when DeFunis was in his 3rd and final year. During oral arguments, counsel for the University of Washington indicated that whatever the Court decided, DeFunis would be allowed to complete his final year. As a result, because the case was not a class action, the Court found it to be moot. In his dissent, joined by Justice William Brennan, Justice William O. Douglas argued that the case was not moot and laid out the basic argument for affirmative action in cases to come.

In the late 1970s, *Regents of the University of California v. Bakke* (1978) was decided by the Supreme Court. Here, Bakke had been rejected from the medical school of the University of California, Davis, on two occasions. He argued that he was denied admission in violation of the Equal Protection Clause of the 14th Amendment and of the Civil Rights Act (1964, Title VI). While rejecting the regents' use of race in admissions decisions due to use of a quota system, the Court upheld the use of race as one factor in admission decisions and noted that colleges and universities have a compelling state interest in diversity among their student bodies. Thus, affirmative action programs that complied with this later principle were legally permissible.

In 1995, the Regents of the University of California voted to end affirmative action in admissions, and the next year California passed Proposition 209 (1996), which abolished all affirmative action in the state (AAAED, n.d). In 2020, another ballot referendum that would have removed this amendment to the California Constitution was rejected by voters (Nieves, 2020).

During the 1990s and early 2000s, a series of affirmative action cases was decided in circuit courts around the country. In the 5th Circuit, *Hopwood v. Texas* (1996) ruled that affirmative action was not a compelling state interest and that affirmative action was thus a violation of the Fourteenth Amendment. However, in the Ninth Circuit, *Smith v. University of Washington Law School* (2000) upheld the legality of affirmative action as laid out in *Bakke,* and this decision was reaffirmed in 2004 (Smith, 2004). These two examples describe the range of opinions on affirmative action.

In order to decide the issue on a national level, the Supreme Court agreed to hear two cases from the University of Michigan: *Gratz v. Bollinger* (2003), which dealt with affirmative action in its College of Literature, Science, and the Arts, and *Grutter v. Bollinger* (2003), which dealt with affirmative action in admission to its law school.

In a 6–3 ruling in *Gratz* written by Chief Justice William Rehnquist, the Court ruled that the admission process in the undergraduate college was not "narrowly tailored" enough to meet the strict scrutiny standard of consideration and was thus unconstitutional (i.e., in violation of the 14th Amendment and Title VI of the Civil Rights Act of 1964). This was true because the admissions policy did not include individual consideration of applicants, but rather put them into categories, which meant that "nearly every" minority applicant was admitted. There were multiple concurring and dissenting opinions in the case.

In *Grutter v. Bollinger* (2003), Justice Sandra Day O'Conner delivered the ruling of a 5–4 Court, holding that neither the 14th Amendment nor Title VI prohibited the use of a narrowly tailored affirmative action plan by the University of Michigan Law School. She noted that it did involve a deeply individualized consideration of each candidate and what the candidate might offer to the diversity of the student body. O'Connor wrote of the need for all races and ethnicities to participate in the civic engagement arena of the United States, and that such inclusion was essential for the realization of the American dream. She cautioned, however, that higher education needed to deal with the issue of diversity and race in admissions and noted that a time would come when affirmative action would no longer be allowed.

In a related case, *Schutte v. Coalition to Defend Affirmative Action* (2014), the Court ruled that the State of Michigan could amend its constitution to prohibit all sex- and race-based preferences (e.g., affirmative action) in public matters such as admissions. Such an amendment would not violate the Equal Protection Clause of the 14th Amendment. This came as a result of a 2006 amendment, which did just that.

In 2012, the Supreme Court heard *Fisher v. University of Texas at Austin* (2013). Here, petitioner Fisher was rejected from admission to the University of Texas. She was not in the top 10% of her high school class, and thus did not qualify to be admitted under the Texas "Top 10 Percent Law," which guaranteed admission to all Texas high school graduates in the top 10% of their high school class. She claimed that the affirmative action process followed by the university unconstitutionally caused less well-qualified minority students to be admitted before her. The lower courts upheld the decision by the university, citing earlier legal precedent. The Supreme Court, however, reversed this decision and sent the case back to the lower courts for reconsideration. It did so because it believed that the lower courts had not appropriately considered the case by not using the concept of strict scrutiny. The latter is necessary to uphold affirmative action policies as being narrowly tailored, as required by previous case law.

The case returned to the Court in 2015 (*Fisher v. Texas*, 2016) and came to be known as "Fisher 2." Justice Anthony Kennedy wrote the opinion for a 4–3 majority (Justice Antonin Scalia had passed away before the opinion and Justice Elena Kagen took no part in the case). Kennedy's opinion indicated that the lower courts had used strict scrutiny in its recent consideration of the UT affirmative action program and rejected Fisher's arguments that the policy violated the 14th Amendment. Thus, the Court upheld the University of Texas policy and affirmative action.

More recently, the 1st Circuit ruled on a case in which Asian students claimed that Harvard College violated Title VI of the Civil Rights Act of 1964 and that, by using an affirmative action admissions process, discriminated against Asian students. Here, the Court ruled in favor of Harvard and said that its admission policies, using race as one factor in admissions, was legal and not in violation of Title VI (*Students for Fair Admissions v. President & Fellows of Harvard College*, 2020). The Justice Department, under President Donald Trump, filed a petition to have the case heard by the Supreme Court, but that petition was withdrawn by the Justice Department, under President Joseph Biden, after the 2020 election. A similar lawsuit is being considered against Yale University, and Students for Fair Admissions (2020) is considering whether it should move forward with its appeal without the support of the Justice Department (*United States v. Yale University*, 2021).

The Randall Kennedy Perspective

Few intellectuals and scholars have been as vocal on the social, political, and legal approaches to race and equality in the United States as Randall Kennedy. With nearly 140 publications on the topic, an academic career could be well spent analyzing his works alone. For the sake of thrift, the majority of this analysis comes from his *For Discrimination: Race, Affirmative*

Action, and the Law (2013). When weighing the evolution of affirmative action in the United States, Kennedy recognizes several stages of historical development and applies them to the pertinent cases mentioned earlier (Kennedy, 2013). During the developmental periods of affirmative action, race theories have changed and challenged policy, both in society and higher education. Throughout his analysis of the relevant issues, Kennedy (2013) skillfully balances the viewpoints of a color-blind constitutionalist who is critical of various aspects of affirmative action and a social realist who recognizes that until America genuinely achieves true equal opportunity, it is a necessity.

Laying the Groundwork: The Constitution, Civil Rights, and Equality

For 155 years, America has attempted to right its path toward equality. That path has seen policies designed to promote equality continuously met with resistance. When the Civil Rights Act (1866) was vetoed by President Andrew Johnson, he claimed that a declaration granting citizenship to all people born in the United States gave "discriminating protections to colored persons" (Johnson, 1866, para. 6). Kennedy (2013) points out that the act was not color-blind. Rather, it was *race-sensitive* in that its primary objective was to specifically help elevate the legal status of African Americans. One could easily determine that this act displayed the foundation of modern-day affirmative action since it was not *race-blind* (Kennedy, 2013).

The debate and progression of America's foundation for affirmative action expanded over the next 70 years, moving from the ratification of the 14th Amendment and issues of citizenship in 1868 to those of economic and employment concerns (Kennedy, 2013). While race segregation under *Plessy v. Ferguson* (1896), with its premise of "separate but equal," was the law for much of the country, federal and state laws were eventually enacted to address racial discrimination in the workplace. President Franklin Roosevelt signed Executive Order 8802 (1941) to prevent discrimination in the defense industry, and 4 years later, New York passed the Ives-Quinn Act (New York Law Against Discrimination, 1945), which prohibited discrimination on the basis of race, creed, color, or national origin in the work place (Kennedy, 2013). This state law applied to all "employers, labor organizations, employment agencies, or other persons" (Lichtash, 1945, p. 170). These race-sensitive policies came complete with government enforcement agencies and were immediately attacked by segregationists and constitutional originalists. The objections asserted that the laws encouraged racial favoritism, quota hiring of African Americans, and discrimination "in favor of the Negro" (as cited in Kennedy, 2013).

The civil rights era spanned the 1950s and 60s, fueled by the end of government-supported segregation, federal prohibition of racial discrimination in the workplace, and federal condemnation of voter disenfranchisement (Civil Rights Act, 1964; Kennedy, 2013; Voting Rights Act of 1965). When the Supreme Court, in *Brown v. Board of Education of Topeka* (1954), determined that separate was "inherently unequal" and in violation of the 14th Amendment, there was a sense of a turning of the tide (although there was no timeframe for compliance). A later ruling in *Brown II* only directed states to act with "all deliberate speed" (*Brown v. Board of Education of Topeka*, 1955; Kennedy, 2013). This lack of guidance proved in practice to be *merely suggestive* as many southern states took a passive approach to desegregation by simply removing race restrictions in public schools. This simple approach resulted in Black students remaining in Black schools and White students remaining in White schools, and required the Supreme Court to address de facto segregation in *Green v. County School Board of New Kent* (1968).

The ruling in *Green* (1968) required the schools in Virginia (and other states with similar legislation and results) to actively address their issues of inequality and segregation with race-conscious policy that would deliver the results of an integrated system that ultimately provided equal opportunities (Kennedy, 2013). As the federal courts and policymakers addressed issues of equality, with a focus on race-sensitive outcomes, much of the United States acknowledged that African Americans for centuries had been "hobbled by chains" and it was improper to simply pass laws declaring equality in the workplace, schools, and in society and expect the results to illustrate that equality (Exec. Order No. 11246, 1965; Kennedy, 2013). The lack of direction from the federal officials generating the policies left state and local agencies to produce affirmative action programs that attempted to achieve equal opportunity.

Quotas and "Goals, Targets, and Timetables"

With little to no guidance from the federal government regarding *how* to successfully create and implement affirmative action programs, universities, employers, and hiring agencies generated their own goals and methods to exhibit their successes in the recruitment and retention of Black employees and students (Kennedy, 2013; Kotlowski, 1998, 2001). Notwithstanding the theories regarding his motives (political gain, impact costs of construction, or sincerity), President Nixon eventually supported some local affirmative action plans and directed federal resources toward them—most notably, the Philadelphia Plan (Kennedy, 2013; Kotlowski, 1998, 2001). The first draft of the plan had requirements from the Labor Department for contractors to meet certain quotas in the hiring of African American workers. That requirement was incredibly unpopular and was later amended (Kotlowski, 1998).

With the model of *quotas with penalties for noncompliance* failing to gain support, the words of Assistant Secretary of Labor Arthur Fletcher harnessed the spirit of affirmative action without offending employers when he said, "We must set goals, targets, and timetables . . . the way we put a man on the moon" (Kennedy, 2013, p. 52). Although the Philadelphia Plan was one model of affirmative action in contractor employment, many others adopted some form of it because it gave credibility to affirmative action with government support and initiated goal-setting policies for government contractors (Kennedy, 2013; Kotlowski, 1998, 2001). By the early 1970s, it appeared that a precedent for the expectations and policies for achieving equality in America had finally been outlined—only to be continuously litigated for the next 45 years.

Policy Discussion

As the United States identified issues of equality in the workplace, education, and social relations, the concept of affirmative action had been tasked with great expectations in the face of shifting sentiments and mission creep. Kennedy (2013) justifies affirmative action by identifying its goals and how they have become entangled with the political and legal realms over the past 60 years. Throughout that time, the path of affirmative action has not followed a direct route, as its policy definitions have been continually recalibrated to pass constitutional muster.

Whether the original intent behind affirmative measures was to make *reparations* for centuries of slavery, segregation, Jim Crow, and permissive racism; to encourage *diversity* in organizations and society; to encourage *integration*; or to *counter ongoing prejudice*, all are viable grounds in the policy debate (Kennedy, 2013). There have been objections and pushback to each of these reasons that have sparked emotions throughout generations. As we have seen, the Court has as much reflected the sentiment of the era as they have helped shape affirmative action. From a broad perspective, Kennedy (2013) believes that affirmative action has been directly and indirectly successful in assisting racial minorities in the United States, and in moving America toward the goal of equality.

Reparations

The concept of "reparations" seems to generate a great deal of opposition and is considered to be "the single most compelling justification for racial affirmative action" (Kennedy, 2013, p. 78). So why the disconnect? If reparations are justified and, on balance, affirmative action has been successful in moving minorities in the United States toward a more equal existence, why the opposition? Much stems from how *reparations* has been defined. Yesterday's wrongs can become tomorrow's wrongs if they are not addressed, regardless of whether reparations are called "rectification, restitution, remediation, correction, [or] compensation" (p. 79).

Much of the contention with reparations stems from the claim that today's beneficiaries of affirmative action are not the *actual* victims of slavery or Jim Crow-era segregation (Karst & Horowitz, 1974; Kennedy, 2013). This objection is often joined by the additional thought that White people who weren't involved in the atrocities of slavery or segregation are somehow victims of *reverse discrimination*, or are paying for the wrongs of prior generations (Kennedy, 2013; Scalia, 1979). However, Kennedy points out that the damaging remnants of segregation are still visible today, and nearly all African Americans in the United States have directly experienced racism or its effects in their lifetimes (Appiah, 2011; Kennedy, 2013).

Another issue that is relevant to reparations is that, in practice, affirmative action programs benefit those in a class more likely to take advantage of its opportunities (Kennedy, 2013). In the case of higher education, minority youth living in poor conditions are unlikely to benefit from most admissions programs since many do not graduate from high school (Kennedy, 2013). Where policies are designed to encourage minority admissions, many elite universities see viable candidates turn down the opportunity in lieu of less expensive schools for several reasons, including debt avoidance (Malamud, 2011). Policies in support of affirmative action should consider not only the racial inequities in the United States, but also socioeconomic status and class differences in order to increase their overall success (Kennedy, 2013; Malamud, 2011). Reparation to make up for injuries that put minorities at a competitive disadvantage is the primary purpose of affirmative action, and Kennedy (2013) believes the supporting discussion far outweighs the opposition.

Diversity

Another purpose or justification for affirmative action programs is the recognition and promotion of the value added to an organization, whether a business or a university, from a diverse population of students, employees, and leadership. Although the concept of diversity existed prior to *Bakke* (1978),

Justice Powell's declaration that racial selectivity in university admissions is justified in the pursuit of the compelling interest of achieving a diverse student body brought the initiative into the limelight in organizational recruitment (Kennedy, 2013). The new focus on *diversity* made discussions of affirmative action more socially acceptable, changing the conversation from yesterday's injustices to tomorrow's goals (Kennedy, 2013; Wood, 2003).

The softer conversation of an inclusive future that produces better goods and services from a united and educated populace invited skeptics and naysayers, but it sounded better than quotas to correct hundreds of years of racism (Kennedy, 2013; Wood, 2003). T.H. Anderson (2004) challenges the tradition of meritocracy that viewed affirmative action beneficiaries as the receivers of special treatment who took the place of those possibly more qualified. Instead, he views it as providing a less stigmatized image of an incredible value added to an organization by contributing diversity to the discussions, ranks, performance, and outcomes.

Kennedy (2013) has doubts regarding the overall impact of diversity initiatives, and his skepticism is not without support. Diversity initiatives are difficult to measure to show overall scientific impact. There are also concerns regarding the candor of the message—that is, is the institution practicing what it preaches? However, whether an institution is sincere in its diversity mission—or whether it is used to fashionably avoid litigation or to sidestep discussions of continuing racial and economic equality—benefits have also been observed. The educational setting has been enhanced by diversity in classrooms and faculty ranks. Uniformity of race, culture, and educational approach can ignore the perspectives of other cultures and customs and make diversity a good (but not great) justification for affirmative action (Kennedy, 2013).

Integration and Countering Ongoing Racism
The race-conscious measures that have emerged from affirmative action are credited as a promotor of racial integration and a means to keep racist policies at bay (E. Anderson, 2010; Kennedy, 2013). These measures are usually not clearly defined, but are hinted at in policy, blanketed by sentiment in speeches, and constitutionally mentioned *in dicta* of judicial opinions (*Grutter v. Bollinger*, 2003; Kennedy, 2013). As new generations of multiple races and ethnic groups learn together, work together, live near one another, and contribute on a similar scale to the advancement of society, then America has indeed moved closer to a more integrated society, partially due to equality initiatives from affirmative action.

Kennedy (2013) notes that antidiscrimination efforts have been marginally enhanced by affirmative action policies and legislation. He further indicates the lack of enforcement of local, state, and federal laws regarding discrimination, combined with the burden of the victims' fight, as grounds for the negligible impact of affirmative action on discrimination. Although the Court in *Grutter* (2003) and *Fisher* (2016) has recognized the need for race-affirmative policy, there are still perceptions of *reverse racism* that are sometimes expressed in terms of serious social costs (Sniderman & Piazza, 1993). In the case of university admissions, it must be recognized that the positive traits often attributed to gaining access (knowledge, intelligence, grade point average, test scores, etc.) are often the result of social, economic, and community conditions that are greater than the individual, and (to some extent) a result of the constructed privilege of being White (Kennedy, 1989, 2013). When an institution chooses to admit candidates who are racial minorities, the achievement is often scarred by an assumption that they took the place of White candidates with greater academic merit (Kennedy, 2013).

Stigma

The blemish on the perceived value of achievement in the face of affirmative action affects accomplished racial minorities *whether or not* they received any benefit from the policy (Kennedy, 2013). Even as universities institute policies to address systemic disadvantages, the feeling of being "the best Black" admitted, promoted, or hired has persisted and caused many proficient scholars and professionals to struggle with the scars of impostor syndrome (Carter, 1991; Hawley, 2019; Kennedy, 2013). To address this stigma in academics and in the workplace, entrance testing should be reevaluated to ensure that knowledge and skill are measured adequately and conditions that continue to display racial disparities are removed (Kennedy, 2013). With better measurables, the student and employee will see greater success and less social and internal stigma.

Conclusion

The path that affirmative action has taken in the United States has merged heavily with considerations of equality and diversity in higher education. Perhaps the road could have been more direct if America were able to fully address the racial atrocities of the past. Ever since *Brown* (1954) failed to reckon with America's history of racism and its support (or permissive allowance) of segregation (possibly to gain greater support and ultimately a unanimous decision), the Court's tacit interest has been in race-affirmative judicial policy-making that blurs the past in order to face less resistance moving forward (Kennedy, 2013, 2019).

History has clearly displayed that when a leave-alone policy is administered with indifference toward racial inequality, the results will always favor White America to the detriment of minority communities. As a procedural tool, constitutional color-blindness can be effective in moving toward goals of equality. However, it is a fallacy to think that a policy for equal access with a goal that disregards race will be successful in effectively achieving its desired outcomes (Kennedy, 2013).

Kennedy (2013) is clear that the *Bakke* decision created a policy in which benign race discrimination was acceptable as one aspect of admissions. The movement toward diversity initiatives was a compromise by Justice Powell that limited the condemnation of a racist history and discussions of reparations and the social fallout that would follow. This accommodation was most likely offered to reduce animosity in the public eye and encourage buy-in moving forward (Kennedy, 2013).

The rulings in *Grutter* and *Gratz* endorsed the diversity discussion from *Bakke* and added the strict scrutiny standard that any program that considered race for the sake of diversity must be narrowly tailored (Kennedy, 2013). The additional focus on scrutiny strengthened *Bakke* and added a sunsetting possibility (potentially enhancing the public relations aspects as well) with the expectation that by 2028 benign discrimination would be unnecessary. In *Fisher* (2016), the Court maintained affirmative action in higher education, but there is some apprehension remaining from the 25-year timeframe mentioned in *Grutter*. Kennedy (2013) is adamant that a time limit stated *in dicta* should not obstruct affirmative action measures, which should continue as long as necessary to achieve the goal of true equality.

References

American Association for Access, Equity and Diversity. (n.d.). *More history of affirmative action policies from the 1960s*. https://www.aaaed.org/aaaed/History_of_Affirmative_Action.asp

Anderson, E. (2010). *The imperative of integration*. Princeton University Press.

Anderson, T. H. (2004). *The pursuit of fairness: A history of affirmative action*. Oxford University Press.

Appiah, K. A. (2011). "Group rights" and racial affirmative action. *Journal of Ethics*, 15(3), 265–280. https://www.jstor.org/stable/pdf/41486914.pdf?refreqid=excelsior%3A89a349b85f88a8d134076f1862e75e9c

Brown v. Board of education of Topeka, 347 U.S. 483 (1954)

Brown v. Board of Education of Topeka, 349 U.S. 294 (1955)

Carlton, G. (2020, August 10). *A history of affirmative action in college admissions*. Best Colleges. https://www.bestcolleges.com/blog/history-affirmative-action-college/

Carter, S. L. (1991). *Reflections of an affirmative action baby*. Basic Books.

Chen, A. S. (2006). The Hitlerian rule of quotas: Racial conservatism and the politics of fair employment legislation in New York state, 1941–1945. *Journal of American History*, *92*(4), 1238–1264. https://doi.org/10.2307/4485890

Civil Rights Act, 14 Stat. 27-30 (1866)

Civil Rights Act of 1964, Pub. L. No. 88-352, 78 Stat. 241 (1964)

Civil Rights Act of 1964, Title VI, 42 U.S.C. § 2000d et seq.

DeFunis v. Odegaard, 416 U.S. 312 (1974)

Exec. Order No. 8802 (1941, June 25)

Exec. Order No. 11246, 3 C.F.R. 395 (1965). https://www.dol.gov/agencies/ofccp/executive-order-11246/as-amended

Fisher v. University of Texas, 570 U.S. 297 (2013)

Fisher v. University of Texas, 579 U.S. ___ (2016)

Gratz v. Bollinger, 594 U.S. 244 (2003)

Green v. County School Board of New Kent County, 391 U.S. 430 (1968)

Grutter v. Bollinger, 539 U.S. 306 (2003)

Hawley, K. (2019). I—What is impostor syndrome? *Aristotelian Society Supplementary Volume*, *93*(1), 203–226. https://doi.org/10.1093/arisup/akz003

Hopwood v. Texas, 78 F.3d 932 (5th Cir. 1996)

Johnson, A. (1866, March 27). *Veto message on civil rights legislation* [Transcript]. https://millercenter.org/the-presidency/presidential-speeches/march-27-1866-veto-message-civil-rights-legislation

Karst, K. L., & Horowitz, H. W. (1974). Affirmative action and equal protection. *Virginia Law Review*, *60*(6), 955–974. https://www.jstor.org/stable/pdf/1072364.pdf?refreqid=excelsior%3A03f9bce059f025139bed666ba3f8c50f

Kennedy, R. L. (1989). Racial critiques of legal academia. *Harvard Law Review*, *102*(8), 1745–1819. https://doi.org/10.2307/1341357

Kennedy, R. L. (2013). *For discrimination: Race, affirmative action, and the law*. Pantheon.

Kennedy, R. L. (2019). Derrick Bell and me. *Harvard Public Law Working Paper*, *19*(13). http://dx.doi.org/10.2139/ssrn.3350497

Kotlowski, D. J. (1998). Richard Nixon and the origins of affirmative action. *The Historian*, *60*(3), 523–541. https://www.jstor.org/stable/24451639

Kotlowski, D. J. (2001). *Nixon's civil rights: Politics, principle, and policy*. President and Fellows of Harvard College.

Lichtash, T. (1945). Ives Quinn Act—The law against discrimination. *St. John's Law Review*, *2*(19), 170–176. https://scholarship.law.stjohns.edu/cgi/viewcontent.cgi?article=5226&context=lawreview

Malamud, D. C. (2011). Class privilege in legal education: A response to Sander. *Denver University Law Review*, *88*, 729. https://digitalcommons.du.edu/dlr/vol88/iss4/6/

New York Law Against Discrimination "Ives-Quinn Act" 1945, NY Exec. Law §§125–136

Nieves, A. (2020, November 4). *California voters reject affirmative action measure despite summer of protest*. Politico. https://www.politico.com/states/california/story/2020/11/04/california-voters-reject-affirmative-action-measure-despite-summer-of-activism-9424555

Plessy v. Ferguson, 163 U.S. 537 (1896)
Proposition 209 (Cal. Constitution, Article 1, § 31, 1996)
Regents of the University of California v. Bakke, 428 US 912 (1978)
Scalia, A. (1979). The disease as a cure: "In order to get beyond racism, we must first take account of race." *Washington University Law Quarterly, 1979*(1), 147–157. https://openscholarship.wustl.edu/cgi/viewcontent.cgi?article=2507&context=law_law-review
Schutte v. Coalition to Defend Affirmative Action, 573 U.S. 291 (2014)
Smith v. University of Washington Law School, 233 F.3d 1188 (9th Cir., 2000)
Smith v. University of Washington Law School, 392 F.3d 367 (9th Cir., 2004)
Sniderman, P. M., & Piazza, T. (1993). *The scar of race.* Harvard University Press.
Students for Fair Admissions vs. President and Fellows of Harvard College, 980 F.3d 157 (1st Cir., 2020)
United States v. Yale University, 3:20-cv-01534 (U.S. District Court of Connecticut, 2020)
Voting Rights Act of 1965, 52 U.S.C. § 10101
Wood, P. (2003). *Diversity: The invention of a concept.* Encounter Books.

16

PATRICIA HILL COLLINS'S
ON INTELLECTUAL ACTIVISM

The Expansion of Our Field of Perspective

Brooke Judie and Stephanie M. McClure

Patricia Hill Collins is an intellectual giant in the field of sociology and Africana studies. Her contributions to theory, especially but not exclusively in the area of intersectionality, which Collins herself identifies as a "field" today in ways it was not when she first published *Black Feminist Thought* (1990), have consistently challenged the often one-dimensional "causal" models dominant in the field of sociology. Her concept of the "outsider within," which draws on the ideas of W.E.B. Du Bois, Margaret Mead, Georg Simmel, and others, provides critical tools to assess the standpoint of hegemonic ideologies that hide behind assertions of neutrality, objectivity, and "letting the data speak."

In the "Fighting Words" essay included in her collection *On Intellectual Activism* (2013), she asks readers to consider how the story of "history" might be changed if we genuinely considered the knowledge and experiences of all the people who have historically served as "props" in a play that centers a cis, White, Christian hero. Social, political, and, by extension, intellectual history has too long focused on telling "our" story from a very limited perspective. We might think of this today in terms of the "nonplayer characters" in the video game of life. This matters on its face, that inequity. Because of course, whose stories matter tells us something about whose lives matter. But it also matters because limited stories lead to bad policy. We cannot solve problems we do not accurately describe. This is true, even as Collins herself too often remains frustratingly lacking in specificity in regard to examples she provides of successful applications of her alternative perspective.

Collins's Life

Patricia Hill Collins was born on May 1, 1948, in Philadelphia, Pennsylvania. She is the only child of Albert Hill, who worked in a factory and was a World War II veteran, and Eunice Hill, who was an office secretary. Collins attended Philadelphia public schools during the 1950s and 1960s, when most schools in northern cities were well-funded avenues for social mobility (Higginbotham, 2012). At an early age, Collins was aware of the fact that she attended a school that was located in a predominantly Black neighborhood, yet gave more attention to White middle-class students. Nevertheless, she was part of a generation of working-class youth who had access to the very educational opportunities that were withheld from their parents. Collins had the distinct experience of attending Philadelphia High School for Girls during the process of desegregation in the 1960s, which significantly contributed to her budding interest in sociology, feminism, and antiracist activism.

She continued on to Brandeis University in 1965 and earned a BA in sociology with honors in 1969. The very next year, Collins proceeded to earn an MAT in social science education from Harvard University (Higginbotham, 2012). She then worked as a teacher and curriculum specialist at three different Boston schools during 1970–1976. Afterward, she was hired as the director of Tufts University's Africana Center and remained there until 1980. Her experiences working as an educator, both in the public school system and at a private university, would enable her to later articulate a standpoint accounting for her race, gender, and class location as she moved across and within various institutions. Collins began her doctoral studies in sociology at Brandeis in 1980, earning her PhD in 1984. She accepted a tenure-track position with the University of Cincinnati's African American Studies Department in 1982 while she was still working on her dissertation. Collins became a full professor in 1994 and went on to chair the department from 1999 to 2002. Three years later, in 2005, she accepted a position as the Wilson Elkins Professor of the University of Maryland's sociology department (Higginbotham, 2012).

Collins's Impact

In considering the impact of Collins's work, we both spent some time reflecting on our own experiences with her writing and how it has influenced us. Given that we come from two different fields, our sense of her impact is definitely shaped by those varying contexts. In the following, each author shares something of these reflections from her own perspective.

McClure

For me, it would be difficult to overestimate the impact Collins has had on the discipline of sociology. Writing from within sociology, I am less able to speak to her impact beyond her field directly, but traditional measures of impact suggest it is equally broad. In her own writing, Collins talks about needing to do the work that she herself needed but could not find in school. Others talk about reading her "on the sly" in their graduate study (Misra, 2012).

For me, she was central and came very early on, first in an undergraduate class taught by Clenora Hudson Weems (1993), where I was introduced to Collins's work. Given my age and educational level, this means that my first introduction to feminism was through the work of Black feminist authors. Having been raised in a rural, multiracial, working-class community, I came to college with a very conservative (honestly defensive) attitude. But my own experiences, questions, and observations about race and racism lead me to Black studies classes. To this day, I am not sure if I would have been as open to feminism if it had not come through those classes. This is because I experienced no small amount of alienation as a working-class woman, among my White peers and in interactions with White women professors, most of whom were from the middle and upper classes (Morgan et al., 2021) and who regularly made me feel broken or wrong or too much for the elite educational environments I found myself wanting to join.

I have personally seen how engagement with Collins's work transforms students' understanding of themselves and our social world over my 15 years of teaching social theory to undergraduate students in Georgia. One student reported to me, upon reading pieces by Collins and bell hooks, "Now I feel like I have to rethink everything I thought I knew about EVERYTHING." That individual transformation is so powerful. In *On Intellectual Activism*, Collins (2013) has collected a set of essays that simultaneously challenges and reaffirms this idea of individual consciousness raising. She repeatedly suggests that "personal revolution" is not sufficient for the kind of social change necessary for society itself to achieve transformation in the direction of greater freedom and social justice. I do not disagree with her, but I often found myself frustrated with how few concrete and specific examples she provided about what *to* do as opposed to what *not* to do.

Of course, this frustration is not unique to Collins's writing. I particularly appreciated her discussion of the limits and constraints and political realities of academic sociology. These mirror exactly my own experiences and observations:

> Many graduate students choose sociology because they are attracted to the vision of an until-now-unnamed public sociology that they encounter in their undergraduate classrooms. Most do not enter graduate programs to become professional or policy sociologists. For many, graduate training resembles a shell game—they look under one shell for the public sociology prize that they anticipated; yet when they pick up the shell, nothing is there. The real prizes, they are told, lie under the remaining shells of professional, policy, and to a lesser extent, critical sociology. They are pressured to choose among types of sociology and to leave behind the idealism of public sociology or the "you'll never get a job if you keep that up" stance of critical sociology. (Collins, 2013, p. 80)

As she so eloquently describes, this issue stems from "the disjuncture between one set of promises within American sociology to place the tools of sociology in service to solving social problems and actual sociological practices that must pay attention to the challenges of paying bills" (p. 85). That effort—to make the discipline "competitive," to make it "profitable," or "high status"—persists almost perpetually in sociology. Here again, I find myself agreeing with her assessment that these "efforts to purify the discipline, in a misguided effort to elevate its status, belie sociology's actual strengths" (p. 107). It is my sense that these frustrations are not unique to sociology, however.

Judie

The first time I encountered Collins's work was during my sophomore year of college. I had recently declared philosophy as a second major and chose to enroll in a Philosophy of Love & Sex course. One of our first readings was of a chapter entitled "The Past Is Ever Present" from *Black Sexual Politics*. I was particularly struck by Collins's systematic analysis of the ways that our nation's structures implicitly relied upon centuries-old, controlling stereotypes about Black people. I distinctly remember reading her discussion about the gender-specific forms of oppression that characterized chattel slavery. It was through this text that I was first introduced to the notion of "every part" of Black women's bodies being used by slave owners via forced reproduction and rape in addition to harsh manual labor. Reading Collins's work allowed me to start building an academic vocabulary I could use to articulate the histories and experiences that informed my philosophical perspective. More importantly, it was partly due to her scholarship that I began to recognize my perspective as worthy of philosophical engagement at all.

The significance of Collins's work is evidenced, in part, by the influence she has had on thinkers across various disciplines. As a philosopher, I can personally attest to the ways that she has impacted my field of study. Philosophy's continental tradition has long grappled with questions of being, being-in-the-world, being-with-others, as well as queries into concepts like existence, freedom, facticity, situation, and oppression. As philosopher Kathryn Belle points out, intersectionality readily engages each of the aforementioned philosophical issues (Gines, 2011). Collins's impact on this field through her contribution to intersectional theory is also significant because those most eagerly recognized as canonical figures are, overwhelmingly, White men. Belle goes on to say that women of color feminists have developed and conceptualized intersectionality, making a theoretical space for such questions to be considered from a viewpoint other than that of White men (Gines, 2011). In this way, intersectionality expands the usual resources for thinking through these philosophical topics beyond figures like Heidegger, Sartre, or Beauvoir, to also include the critical contributions of philosophical thinkers like Collins.

Although Collins's work has impacted us in unique ways, we both believe in and share her commitment to teaching for transformation. We need to develop critical consciousness in our students about the actual realities of systemic oppression while working to develop classroom pedagogies that empower students and help them develop "the tools to envision a more socially just community as well as a skill set that might move the communities they build for their children closer to this valued social ideal" (Collins, 2013, 129).

One example of how I have been able to practice teaching for transformation in my ethics course is by helping my students see connections between John Locke's concept of "the right to kill" in the *Second Treatise of Government* and the current "Stand Your Ground" laws. Locke's work on social and political philosophy has been hugely influential to the formation of American government, especially its impact in helping draft South Carolina's slave codes—the *Fundamental Constitutions of Carolina* (Bernasconi, 1992). Many of my students reported that they were never taught about these aspects of American history and, thus, are now better equipped to identify and critique newer iterations of systemic racial oppression.

McClure

Like me, she recognizes that "since so many white students are already in racially segregated classrooms, we must make them aware of how they got to that classroom and how they might get to another type of classroom that contains people who don't all look like them" (Collins, 2013, p. 134). Given the racial composition of the classrooms I regularly find myself in (teaching about racial segregation and sundown towns to a classroom with 22 White students and two students of color), being empowered to encourage students to ask these questions, which I have myself been asking for years, means that our education is not just about content knowledge but about critical reflection on the actual conditions that we experience.

Collins's Work

One of Collins's earliest key pieces was an article entitled "Learning From the Outsider Within," first published in 1986 (Higginbotham, 2012). This text was important to Black feminist scholars in their critique of essentialism within women's studies. The essentialism referenced here is the tendency of women's studies scholars to represent the perspective of White women as the universal viewpoint of all women. Collins's critique of women's studies demonstrates the desire many Black feminists had to contribute to the movement while thinking about how gender *and* race would provide an avenue to explore the lives of Black women (Higginbotham, 2012).

Collins then published her first book, *Black Feminist Thought* (1990), which has gone on to become a canonical text within Black feminist theory. In fact, Elizabeth Higginbotham (2012) says that "the clarity of her discussion of power, including how oppressed people understand the power that engulfs them and develop alternative self-definitions of themselves and their situations, has turned the tide of theoretical analysis" (para. 10). As Collins writes, the patterns of knowledge validation in the academy utilize "criteria [that] ask African-American women to objectify themselves, devalue their emotional life, displace their motivations for furthering knowledge about Black women, and confront, in an adversarial relationship, those who have more social, economic, and professional power than they" (Collins, 1989, pp. 754–755). In this critique she creates space for a more inclusive understanding of epistemology and ontology that reflects the best of Weberian *verstehen* and social constructionism's emphasis on intersubjectivity.

Not only did Collins expose many to new work being produced by Black women scholars with this book but she also drew upon the historical legacy of Black women thinkers from the 19th and early 20th centuries.

This includes the work of Anna Julia Cooper and Ida B. Wells-Barnett, who understood that "African American women's subordination relied on race/gender ideologies that explained practices as diverse as eugenics and lynching" (Collins, 2015, p. 7). Other key inspirations include Audre Lorde's (1984/2007) analysis of difference in *Sister Outsider*, Gloria Anzaldua's (2012) *Borderlands/La Frontera*, and Angela Davis's scholar-activism in her work on the prison system. Referencing R.D.G. Kelley's (2003) "radical imagination," Guinier and Torres's (2003) "magical realism," and C. Wright Mills's (1959) "sociological imagination," Collins (2013) writes that she draws "on these ideas via the concept of visionary pragmatism within Black women's oppositional knowledge, a creative tension that links visions for a better society and pragmatic strategies for how to bring it about" (p. 81).

Two years later, Collins coedited *Race, Class, and Gender: An Anthology* with Margaret Anderson (now in its 10th edition; Anderson & Collins, 1992/2020). This text includes readings from a wide range of contributors, in and out of the academy (Glenn, 1992). Since its first publication, the reader has consciously centered the voices of those often left out of academic discourse, in ways that are both accessible to a lay audience and stand up to the scrutiny of scholarly audiences. It has been widely adopted by classroom instructors seeking to help students better see and understand the importance of intersectionality in thinking about contemporary inequality.

In 2004, she released *Black Sexual Politics,* which examines how racist stereotypes have been weaponized against Black Americans in order to perpetuate notions of Black sexual deviancy. Collins (2013) continues to critically analyze contemporary discourse about the hegemonic ideology of color-blindness. She says,

> Given the visibility of trends such as African American hyper-ghettoization in cities and the racial resegregation of American public schools, I wonder how people come to ignore these and other contemporary forms of racial resegregation. . . . If the work of Eduardo Bonilla-Silva is to be believed, many white Americans genuinely believe that racism ended in 1965. How do they come to think this way? (p. 34)

Here, Collins thinks through the conditions that enable Whites to believe in a "postracial" society while also being complicit in the perpetuation of White supremacy. Furthermore, by pushing us to recognize that anti-Black oppression is still alive, she calls us to be vigilant in refining our theories in order to understand its current structure.

Critiques

One of *On Intellectual Activism*'s drawbacks is that a number of the essays are repetitive, as they are reprints from previous works. Despite talking about writing for a nonacademic audience, both of us, as academics, find Collins's writing very dense; this is at least partly due to the various overlapping layers of content from this collection of written and spoken pieces. Another reason her writing is so dense is that she takes quite a while to clarify, to explain why she is saying what she is saying by providing the reader with examples. In general, Collins seems to focus more on naming concepts than on providing examples for how they might practically function, sharing the results of engaged work (activism), or testing ideas about what works and what doesn't. Although we believe in intersectional analysis and agree with her on its necessity, she spends most of her time saying *what* it is (relational, inclusive, antiessentialist) without giving clear examples of what this looks like in real life. She talks about this in her "Definitional Dilemmas" piece as well. For instance, her discussion of coalition building mainly focuses on the challenges to doing such work and the barriers that have to be overcome, rather than providing a clear explanation of *how* to properly execute it.

This is so common and it is where critical perspectives can overlap with postmodernist ideas, which quickly devolve from deconstruction to nihilism. "Let's do this." "Here's how that is oppressive." "Let's do this." "Here's who you are leaving out." This is easy to do. Local, concrete, specific examples of successful movements are what is essential (see, e.g., the voting rights organizational efforts in Georgia in 2017–2021). Collins also critiques this herself when she examines rampant individualism. Although our goal is freedom, as we seek to name ever more categories, we find ourselves more and more all alone. People feel better when they are part of something larger, even as that often means sharing space with folks who may have very different backgrounds than your own (Collins, 2013).

This deconstructive impulse is strong in the discipline of sociology and has been from the very beginning. We are a field oriented toward debunking, questioning conventional wisdom, challenging the taken-for-granted. We are not looking to be liked, which makes things tough in the neoliberal market of higher education today. Collins talks about this issue as she explores her own long career in Africana studies at the University of Cincinnati (where she spent 23 years; she left in 2005 for the University of Maryland). She stayed there a long time, even with lots of other opportunities, committed to the institution, her program, its students, and the community. In an age when many critical race scholars (mainly men) seem to constantly be on the move to the next "big" job, even as they critique institutional and systemic racism, her commitment to place speaks to her commitment to activism. It is hard to build community if you are constantly relocating to a new community. And she could be making much more money had she made those moves. That is part of the paradox of intellectual activism. What works best is concrete, local, and specific. What makes academic headlines is abstract, national, global, and general.

However, many question how engaged she is beyond the academy (Collins, 2012). In one of the essays in *On Intellectual Activism*, she talks about doing Black talk radio and how she had to think through what her message truly was as she engaged with the audience. But most of the rest of the essays were originally presented to academic audiences of some type. If we consider intellectual activism in the 21st century, that certainly includes a social media presence, and we have models for that in Jessie Daniels, Crystal Fleming, Roxane Gay, and Tressie McMillan-Cottom, all of whom show a very different model of public engagement through social media (which, as they regularly note, has many drawbacks; see Daniels et al., 2017). Certainly, however, all of these activists use Collins in their own work.

Given Goldrick-Rab's (see chapter 12 in this volume) definition of *scholar-activism*, it is not immediately clear what elements of Collins's research have been translated into action or policy. One can think of Seamster and Charron-Chénier's (2017) and Baradaran's (2018) work on the racial wealth gap that became part of the banking and college student debt forgiveness policies under consideration at the national level today. Nonetheless, it is doubtful there is a serious person (inside or outside the academy) writing about, thinking about, talking about, or advocating for social equality, social justice, or social change we could identify today who has not, in some meaningful way, been influenced by Collins's ideas.

Conclusion

Whatever might be the limits of Collins's work, we continue to be inspired by the challenges she provides.

> Academics know that the test of so-called truth is in its "telling"; yet when we present our ideas, in writing or orally, to small groups of homogeneous practitioners within our disciplines, we limit our truth-telling. We often do not speak the truth to power, but rather collude with existing power relations. (Collins, 2013, p. xxi)

This is certainly true on an almost daily basis, and is particularly frustrating as we look at the nature of "diversity regimes" in higher education

(Thomas, 2020). Collins (2013) writes, "Stated differently, new power relations predicated on token inclusion need an array of visible difference at the top to legitimate the continuation of business as usual at the bottom" (p. 73). This is exactly what we see so often in higher education today, where Whiteness continues to predominate in positions of power but with visible/celebrated/siloed exceptions and then a striking homogeneity at the bottom (in maintenance, grounds, food service, etc.). Collins reminds us that Black visibility does not necessarily translate to Black empowerment.

Given this, she charges her students (and by extension, her readers) with a responsibility for action that we believe is a great way to close this reflection on her life and work.

> Existing social problems—whether school performance, poverty, HIV, voter apathy, the gendered contours of the new racism, or other issues you care deeply about—are responsive to your thoughts and actions. Every single person has a choice. You do not have to leave the world as you found it. You need not move through the world thinking, "There's nothing I can do. I've been socialized this way." Because if you think of yourself that way, you uphold social injustice. It is your choice. I encourage you to choose the difficult path of social justice, to imagine new possibilities, and to act. (Collins, 2013, p. 39)

References

Andersen, M. L., & Collins, P. H. (1992/2020). *Race, class, and gender: An anthology.* Cengage.

Anzaldua, G. (2012). *Borderlands/La frontera: The new mestiza* (4th ed.). Aunt Lute Books.

Baradaran, M. (2018). *How the other half banks: Exclusion, exploitation, and the threat to democracy.* Harvard University Press.

Bernasconi, R. (1992). Locke's almost random talk of man: The double use of words in the natural law justifications of slavery. *Perspektiven der Philosophie, 18,* 293–318. https://doi.org/10.5840/pdp19921818

Collins, P. H. (1989). The social construction of Black feminist thought. *Signs, 14*(4), 745–773. https://psycnet.apa.org/doi/10.1086/494543

Collins, P. H. (1990). *Black feminist thought: Knowledge, consciousness, and the politics of empowerment.* Routledge.

Collins, P. H. (2012). Looking back, moving ahead: Scholarship in service to social justice. *Gender and Society, 26*(1), 14–22. http://www.jstor.org/stable/23212234

Collins, P. H. (2013). *On intellectual activism.* Temple University Press.

Collins, P. H. (2015). Intersectionality's definitional dilemmas. *Annual Review of Sociology, 41,* 1–20. https://doi.org/10.1146/annurev-soc-073014-112142

Daniels, J., Gregory, K., & McMillan Cottom, T. (2017). *Digital sociologies*. Policy Press.

Gines, K. (2011). Black feminism and intersectional analyses: A defense of intersectionality. *Philosophy Today*, 55(Suppl.), 275–283. https://doi.org/10.5840/philtoday201155Supplement68

Glenn, E. N. (1992). Race, class, and gender: An anthology by Margaret L. Andersen and Patricia Hill Collins [Review]. *Gender and Society*, 6(3), 525–527.

Guinier, L., & Torres, G. (2003). *The miner's canary: Enlisting race, resisting power, transforming democracy*. Harvard University Press.

Higginbotham, E. (2008). A new perspective with Patricia Hill Collins. *Footnotes*, 36(7). 1, 6–7. https://www.asanet.org/sites/default/files/fn_2008_07.pdf

Higginbotham, E. (2012). Reflections on the early contributions of Patricia Hill-Collins. *Gender and Society*, 26(1), 23–27. https://doi.org/10.1177/0891243211426723

Kelley, R. D. G. (2003). *Freedom dreams: The black radical imagination*. Penguin Random House.

Lorde, A. (2007). *Sister outsider: Essays and speeches*. Ten Speed Press. (Original work published 1984)

Mills, C. W. (1959). *The sociological imagination*. Oxford University Press.

Misra, J. (2012). Introduction: Well, how did I get here? *Gender & Society*, 26(1), 5–13. https://doi.org/10.1177/0891243211429683

Morgan, A., Clauset, A., Larremore, D., LaBerge, N., & Galesic, M. (2021, March 24). *Socioeconomic roots of academic faculty*. https://doi.org/10.31235/osf.io/6wjxc

Seamster, L., & Charron-Chénier, R. (2017). Predatory inclusion and education debt: Rethinking the racial wealth gap. *Social Currents*, 4(3), 199–207. https://doi.org/10.1177/2329496516686620

Thomas, J. T. (2020). *Diversity regimes: Why talk is not enough to fix racial inequality at universities*. Rutgers University Press.

Weems, C. H. (1993). *Africana womanism: Reclaiming ourselves*. Routledge.

17

THE FIGHT FOR THE PUBLIC

Henry Giroux, the Neoliberal Project, and the Limits of Critical Pedagogy

Dana Morrison

In March of 2020, colleges and universities across the country were struck by the reality of the COVID-19 pandemic. This crisis sent many public institutions of higher education into an operational and budgetary tailspin. As campuses were closed to stem the spread of the virus, adjunct faculty and staff were laid off *en masse* (Valbrun, 2020). Many institutions, dealing with years of austerity and subsequent loan debt (Marcus, 2017; Shirmer, 2020), sought reckless reopening plans in order to pay their creditors the only way they knew how—by getting bodies in desks. These plans led to increasing levels of community spread (Burke, 2021) as well as horror stories from students forced into quarantine housing (Marowski, 2020; Wells, 2020). Other public institutions proposed massive cutbacks to tenured faculty and academic programs, particularly those in the humanities, social sciences, and service fields, stating that they were simply responding to the needs of the market in light of the crisis (Indiana University of Pennsylvania, 2020; Ritchel, 2020). Some particularly vulnerable public institutions were threatened with being merged into others (Whitford, 2020) or closed forever (Duffort, 2020).

What happened to these schools—and numerous others—however, is a part of a larger project to remake the university, a project that scholar and critical pedagogue Henry Giroux has been naming and critiquing for decades. This project, which Giroux (2014) termed the *neoliberal war on higher education*, has sought to turn our shared interest in a robust system of higher education into a private matter, pushing publicly held goods, like many colleges and universities, into the marketplace and out of the realm of collective responsibility. In his words, what were once "public concerns are now understood and experienced as utterly private miseries" (Giroux, 2009, p. 32), leaving public institutions of education to fend for themselves in a relentless framework of austerity.

Giroux's scholarship then, which has openly challenged this neoliberal attack on higher education, can best be characterized as a foundational contribution to the ongoing fight for the public. Centering on detailed cultural and political analyses of the neoliberal project as well as the promise of critical pedagogy in combating it, Giroux's writing on the state of higher education in the 21st century has provided those who struggle against neoliberalism with much needed theorization and hope. As someone who identifies as being a part of this struggle, my view of Giroux has been as an intellectual mentor and ally whose texts have shaped my understandings, my pedagogy, and my identity as a scholar and an educator. Yet as an *organizer*, I've come to question whether academic critique and critical pedagogy are enough. In this chapter I will explore Giroux's analysis of higher education in the neoliberal era as well as the critical pedagogy he often centers as a solution. To conclude, I will share some thoughts on the limits of critique and pedagogy as we fight to save the public.

Henry Giroux

An educator for over 50 years, Henry Giroux is the current chair for scholarship in the public interest at McMaster University in Ontario, Canada. Although Giroux has taught at some of North America's most respected universities, he began his career as a high school social studies teacher in 1968. It was during this time that Giroux discovered the critical pedagogy of Paulo Freire. As Giroux once recounted, after struggling to defend democratizing classroom practices to an overbearing principal, he picked up a copy of *Pedagogy of the Oppressed*. In his words, "I was so frustrated that I went home, read the book. I stayed up all night, got dressed in the morning, went to school, I felt my life had literally changed" (Kincheloe, 2007). This life-changing experience inspired Giroux to submit a review of the text, which eventually caught the attention of Freire himself. Inspired by Giroux's review, Freire contacted him, igniting a decades-long friendship as well as Giroux's academic career.

Giroux has since established a vita containing hundreds of articles and over 70 authored or coauthored books in the fields of cultural studies and critical education. This chapter will focus primarily on Giroux's texts on higher education, which make essential contributions to the discourse on postsecondary schooling. In these publications, Giroux provides in-depth cultural and political critiques of the neoliberal project in higher education, contextualized by discussions of critical happenings in the United States and around the globe. Yet these publications also exemplify Giroux's commitment to critical education by centering on the contention that a critical pedagogy—facilitated by public intellectuals and protected by the university—is an essential weapon in the fight against the oppressive neoliberal regime.

Giroux and the Neoliberal Project in Higher Education

Scholar and activist Pauline Lipman (2011) has characterized neoliberalism as an ideological project to "change the soul" (p. 10). Constituting both sociocultural and political elements, the neoliberal project has redefined democracy and freedom around notions of individual choice within the private marketplace, altering not only concrete policy decisions but also our very conceptualization of *the public*. It is this aspect of the neoliberal transformation applied to higher education that undergirds much of Henry Giroux's analysis of postsecondary institutions in the 21st century. As Giroux (2002) has explained, neoliberalism's growing influence in the United States has signaled a radical shift in what constitutes "the meaning of citizenship and the defense of the public good" (p. 429). In place of communal notions of democratic participation in a mutually beneficial and collectively governed public sphere, we have "substituted the language of personal responsibility and private initiative" (p. 430).

This neoliberal prioritization of the freestanding individual has deeply impacted the dominant purpose of higher education. For decades it was widely accepted that foundational to the university's mission was a commitment to a broad liberal arts education. As John Dewey (1944) argued, a liberal arts education was necessary in a democratic society as it demanded that any vocational preparation be accompanied by a "deep sense of the social foundations and social consequences of industry" (p. 393). In brief, Dewey suggested that a robust and socially contextualized higher educational experience would foster an essential criticality of the modern industrial world that would serve the democratic foundation. Yet as explained by Giroux (2002), in the neoliberal era "many students and their families no longer believe that higher education is about higher learning, but about gaining a better foothold in the job market" (p. 435). What's more, according to Giroux, even colleges and universities have bought into this mission, perceiving and promoting themselves as "training grounds" for corporate interests (p. 435).

A recent example of this comes from Indiana University of Pennsylvania (IUP). Facing dramatic fiscal and enrollment challenges after years of state funding losses, President Michael Driscoll proposed changes to the university structure that would reflect the needs of the 21st century corporate economy. Under the "NextGen" plan, the university, originally modeled around the liberal arts tradition, would adopt new "areas of focus" based expressly on "employer demand" (IUP, 2020, p. 5). Citing projected employment growth categories, the restructuring would primarily emphasize STEM fields as well as those connected to health care and business. Although the institution claimed that this plan would not abandon important coursework outside of these areas, a full 74 tenured or tenure-track faculty members were subsequently laid off from programs that were cut or consolidated by the restructuring plan (Cloonan, 2020).

The underlying logic of IUP's restructuring, of course, is a key ideological component of neoliberalism's war on higher education. As explained by Giroux (2014), the neoliberal project articulates the value of higher education as exclusively tied to the need for credentials, meaning that "disciplines and subjects that do not fall within the purview of mathematical utility and economic rationality are seen as dispensable" (p. 60). Thus, in shifting our conceptualization of higher education from democratic public good to individual consumer commodity, we impose on the university the tenets of "corporate culture" (Giroux, 2002). Centering economic principles like competition and profitability, corporate culture has become an "all-encompassing horizon for producing market identities, values, and practices" in higher education (p. 429). Quite practically, corporate culture refashions colleges and universities into businesses that—even when nonprofit public entities—operate with a strict commitment to the "bottom line."

This adoption of corporate culture has had dramatic material consequences in higher education, especially for public colleges and universities, the students they serve, and the faculties they employ. Public higher education workers, in particular, have been living through an era of adjunctification, with a full 75% of college faculty having no path to the job security provided by tenure. As universities turn toward corporate management models, they are increasingly drawing on adjunct faculty who lack benefits and are paid salaries that qualify them for food stamps (Giroux, 2014). Although this precarity undermines the stability of the academy, it is desired by administrators who seek the employment flexibility espoused by neoliberal corporate culture.

Giroux's work shines a bright light on the ways that colleges and universities across the United States have adopted the organizational characteristics of businesses. This appropriation of corporate culture has engendered the neoliberal push toward the wholesale privatization of the public; for if schools are businesses, the rationale goes, they should be able to fund themselves through the payments of their private customers. It should come as no surprise, then, that between 2008 and 2018 state funding for 2- and 4-year institutions dropped by $6.6 billion nationally (Mitchell et al., 2019). In that same time, colleges responded "by increasing tuition, reducing faculty, limiting course offerings, and in some cases closing campuses" (p. 1). For many state systems, this has placed vulnerable schools in an inevitable financial tailspin—fewer students wanting to attend institutions with limited programs and services and fewer students able to attend institutions with increasingly higher costs.

In the Pennsylvania State System of Higher Education (PASSHE), for example, a decade of stagnant funding followed a $150+ million cut initiated by Governor Tom Corbett in 2011. Now, with increasing costs, level funding, and falling enrollment, several institutions are nearing their fiscal cliffs, and PASSHE is being forced into a dramatic "redesign" by Chancellor Dan Greenstein, who plans to consolidate six of the system's 14 universities (McKenzie, 2020). What's more, Cheyney University, the system's only HBCU, has been pressured into forming a strategic relationship with a for-profit real estate development firm, Mosaic Development Partners, in order to attract businesses to form private partnerships (Cheyney University of Pennsylvania, 2021).

Giroux's work in higher education takes care to document and theorize concrete examples like this, shining a spotlight not only on the material consequences of the neoliberal project but also its underlying logic. In each of his texts, he provides critical analyses of the forces that have driven the relentless attacks on the public. Thus, Giroux's work supplies those of us who seek democratic alternatives to neoliberalism with the sharp theorization necessary to inform efforts for change.

Giroux and the Promise of Critical Pedagogy

Giroux's work on higher education, however, provides more than just analysis. A consistent thread throughout his writing is a clear commitment to the promise of critical pedagogy in the fight against the neoliberal project. Critical pedagogy, in the words of Joe Kincheloe (2008), "maintains that the classroom, curricular, and school structures teachers enter into are not neutral sites," but contested, political spaces (p. 2). In an ideally democratic society, this means that educators and institutions mustn't shy away from questions of politics and power, but openly explore them with students in their preparation as critical citizens. As argued by Giroux (2014),

> Democracy places civic demands upon its citizens, and such demands point to the necessity of an education that is broad-based, critical, and supportive of meaningful civic values, participation in self-governance, and democratic leadership. Only through such a formative and critical educational culture can students learn how to become individual and social agents, rather than merely disengaged spectators. (p. 142)

This critical educational culture must be fostered by educators who recognize that "pedagogy always represents a commitment to the future" and who seek to ensure "that the future points the way to a more socially just world" (p. 98).

A key component of this critical pedagogy is the facilitation of a process wherein students learn to read the world (Freire, 1985). As Giroux (2009) explained, "Pedagogy in this instance works to shift how students think about the issues affecting their lives and the world at large" (p. 14). In essence, education becomes a practice of consciousness raising, providing students with the conditions to engage in robust, rigorous, and critical forms of questioning (Giroux, 2009). In an era of education as job training, critical pedagogy envisions students—and their educators—as "autonomous, self-reflective, and socially responsible" individuals who are committed to an ongoing analytical engagement with each other and with the world (Giroux, 2014, p. 147).

Yet as argued by foundational theorist Paulo Freire, it is not enough to simply *read* the world. The true promise of critical pedagogy is grounded in the belief that understanding the world is a precondition to *engaging* in it (Freire, 2012). Thus, in Giroux's (2014) words, critical pedagogy asks students to critically examine the issues affecting their lives in the hope of energizing them to seize crucial moments "as possibilities for acting on the world" (p. 14). Particularly as the neoliberal project encroaches on democratic governance and concerns for the collective good, Giroux (2009) argues that a critical pedagogy in higher education is a "cornerstone" in the fight for the public (p. 21).

The Public Intellectual

An essential component in the realization of critical pedagogy in higher education is the public intellectual. These "citizen-scholars" are college and university faculty committed to a project of questioning, investigation, and analysis of the dominant structures of society. They draw fundamental connections between their scholarship and the politics impacting society at large, perceiving their research not as a disconnected endeavor but as an essential contribution to the fight for the public. In Giroux's (2002) conceptualization, public intellectuals recognize their work as a "civic duty" (p. 451). As he has argued, "the role of engaged intellectuals is not to consolidate authority but to understand, interpret, and question it" (Giroux, 2009, p. 22).

Drawing on Edward Said's configuration of public intellectuals as *exiles*, Giroux (2009) contends that academic faculty must live on the border of the institution by carving out a space in which critique can endure in spite of the pressures to conform to the established neoliberal order. Giroux recognizes, however, that many structural and institutional forces push against the development of such academics. As he explained, many scholars are quite "secure in their professed status as specialists and experts," and thus retreat into the confines of the academy, showing little interest in how power is used in their institution or social life more broadly (p. 21).

Yet throughout his texts, Giroux makes powerful arguments for the public intellectual, providing clear examples of scholars who have refused to retreat and instead have embodied the role of citizen-scholar. These thinkers, many of whom are showcased in this very book, have chosen to use their work to uncover, theorize, and draw attention to critical issues facing the public. Giroux argues that if we hope to realize the promise of critical pedagogy, we need more academics willing to do the same. In his words, this type of pedagogy needs scholars who are "neither afraid of controversy or the willingness to make connections that are otherwise hidden, nor are they afraid of making clear the connection between private issues and broader elements of society's problems" (Giroux, 2014, p. 148).

The University as Democratic Public Sphere

Another essential element of realizing the promise of critical pedagogy is the affirmation of the university as a democratic public sphere. Throughout Giroux's writings he frames colleges and universities as vital resources to the democratic and civic life of the nation (Giroux, 2002). Giroux perceives these institutions as spaces where critical discourse can flourish and, thus, a necessity for any democratic society. As he contends, "Democracy necessitates a culture of questioning and a set of institutions in which complicated ideas can be engaged, authority challenged, power held accountable, and public intellectuals produced" (Giroux, 2014, p. 59).

Giroux posits the university as one of the few institutions in which these things remain possible. In particular, he highlights the tradition of academic freedom within the academy as a mechanism that, if protected, could facilitate the promise of critical pedagogy. Academic freedom, or the legal protection that allows faculty to freely express their views without fear of censorship or repercussions, has been a cornerstone of the university. Although Giroux takes care to document the calculated attacks on academic freedom from right-wing sources, he also holds up the security that it affords faculty as they pursue critical scholarship and pedagogy.

The foundation of academic freedom provides the potential for higher education to act as a safe harbor for critical pedagogy. It is for this reason that Giroux (2009) has argued for the university to be understood and protected as a necessary public arena, noting that

> higher education must be embraced as a democratic sphere because it is one of the few public spaces left where students can learn the power of questioning authority, recover the ideals of engaged citizenship, reaffirm the importance of the public good, and expand their capacities to make a difference. (p. 450)

The Limits of Critique and Critical Pedagogy

As detailed previously, Giroux's work in higher education can be characterized by its emphasis on academic critique and critical pedagogy. Throughout his texts he consistently posits these activities as potential weapons against the wide-ranging neoliberal attacks both inside and outside of postsecondary institutions. His calls for duty-minded faculty to engage in both critique and critical pedagogy are, in his words, an appeal "to collectively address material inequities involving resources, accessibility, and power in both education and the broader global society" (Giroux, 2009, p. 14). Thus, although Giroux often mentions the importance of mass movements in bringing about change, he focuses the majority of his attention on these ideological activities as the means for confronting concrete social, political, and economic issues.

As an educational scholar and a teacher-educator, Giroux's contributions in this regard have been crucial to my research and my teaching. Particularly in the beginning years of my career, they provided me with the wide-eyed hope that I could change the injustices of the world by simply fulfilling my duty as a member of the academy. Yet with my growing role as an organizer of public higher education workers, I've been pushed to question the extent to which these activities are enough to save our public institutions.

Instead of adhering to Giroux's theory of change, which assumes that the raising of consciousness through critique and critical pedagogy will lead to action, I've taken on what many scholar-activists have called an *organizing theory of change*. As explained by labor scholar Jane McAlevey (2016), an organizing theory of change envisions transformation as a process brought about by a "continually expanding base of ordinary people" who seek to "transfer power from the elite to the majority" (p. 10). As our schools face an onslaught of concrete layoffs, cutbacks, consolidations, and closures, I argue that centering the work of grassroots organizing is essential for critical scholars in higher education.

An Organizing Theory of Change

An organizing theory of change centers on two key beliefs. The first of these beliefs is that the primary mechanism for genuine social change is the collective, mass movement. Particularly as the neoliberal project has replaced formerly democratic structures of governance with top-down, corporate models of decision-making, higher education stakeholders are left with few tools to engender change. One of the tools remaining in the tool chest, however, is organized actions taken by the many. An organizing theory of change centers on the belief that "power concedes nothing without a demand" (Douglass, 1857, p. 22) and thus that collective movements are our most effective weapon against assaults on the public.

The second of these beliefs, however, is that such movements are born, not merely out of consciousness raising in the publishing house or in the classroom, but out of careful and time-intensive work at the grassroots. Although critical theorization and political education remain essential components of this theory of change, they are not the only steps. More importantly, they are conceptualized as happening continuously within the movement, not merely as a precondition to it. As labor scholar Jane McAlevey (2016) has explained, an organizing approach entails teaching people about their potential power by involving them as central actors in the theorization and development of a campaign for change.

The Need for Movement-Relevant Scholarship

Although critique and critical pedagogy are essential, so too is the daily activity of building an expanding base of people who will work collectively toward democratic aims. Giroux's work, however, by continually emphasizing the former, often obscures the latter. Take, for instance, Giroux's (2014) discussion of the 2012 Québec student strike, which took place in opposition to a proposed 75% tuition increase from the provincial government. As Giroux (2014) details:

> In February 2012, after the government refused to negotiate with organizations representing student interests, the student leaders called for a strike. Tens of thousands of students responded immediately by boycotting their classes. Many of the province's colleges and universities were shut down as a result. (p. 168)

This account, which reports a bird's-eye view of the conflict, says nothing about the painstaking on-the-ground efforts that led to "tens of thousands of students" responding to the calls for a strike. The mass action, however, was the result of a 3-year mobilization campaign organized by members of the Association pour une Solidarité Syndicale Étudiante (ASSÉ), the largest of the student organizations involved in the 2012 strike coalition. In spite of this, Giroux spends much of the text detailing the actions and perspectives of Québec's neoliberal politicians, not the student movement.

With public higher education in the United States facing similar neoliberal attacks, we need scholarship that provides us with what Bevington and Dixon (2005) call "movement-relevant" theory. Such theory puts the needs of social movements at its heart and takes seriously the task of revealing and analyzing change-seeking efforts in order to demystify the development of collective actions. In brief, critical scholarship of higher education must push beyond theories of consciousness raising to those that reveal and advance the inner workings of movements.

More than this, however, those of us in the field of critical education must be honest with ourselves about the often-outweighed role that critique and critical pedagogy play in our theories of change. This is not to say that critical scholarship and teaching should be forgotten; for any movement to be successful, it will need careful analyses of the structures of power in order to make effective inroads against the entrenched neoliberal regime. Likewise, we need educators to foster a culture of learning that will increase the likelihood that critically minded citizens who seek change will exist in great enough numbers to make a difference.

What we must contend with, though, are the risks we run when critique and critical pedagogy assume a disproportionate role in our work. Placing undue emphasis on these areas not only puts a tremendous social burden on academics but also tends to turn our attention inward, so that even when writing and teaching about the world, our efforts become more individualized and contained within the academy. Perhaps even more damaging, however, is how this overemphasis might prevent a more radical theory of change from developing among faculty, by placating us with the promise of incremental progress that will one day come from our academic work—hopefully.

Particularly at a time when K–12 educators in the United States are leading some of the most promising mass movements against the neoliberal regime (Dyke & Muckian Bates, 2019), we must take care to conceptualize institutions of education in a manner that does not divert attention away from the need for collective action outside of the classroom. As argued by David Backer (2016), "Education's real promise is that it is one site among many others in the struggle to transform the social structures that create inequality" (p. 1). Thus, Backer encourages us to think of education as a space that can contribute to the larger fight against neoliberal capitalism, rather than as a "compensatory panacea for capitalism's shortcomings" (p. 1).

Conclusion

When reading Henry Giroux's work on postsecondary schooling in the 21st century, his status as a foundational figure in the field of critical education can be easily understood. Not only are his contributions prolific, but they also provide a level of analysis that few scholars have been able to replicate in such volume. Yet as our public institutions of higher education face a new onslaught of neoliberal austerity ignited by the COVID pandemic, we are in need of scholarship that reimagines the work of foundational thinkers like Giroux for this urgent moment. In brief, if the next generation of critical educators are to take up a genuine fight for the public, we must be willing to contend with the promises *and limitations* of critique and critical pedagogy. Our institutions depend on it.

References

Backer, D. I. (2016, November 15). The false promise of education. *Jacobin Magazine.* https://www.jacobinmag.com/2016/11/education-reform-inequality-jobs-economy/#:~:text=Education's%20real%20promise%20is%20that,more%20equal%20economy%20and%20society

Bevington, D., & Dixon, C. (2005). Movement-relevant theory: Rethinking social movement scholarship and activism. *Social Movement Studies, 4*(3), 185–208. https://doi.org/10.1080/1472830500329538

Burke, L. (2021, January 13). Are colleges superspreaders? *Inside Higher Ed.* https://www.insidehighered.com/news/2021/01/13/college-openings-led-increase-community-cases-research-says

Cheyney University of Pennsylvania. (2021). *Strategic partners.* https://cheyney.edu/strategicpartners/

Cloonan, P. (2020, December 4). Fewer faculty face retrenchment. *Indiana Gazette.* https://www.indianagazette.com/news/fewer-faculty-members-face-retrenchment/article_4c34808c-364a-11eb-90f3-cb4c2b931c1e.html

Dewey, J. (1944). The problem of the liberal arts college. *The American Scholar, 13*(4), 391–393. http://www.jstor.org/stable/41206764

Douglass, F. (1857). *Two speeches, by Frederick Douglass: One on West India emancipation, delivered at Canandaigua, Aug. 4th, and the other on the Dred Scott decision, delivered in New York, on the occasion of the anniversary of the American Abolition Society, May, 1857.* CP Dewey.

Duffort, L. (2020, April 17). *Vermont state colleges chancellor to recommend closing three campuses.* VT Digger. https://vtdigger.org/2020/04/17/vermont-state-colleges-chancellor-to-recommend-closing-three-campuses/

Dyke, E., & Muckian Bates, B. (2019). Educators striking for a better world: The significance of social movement and solidarity unionisms. *Berkeley Review of Education, 9*(1). https://escholarship.org/uc/item/7zk5p5sw

Freire, P. (1985). Reading the world and reading the word: An interview with Paulo Freire. *Language Arts, 62*(1), 15–21. http://www.jstor.org/stable/41405241

Freire, P. (2012). *Pedagogy of the oppressed* (30th anniversary ed.). Bloomsbury.

Giroux, H. (2002). Neoliberalism, corporate culture, and the promise of higher education: The university as a democratic public sphere. *Harvard Educational Review, 72*(4), 425–464.

Giroux, H. A. (2009). *Global neoliberalism and education and its consequences.* Routledge.

Giroux, H. A. (2014). *Neoliberalism's war on higher education.* Haymarket Books.

Indiana University of Pennsylvania. (2020, October 28). *Academic restructuring plans.* https://www.iup.edu/news-events/academic-restructuring-plans/

Kincheloe, J. (2007, December 7). *Henry Giroux: Figures in critical pedagogy* [Video]. https://www.youtube.com/watch?v=UvCs6XkT3-o

Kincheloe, J. L. (2008). *Knowledge and critical pedagogy: An introduction* (Vol. 1). Springer.

Lipman, P. (2011). *The new political economy of urban education: Neoliberalism, race, and the right to the city.* Taylor & Francis.

Marcus, J. (2017, March 10). Why colleges are borrowing billions *The Atlantic.* https://www.theatlantic.com/education/archive/2017/10/why-colleges-are-borrowing-billions/542352/

Marowski, S. (2020, October 16). *Quarantine, isolation housing occupancy nearing 50% at University of Michigan.* Michigan Live. https://www.mlive.com/news/ann-arbor/2020/10/quarantine-isolation-housing-occupancy-nearing-50-at-university-of-michigan.html

McAlevey, J. (2016). *No shortcuts: Organizing for power in the new gilded age.* Oxford University Press.

McKenzie, L. (2020, July 17). Rethinking the Pennsylvania state system. *Inside Higher Ed.* https://www.insidehighered.com/news/2020/07/17/pennsylvania-university-system-proposes-plan-redesign

Mitchell, M., Leachman, M., & Saenz, M. (2019, October 24). *State higher education funding cuts have pushed costs to students, worsened inequality.* Center on Budget and Policy Priorities. https://www.cbpp.org/research/state-budget-and-tax/state-higher-education-funding-cuts-have-pushed-costs-to-students

Ritchel, M. (2020, December 28). How the pandemic is worsening the working-class college. *The New York Times.* https://www.nytimes.com/2020/12/28/us/college-coronavirus-tuition.html

Shirmer, E. (2020, November 20). It's not just students drowning in debt. Colleges are too! *The Nation.* https://www.thenation.com/article/society/student-debt-university-credit/

Valbrun, M. (2020, July 6). CUNY layoffs prompt union lawsuit. *Inside Higher Ed.* https://www.insidehighered.com/news/2020/07/06/economic-fallout-pandemic-leads-layoffs-cuny-and-union-lawsuit

Wells, K. (2020, September 11). *"They gave me a bag of chips for dinner": One Michigan student's quarantine experience.* Michigan Radio. https://www.michiganradio.org/post/they-gave-me-bag-chips-dinner-one-michigan-students-quarantine-experience

Whitford, E. (2020, September 15). Pennsylvania system surprised with new integration proposal. *Inside Higher Ed.* https://www.insidehighered.com/news/2020/09/15/pennsylvania-state-system-plans-integrate-three-universities-departing-earlier

ABOUT THE CONTRIBUTORS

Cassie L. Barnhardt is associate professor of higher education, Department of Educational Policy and Leadership, University of Iowa.

Dan Bauer is dean of the College of Liberal Arts at Slippery Rock University of Pennsylvania.

Deron Boyles is distinguished university professor in the Department of Educational Policy Studies, Georgia State University.

Cheron H. Davis is associate professor of elementary education and coresearch director of FAMU Freedom School and North Florida Freedom Schools at Florida Agricultural and Mechanical University.

Joseph L. DeVitis is a retired professor of social foundations of education and higher education who taught at five universities in his 40-year career.

John M. Elmore is professor and chair of Educational Foundations and Policy Studies, West Chester University of Pennsylvania.

Carrie Freie is associate professor of education at Pennsylvania State University, Altoona.

Timothy Glander is professor of education at Nazareth College, Rochester, New York.

Dennis E. Gregory is associate professor of higher education and community college leadership at Old Dominion University.

Adriel A. Hilton is vice chancellor for Student Affairs and Enrollment Management at Southern University at New Orleans (SUNO).

Spoma Jovanovic is professor of communication studies at the University of North Carolina, Greensboro.

Brooke Judie is a doctoral student in philosophy and African American and diaspora studies at Pennsylvania State University.

Daniel P. Liston is professor emeritus of education at the University of Colorado, Boulder.

Marshall Martin is a doctoral student in rhetoric and composition at the University of South Florida.

Stephanie M. McClure is professor of sociology at Georgia College.

Dana Morrison is assistant professor of educational foundations and policy studies at West Chester University of Pennsylvania.

Kevin Murray is associate director of academic success at Colby College.

William Nuckols is director of community outreach and engagement and adjunct professor of higher education, Old Dominion University.

J. Todd Ormsbee is associate professor and coordinator of American studies, San Jose State University.

Sabrina N. Ross is professor of curriculum studies at Georgia Southern University.

Dan Sarofian-Butin is professor in the Department of Education and Community Studies, Winston School of Education and Social Policy, Merrimack College.

Pietro A. Sasso is assistant professor of higher education at Stephen F. Austin State University.

Greg Seals is associate professor of social foundations of education at the College of Staten Island/City University of New York.

INDEX

academic freedom, 59, 98, 100, 102–104, 122, 164, 243–245
academic labor, 71, 106ff., *see also* labor
access, in higher education, 7, 30, 74, 85ff., 94, 116–119, 134, 156–157, 165, 171–174, 191, 200–202
achievement
  physical, 49–50
  social, 69, 72, 75–76, 79–80, 163
accreditation, 100, 124–125, 129
activism, 37, 171, 176–178, 184, 201–202, 209, 233–236
Addams, Jane, 42–46, 52
administration, in higher education, 101–103, 112–116, 124, 133–135, 141, 144, 191–194, 203–205, 210, 242
adolescence, 49, 107
advocacy, 27, 42, 177, 198, 200, 209
affectionate interpretation, 44, 52, *see also* Michael Roth
affirmative action, 4, 7, 146, 198, 214ff.
affordability, in higher education, 7, 171, 174, 178
African-American higher education, 4, 7, 183ff., 197–203, 230, *see also* historically black colleges and universities (HBCUs)
African-American history, 207–208, 218
agency, personal, 69, 75–78, 93, 140
allyship, in college students, 191–192
American Association of University Professors (AAUP), 98, 104
Anderson, James D., 197, 202–203

Arnold, Matthew, 22
Aronowitz, Stanley, 5–7, 13, 119–130
Arroyo, Andrew T., 199–200
Arum, Richard, 144, 171–172
Ashman Institute, 199, *see also* Lincoln University (PA)
athletics, in higher education, 49–50, 94
authoritarianism, 28, 94, 121, 129, 159
autonomy, 43, 76, 93, 108, 128–129, 140, 143

Backer, David I., 30, 87, 247–248
Bard Prison Initiative, 42, 53n3
Bauer, Dan, 107, 110, 113
Belle, Kathryn, 231
belonging, 86, 188, 200, 234
Bensimon, Estela M., 141, 198, 200
Berube, Michael, 5, 13, 97–105
Biden, Joseph R., 82, 217
biography, in research, 22, 24–25
Black Lives Matter, 27
Black students, in college, *see also* historically black colleges and universities (HBCUs)
  females, 184ff., 197, 230–233
  males, 188, 197
Black studies, 224, 230
Boler, Megan, 42 *see also* Michael Roth
border crossing, in research, 44, 84, 244
Bousquet, Marc, 106–118
Bowles, Samuel, 42
Bowman, Nelson, III, 203
Brown v. Board of Education of Topeka, Kansas, 223
Burris, Val, 139

Busch, Lawrence, 100, 119–120
Bush, George W., 108, 201
business, 35, 38, 70, 87–88, 90, 98–100, 108, 112, 124–125, 153–154, 161, 167n6, 205, 221–222, 241–243
Cabrera, Nolan L., 146
California, University of, system, 4, 11, 57, 85, 138
capitalism, 7, 22, 24, 68, 78, 87–90, 107, 119–121, 135, 160, 191, 248
Center for Minority Serving Institutions, 205–206, *see also* Marybeth Gasman, Rutgers University, University of Pennsylvania
Chicago, University of, 20, 88
Chomsky, Noam, 13–14, 89, 126–127
Cincinnati, University of, 228, 234
City University of New York, 13, 120
civic education, 2, 5, 17, 33, 35–36, 46, 56, 58, 85, 87, 90–95, 124–127, 134, 140, 244–247
civil liberties, 7, 14, 126, *see also* freedom, liberties
Civil Rights Act (1964), 88, 90, 166–167
citizen-scholar, 243–245, *see also* Henry A. Giroux
class
   as social status, 22–23, 28, 193–198, 207, *see also* status-seeking
   lower-, *see also* low-income students; poverty, 86, 116, 156–157, 172–174, 176–177, 201–202
   middle-, 90, 100–101, 134, 156, 171–172, 174
   ruling, 73–75, 127
   upper-, 73, 229, *see also* wealth
Cold War, 155, 159–160, 163–164
Collins, Patricia Hill, 7, 184, 227–237
Columbia University, 74
commercialization, 11, 14–15, 135, 167, *see also* marketization

common good, 5, 90–91, 125, 128, 155, 159–163, 174, 176, 216, 238, 244, *see also* public good
community, 34, 47, 58, 108, 137, 166, 167, 185, 231, 234–235
   colleges, 86, 157, 174–117
   interpretive, 58–61, 63–64
   of scholars, 88–90, 166–167, *see also* Paul Goodman
communism, 24, 119, 122, 130
community engagement, in higher education, 62, 64, 216
composition, teaching of, 107, 110–116
consciousness-raising, 138, 243, 245–247
conservatism, Rightism, 26–27, 42, 52, 61, 124–125, 134–135, *see also* neoconservatism, Rightism
consumerism, 15, 17, 71, 75–79, 88–90, 112, 119–129, 124–125, 152–154, 157–159, 160–165, 241
corporativism, 5–6, 70–71, 100, 103, 106, 113–114, 120, 124–125, 127, 129–131, 167, 241–242, *see also* marketization
costs, of college, 101, 124, 177, 201, 243, *see also* affordability, in higher education
cosmopolitanism, 19, 104
Covaleskie, John F., 4
COVID-19 pandemic, 5, 31, 68, 100–101, 106, 108–110, 117, 209
creativity, 12, 32, 34, 36, 46, 64, 134
credentialing, 14, 71, 163
Crenshaw, Kimberle W., 184–185, 207
critical
   pedagogy, 7, 33, 121, 183, 203, 230, 238–240, 243–248
   race theory (CRT), 146–147, 183–187, 203–207, 234–235, *see also* Kimberle W. Crenshaw
   studies, 98

theory, 56, 62, 121, 183, 203, 230, 238–239, 243–244, 244–248
thinking, 12, 14, 26, 32, 35–36, 46–48, 52, 70, 198, 120, 124, 127–130, 134–137, 146, 154–155, 165, 230–232, 243–244, 247
critical university studies (CUS), 142–143, 146, *see also* Christopher N. Newfield
Croom, Natasha, 185–187
cultural
   capital, 69, 74–75, 86, 116, *see also* social capital
   chauvinism, 21–22
   pluralism, 20, 33, 79, 134–135, 137, 166, 222, *see also* political pluralism
   studies, 97, 140, 238–239
   transmission, 6, 80, 88, 146, 161–163, 200–201
culture, 17–19, 24–25, 28, 42, 59, 77, 140–141, 146, 155
   African-American, 183–184, 190–191, 222
   consumer, 153–154
   corporate, 122, 141–142
   neoliberal, 75–79, 140
   war, 18–19, 52, 98, 141–142
curriculum, 5–6, 18–20, 42–43, 59, 108, 113, 122, 124, 130, 134–135, 161–162, 164, 166n3, 191–192
   common, 18–20
   cosmopolitan, 19–20
   delivery, 134
   Great Books, 98
   hidden, 61
   liberal arts, 42–43, 61, 134
   STEM, 203
   vocational, 119–120, 125, 141–142, 176, 199, 203, 240–241

Davis, Lori Patton, 7, 183–196, *see also* Lori D. Patton

debt, student, 5, 86, 124, 128, 130, 144, 172, 174–176, 209, 221, 235, 238
deficit model, 183–187
democracy, 22, 27, 30ff., 44–45, 64–65, 73, 78, 87, 91, 106, 117, 120–121, 125–127, 134, 137, 140, 148, 152, 167n5, 172, 240, 244–245
   deliberative, 30ff., 91, *see also* Amy Gutmann
Deresiewicz, William, 3, 68–81
Dewey, John, 13, 19, 27, 33, 43–43, 46, 64, 154, 240
disability studies, 28, 104–105
disciplinary knowledge, 41–42, 45–47, 58–62, 113–116, 138, 140, 145, 164, 235
discrimination, 218–219, 222–224, *see also* Jim Crow Laws, *Plessy v. Ferguson*
   reverse, 221, 223
diversity, 26–28, 32, 36–38, 52, 58, 61, 73–74, 79, 87, 134–135, 166n3, 172, 191, 206–208, 215–216, 221–223
Donoghue, Frank, 2, 141
donors, college, 73, 75, 78
Dorn, Charles, 167
dropouts, college, 85–88, 91, 94–95, 121
D'Souza, Dinesh, 122
Du Bois, W. E. B., 16, 42–43, 45, 199, 2270
Durkheim, Emile, 18

Early, Gerald, 15
economics, influence of, 14, 20, 21, 24, 28, 32ff., 45–46, 60, 68, 72ff., 80, 86–87, 90ff., 103, 110–114, 127, 134ff., 140–142, 146, 152–156, 160–162, 166n3, 172, 176, 200, 218, 222, 232, 241–242, 245
Edmundson, Mark, 47–49, 50ff.

Education
  developmental, 86, 116, 201
  elementary, 73, 85, 144, 173–178, 202–203, 221, 229
  higher (postsecondary), 32ff., 42ff., 45–46, 56, 69ff., 78–80, 85ff., 91–92, 94, 97ff., 106, 108, 112ff., 130, 132ff., 152ff., 171ff., 183ff., 196, 197ff., 214ff., 229–237, 238ff.
  liberal, 2–3, 14, 16–19, 34, 36, 41, 55, 68–69, 97–105, 125, 128, 135, 138, 142, 147, 152–153, 155, 158, 161–162, 175, 199, 203, 240
  secondary, 49–51, 53, 73, 77, 111, 144, 154, 173–178, 202–203, 217–218, 228, 234, 247
  vocational, 16–17, 45, 108, 120, 124, 141–142, 176, 199, 240–241
efficiency model, in higher education, 6, 100, 112–113, 126, 160
egalitarianism, 22, 73, 156
ELEVATE Program, 205–208, *see also* Marybeth Gasman, Rutgers University
elitism, 1, 6–7, 15, 22, 45, 68–69, 72ff., 80, 98, 117, 123–124, 127–128, 135, 139, 147, 156, 158, 175, 221, 229
emotion, 46–50
empathy, 43, 49, 52–53, 162
empiricism, 98, 122, 140–141, 147, 193
enrollment, in college, 32–33, 159, 191, 178–179, 209, 243
epistemology, 115, 133, 160, 185, 232
essentialism, 185, 232, 234
equality, 22, 30, 34, 37, 64–65, 93–94, 156, 178, 217ff., 235
equity, 98, 156, 174–175, 178, 183–186, 191–192, 198, 200–201, 207
ethics, 31–33, 36–38, 61–62, 72, 88–89, 160, 220–221, 227

ethnicity, 126–127, 142, 172, 216
ethnic studies, 17, 142
expertise, 12–13, 244

faculty, college, 5–6, 12, 14, 26, 35–37, 56ff., 68–71, 99–104, 106, 111, 115, 124–125, 136–139, 142ff., 157–158, 161–162
  contingent, 5–6, 71, 100–106, 109–113, 120, 125, 127, 129–130, 144, 164, 201, 204, 222, 238, 241, 244, 247
  of color, 204, 206–208
  tenure-track, 5, 57, 71, 98, 101–104, 109ff., 138–139, 144, 157–158, 178, 185–186, 241, *see also* tenure
families, 6, 33, 48–49, 72–74, 79, 97, 171–173, 186, 197, 202
  low-income, 33, 172–173, 186
  middle-income, 33, 172–173
  upper-class, 73, 229
  white-collar, *see also*, C. Wright Mills, 76, 157
  working-class, 6, 22–23, 33, 72, 94, 121–124, 127–128, 162, 171–172, 229
Faculty Inclusion Report, *see also* University of Pennsylvania, 37–38
Felber, Garrett, 115
feminism, 33, 50, 62, 64, 187, 193, 197, 206, 223–224, 232–233
  Black, 228–229
financial aid, 32–33, 88–89, 172–177, 201, *see also* Pell Grant
final narratives, 47–51, *see also* Mark Edmundson, Richard Rorty, Michael Roth
Fisher v. University of Texas (2013), 216–217, 223–224
Fish, Stanley, 1–3, 56–67
Fisk University, 203
Florida, University of, 4
food insecurity, in college students, 7, 172–173, 176–179

Fordism, 68, 78–79
Foerster, Norman, 163
for-profit colleges, 109, 175
Franklin, Benjamin, 45
fraternities, *see also* sororities, 201–204
Frederick Douglass Global Fellowship Program, 205, *see also* Marybeth Gasman, Rutgers University
freedom, 33, 36, 43, 62–65, 76, 78, 92–95, 100, 120–121, 129, 140, 148, 230–231, *see also* liberties, civil liberties
free speech, 34–37, 42, 58, 63–64, 120–122
Free University of New York, 122
Freire, Paulo, 239, 243
Fries-Britt, Sharon, 198, 200
Fromm, Erich, 167n5
functionalism, 156, 166
funding, in higher education, 33–34, 57, 68, 71, 73, 75, 78, 97–98, 101, 116, 173, 177–178, 209–210, 243
Gallagher, Chris, 114–115
Gasman, Marybeth, 7, 197–212
Gates, Henry Louis, 15
gay studies, 62, 64, *see also* queer theory
gender, 7, 28, 50, 61–62, 73, 98, 187–189, 194, 214, 230, 233
GI Bill, 4
Gintis, Herbert, 42
Giroux, Henry A., 6–7, 15, 38, 79, 89, 119–120, 125–127, 238–250
globalism, 111–113, 153, 245
Goldrick-Rab, Sara, 7, 171–182
governance, in higher education, 102–103, 115, 117, 125, 133–134, 140–142, 203, 244, 246
government, 36, 73, 87, 106, 141, 144, 153, 159, 219–220, 246
Great Books, 20, 42, 98, *see also* curriculum
Great Depression, 4, 159
Great Recession, 98–99

Grutter v. Bollinger (2013), 216, 223–224
Gutmann, Amy, 3, 30–40

habits of mind, 41, 45, 53n1
Harper, Shaun R., 200, 203
Harvard University, 3, 15, 72, 124, 157–158, 167n6, 171, 217, 228
Harvey, David, 5, 79, 89
health care, 32, 36, 86, 93–94, 241
Higgonbotham, Evelyn B., 228, 232
Higher Education Act (1965), 4, 199, 201
Historically Black colleges and universities (HBCUs), 7, 187–189, 197–199, 200ff.
history, influence of, 20, 49, 72, 89, 92, 97, 100–102, 109, 115, 138–140, 146–147, 156ff., 161–162, 166n2, 200, 207–209, 214, 218, 224, 230–231
Hitchens, Christopher, 129
hooks, bell, 229
Hope Center for College, Community, and Justice, 177–179, *see also* Temple University
Horowitz, David, 104–105, 119, 122
housing shortage, in college, 7, 119, 123, 172–174, 178, 238
human flourishing, 22, 24–25, 34, 43, 45–49, 60, 86, 134, 140
humanities, 46, 48–49, 57, 63–64, 69–72, 60, 97ff., 109–110, 112, 116–117, 134–135, 138ff., 162, 168, *see also* liberal arts curriculum, liberal education

identity, 7, 26, 42, 52, 142, 147, 184, 186–189, 194, 198
  politics, 26, 42, 142, 147, 184, 187, 192

ideology, 26, 35, 42, 52, 58, 72, 78–80, 107, 112–113, 116–117, 123–124,

134, 140, 160, 163–164, 183–184, 227, 233, 245
imagination, 44, 48–49, 52, 167n6
immigrants, 72, 74
independent thinking, 13–14, 26
Indiana University of Pennsylvania, 238, 241
Indiana University-Purdue University, Indianapolis (IUPUI), 194, *see also* White Racial Literacy Project
individualism, 21, 26–28, 33–34, 69–72, 75–80, 160, 166n3, 239, 241, 247
inequality, 4, 22, 28, 36–38, 74, 77, 80, 109, 122, 132, 134, 156, 172, 175, 183–184, 224
innovation, 32, 35–36
instrumentalism, 17–18, 57–58, 62, 76, 146–148, 153–154
interdisciplinary studies, 36, 41–42, 147–149
interpretive community, 58–61, 63–64
intersectionality, 7, 183ff., 198, 231, 234. *See also* Patricia Hill Collins
Institute for the Arts and Humanities, 98, *see also* Michael Berube, Pennsylvania State University
Intolerance, 34–35, 48, 52, 64

Jacoby, Russell, 3, 11–28, 57
James, William, 42–46
Jayakumar, Uma M., 198
Jim Crow laws, 4, 201, 221
job training, 43, 77, 97–98, 125–127, 176, 240, 243, *see also* vocational curriculum, education
Johns Hopkins University, 2, 133–134
Johnson, Lyndon B., 4, 214
Judie, Brook, 230–231

Kennedy, John F., 214
Kennedy, Randall, 7, 15, 214–226
Kezar, Adrianna, 6, 141
Kirp, David, 5, 85–96

knowledge
 dissemination, 59
 factory, 122–126, *see also* Sidney Aronowitz
 of ourselves, 70, 98
 production, 57
 transmission, 61

Labaree, David F., 1, 6, 57, 152–168
labor, 71, 76, 106ff., 120, 218, 230–231, 245–246, *see also* work
 academic, 71, 106ff., 245–246
land-grant colleges, 3–4, 201, *see also* Morrill Act (1862), Morrill Act (1890)
language, 107–108, 110, 142, 153
Latinx studies, 62, 197, 200
laws, influence of, 70, 80, 108, 147, 214, 144–145
Leftism, 15, 20–21, 26, 42, 48, 58, 68, 104, 119–124, 129
legal analysis, 146, 217–218
legislatures, 72, 79–80, 102, 124–125, 210, 214
Lewis, John R., 7
LGBTQ+ students, 187–188, 194, *see also* gay students
liberalism, 18, 92, 119, 122, 142, 152, 156, 160, *see also* liberalism, neoliberalism
 classical, 135, 240
liberation, 107–108, 190, 198
liberties, 7, 32, 87, 92–94, 138, 140, 156, *see also* civil liberties, freedom
Lincoln University (PA), *see also* Ashman Institute, 199
Lipman, Pauline, 87
literary
 studies, 115–116, 140
 theory, 62, 116, 146
literature, 62–63, 109–110, 140, 143–144
loans, student, 90
Lorde, Audre, 233

low-income students, 86, 116, 156–157, 172–177, 201–202, *see also* poverty
loyalty oaths, 164

McAlevey, Jane, 245–246
McClure, Stephanie M., 229–230, 232
Malcom, Lindsey E., 198, 200
managerialism, 79, 100, 108ff., 116, 134–135, 241–242
marketing, 15, 70, 87, 90–91, 241
marketization, 20–24, 70, 78–79, 87–91, 94–95, 98, 100, 111–113, 119, 152, 156–157, 160–161, 234, 238, 240–241
mass movements, 245–247
Marx, Karl, 24, 122
Maryland, University of, 228, 234
Maslow, Abraham H., 177
Mattson, Kristen, 23
media, 13, 116, 185, 187, 210, 235
mentoring, in college, 71–72, 185–186, 198, 201, 205–206
meritocracy, 69–70, 72–75, 88, 186, 222
#Me Too movement, 27, 50
Mettler, Suzanne, 4
Michigan, University of, 158, 216
Miller-Adams, Michelle, 173–175
Mills, C. Wright, 7, 13, 76, 78, 121, 128–129, 233
Milton, John, 56, 63
minority-serving institutions (MSIs), 197–199, 201ff.
  Alaskan Native-Serving Nontribal Institutions (NASNTIs), 199, 201
  Asian-American Pacific Islander-Serving Institutions (AANAPISIs), 199, 201
  Hispanic-Serving Institutions (HSIs), 199, 201
  Native American-Serving Nontribal Institutions (NASNIs), 201

  Native Hawaiian-Serving institutions (HSIs), 199
Mississippi, University of, 115
monoculturalism, 20–21
morality, 3, 13, 25, 30, 37, 46, 58, 70, 73, 86, 90–91
Morrill Act (1862), 3–4
Morrill Act (1890), 4, 201
Morrison, Dana, 245–246
multiculturalism, 21, 27, 30, 134, 142, 229
Museus, Samuel D., 198, 200

narcissism, 162, 165, 167n5
National Pan-Hellenic Council (NPHC), 203–204, *see also* fraternities, sororities, 203–204
neoconservatism, *see also* conservatism, 134–135
neoliberalism, 5–6, 14–15, 35, 38, 68–ff., 87, 89, 97ff., 111–114, 119–124, 128, 134, 234, 238–240, 243ff., *see also* liberalism
Newfield, Christopher N., 6, 132–151
New York Excelsior Scholarship, 174–175
New York Law Against Discrimination (1945), 209–210
Nguyen, Thai-Huey, 203
Nixon, Richard M., 214–215, 219–220
North, Peter, 115
Nussbaum, Barbara, 46, 49, 53n3, 72, 104, 162

Obama, Barack H., 32
Okun, Arthur, 87–88
online instruction, 68, 109, 175
openness, 2, 44, 52, 88
opportunity, 32, 37, 73, 106, 117, 156, 171, 179, 198–199, 207, 214, 221
oppression, 87, 127, 184, 188, 191–193, 200, 204, 230–234, 240
organizing theory of change, 245–246, *see also* social change

Paley, William, 25
Palmer, Rober T., 201
Parents, 3, 33, 48, 69ff., 80, 101–102, 173, 202, *see also* families
Pascarella Ernest T., 143, 172
Patton, Lori D., 146, 183–196
Pell Grant, 176, 198, 201, *see also* financial aid
Pennsylvania State System of Higher Education (PASSHE), 115, 242
Pennsylvania State University, 97–98
Pennsylvania, University of, 30, 32–33, 37, 158, 205–206, 208, *see also* Marybeth Gasman, Amy Gutmann
    Penn Biden Center for Diplomacy and Global Engagement, 32
people of color (BIPOC), in college, 198, 207–208
Perna, Lauren, 203
Pettit, Phillip, 85, 87, 92
Philadelphia (PA), 199, 206, 228
    High School for Girls, 228
    Plan, 219–220
philanthropy, 198, 203, 206, 209, *see also* Marybeth Gasman
philosophy, 13, 30, 46, 49, 58, 92, 97, 100, 122, 140, 144, 154, 160–161, 230–231
Pierce, Charles S., 19
pluralism, political, 21, 30, 33–34, 134–135, 137, 144, *see also* cultural pluralism
Plessy v. Ferguson (1896), 218
poetry, in philosophy, 13, 49, *see also* Richard Rorty
political correctness, 11, 70, 134, 142, 191
politics, influence of, 32ff., 42, 52, 57–58, 61, 63, 78–80, 89, 91, 93–94, 98, 104–105, 112, 117, 120, 126–127, 134, 137, 140, 142, 146–147, 153, 156, 164, 186, 198–199, 200, 227, 230, 239, 243–47

Posselt, Julie, 6
power
    elites, 7–8, 72–74, 108, 147, 184, 186, 232, 235–236, 243–247, *see also* C. Wright Mills
    relations, 7–8, 72–74, 108, 147, 184, 186, 191–192, 232, 235–236, 243–244
postmodernism, 104, 234
poststructuralism, 99, 146–147
poverty, 23, 28, 58, 72, 74, 77, 86, 101, 114–117, 156, 171ff., 207, 221, 236, *see also* lower-income class
pragmatism, 19, 24, 46, 57–58, 119, 233
predominantly White institutions (PWIs), in higher education, 193, 197–198, 200–202, 207, 209
prestige, 154, 158–159, 163–164, *see also* status-seeking
privatization, 6, 12, 14–15, 100, 119–120, 134, 159–163, 166n3, 238–239, 243–244
privilege, 3, 73, 109, 112, 134, 147, 156, 171, 175, 192, 198
professionalization, 2, 15, 49, 71, 76, 208
progressivism, 42, 114
psychology, 142, 157, 200
public good, 5–6, 34, 38, 112, *see also* common good
public intellectuals, 1–3, 11, 132–151, 171–182, 183–196, 197–212, 214–226, 238–250

quantification studies, 142, 162, 174
queer theory, 99, 146–147, *see also* gay studies
quota system, 215, 218–219, *see also* affirmative action

race, 28, 31, 37, 73, 98, 142, 183ff., 190–191, 198, 201–202, 207, 214ff., 231–233

racial justice, 31, 37, 172, 186, 216, 223–224
racial relations, 142, 218–219, 223, 232–233
racism, 7, 31, 37, 58, 183–184, 190, 200–201, 215, 218, 232–236
  systemic, 186–187, 190–192, 194, 201, 215, 231, 234–235
radicalism, 42, 99, 114–115, 127, 247
reading, *see also* Henry A. Giroux, 48–49, 114
Reagan, Ronald W., 4, 14, 79, 124, 142
#Real College, 171, 173–179, *see also* Sara Goldrick-Rab
Regents of the University of California v. Bakke (1978), 215–216, 221–224
relativism, 45, 63
religion, 3, 38, 48, 93, 158–160, 166n5, 214
Renn, Kristen, 141, 145
reparations, 221
republicanism, 85, 90–95
research, scholarly, 133–135, 141, 147, 157–159, 163–164, 176, 178, 189–190, 193–194, 210, 245
retention, in college, 71, 172, 176, 209
rhetoric, 109–111, 114–115
Rhoades, Gary, 141, 143
Rightism, 48, 52, 58, 68, 104, 120, 122, 124, 245, *see also* conservatism, neoconservatism
Roksa, Josipa, 171–172
Roosevelt, Franklin D., 94
Rorty, Richard, 13, 42–43, 46, 48, 63–65, 98
Rotfield, Herbert, J., 125
Roth, Michael, 5, 41–55
Ruth, Jennifer, 99, 101–103

safety, on college campuses, 32, 50–51, 93, 164, 200
Sanchez, Berenice, 191–192
St. John's College (MD), 53n2

Sartre, Jean-Paul. 231
Sasso, Pietro A., 197–199
scholar-activism, 227, 229, 234–235, *see also* activism, advocacy, Patricia Hill Collins
scholarship, academic, 12–13, 18, 62, 64, 71, 85–89, 95, 115–117, 139ff., 153, 161–162, 171, 173, 183–185, 193, 198, 202, 206–208, 210, 230–231, 243–245, 247–249, *see also* scholarly research
scholasticism, 42, 57
schooling, 152, 155, 160–164, *see also* education
Schutte v. Coalition to Defend Affirmative Action (2014), 216
Schutz, Alfred, 24–25
Scialabba, George, 23
science, 100, 108, 137, 142, 166n1, 167n5, 222
Sedgwick, Katherine, 203
segregation, 4, 73, 221–232
self-actualization, *see also* Abraham H. Maslow, 177
self-determination, *see also* autonomy, 30, 108
self-reflection, 47–49, 243
separate but equal doctrine, 218, *see also* *Plessy v. Ferguson* (1896)
service-learning, 47, 61–62
Silber, John, 15
Sizer, Theodore R., 41–42, 53n1
Slaughter, Sheila, 143
slavery, 199, 207, 221, 230–231
social capital, 5, 69, 73–74, 86, 116, *see also* cultural capital
social change, 6–7, 14, 38, 42–43, 58, 229, 235, 243–248
socialization, 24, 236
social justice, 3, 27, 31, 35, 42, 44, 52, 59, 61, 74, 78–80, 91, 95, 98, 188–194, 198, 206–207, 230–231, 235–236
social media, 61, *see also* media

social reproduction, 34, 68, 71, 73–75, 77, 79, 147, 165, 191, 200, 235
Social Science Research Council, 133
social sciences, 100, 163, 177, 238
social stratification, 147, 156, 160, 175
sociological imagination, 77, 233, *see also* C. Wright Mills
sociology, 156, 161, 165, 177, 227–230, 234, 238
solidarity
　mechanical, 118
　organic, 18–20, 23–24
sororities, 202–204, *see also* fraternities
specialization, academic, 12–13, 17–18, 61, 115–116, 142, 244
status-seeking, 14–15, 73, 76–78, 153, 156ff.
STEM, 100, 108, 201, 203, 241
stereotypes, 185, 192, 230
Stoneman Douglas High School, Parkland (FL), 27, *see also* activism, advocacy, student protest
storytelling, in scholarship, 26, 48–50, 140, 184, 194
Strickland, Ronald, 134–135, 139–140, 142
students
　first-generation, 32–33, 86, 94, 171
　graduate, 1, 100
　low-income, 86, 94, 116, 171, 176–177
　nontraditional, 57, 86, 94
　of color, 5, 216–217
　undergraduate, 14, 32–35, 42, 45ff., 59, 69ff., 94, 99, 100ff., 122ff., 136, 139, 144–147, 153–154, 159, 161ff., 187–194, 197–199, 200–203, 216–217, 228ff., 238, 240, 245–247
Student Non-Violent Coordinating Committee (SNCC), 14, *see also* activism, advocacy, student protest
student protest, 27, 42, 246–247

Students for a Democratic Society (SDS), 14, *see also* activism, advocacy, student protest
success
　as life goal, 15, 80, 86, 182–163, 200, 221
　student, 86–87, 203

teaching, 42, 44, 46–47, 49–52, 58–60, 63–65, 70–73, 108, 115–116, 157–158, 245–246
technology, 19, 88, 108, 125, 135, 137, 142–144, 162–164
Teitelbaum, Kenneth, 27
Tennessee Promise Scholarship, 174–175
tenure, 5, 57, 71, 98, 100–104, 109ff., 138–139, 144, 157–158, 178, 185–186, 241, *see also* tenure-track faculty
Texas, University of, 216–217
Thayer-Bacon, Barbara J., 30, 33, 37
Thoreau, Henry D., 72
Tierney, William, 141
tolerance, 64, 166n3
traditionalism, 114–116
transformative intellectuals, 6, 7, 58, *see also* Henry A. Giroux
tribalism, 42, 53n6
Trotsky, Leon, 22
Trump, Donald J., 7, 217
truth, 2, 13, 34, 51, 57, 60–63, 88, 129, 184, 235
tuition, 5–6, 33, 38, 78, 89, 101, 119, 123–125, 128, 159, 172–175, 210, 243, 246, *see also* college costs
Turner, Bridget, 200

unions, 112–113, 115, *see also* labor
United States v. Yale University (2021), 217
utopia, 11, 20–26

values, influence of, 47, 49, 52, 57–58, 68–69, 71–72, 76–80, 94, 126, 133–134, 137, 140, 154, 160–164
variety, 26, 48, *see also* Russell Jacoby

Washington, Booker T., 199
Washington, University of, 215
wealth, 73–74, 77, 87, 153, 156
Wells-Barnett, Ida B., 233
West, Cornel, 15
white ethnic groups, 126–127, 144, 202, 227–229, 232–233, *see also* ethnicity
Whitehead, Alfred North, 167n6
Whiteness, 204, 227, 233, 236
White Racial Literacy Project, 194, *see also* Indiana University-Purdue University, Indianapolis (IUPUI)
white students, in college
 females, 187, 194, 202, 206–209, 229
 males, 192, 194
white supremacy, 190–191, 193, *see also* racial relations, racism

Williams, Jeffrey J., 56, 62, 145–146
Williams, Krystal L., 187
Williams, Raymond, 22
Wills, Katherine, 106–108
Wisconsin, University of, Madison, 172, 175, 178
Wisconsin, University of, Milwaukee, 175
women's studies, 232–233, *see also* Black feminism, feminism
work, 45, 76, 112, 120, 125, 127–128, 135, 162, 172–175, 192, 202, 220, 228, 230–231, *see also* labor
Workforce development, 135, 139, 146, *see also* job training
World War II, 14, 45, 155, 159–160, 163–164, 228
Worthen, Helena, 176

Xavier University of Louisiana, 207–208

Yale Report (1828), 45
Yale University, 3, 45, 69, 73, 109, 158, 217